SUBMERGED

*Ryan Widmer, his drowned bride
and the justice system*

Janice Hisle

Submerged

Ryan Widmer, his drowned bride and the justice system

© 2018 Janice Hisle

ISBN: 978-0-9740602-7-9

Chilidog Press, Loveland, Ohio

For information, contact the author:

Janice Hisle

P.O. Box 219

Morrow, Ohio 45152

www.janicehisle.com

Published by:

Chilidog Press LLC

Loveland, Ohio

www.chilidogpress.com

Cover: David Juergens

Book design: Andy Melchers

Truth only reveals itself when
one gives up all preconceived ideas.
~ *Shoseki*

For Michael and Betty,
who believed in me more than I believed in myself.

&

For everyone who helped reveal the untold story.

Table of Contents

Introduction

The law isn't justice. It's a very imperfect mechanism. If you press exactly the right buttons and are also lucky, justice may show up in the answer. A mechanism is all the law was ever intended to be.

Raymond Chandler

If Chandler wrote the story of the Widmer case, there would be a mysterious blonde, a jilted lover, a missing diamond and a dogged detective as stubborn as a migraine, who ties all of the strings together to solve it.

But flesh and blood are not fiction. The strings cannot be untangled. There is no satisfying conclusion.

The Widmer case is more like a black box. A man and his wife are alone in their house. She drowns in a tub. He cries "innocent." And after three trials, we can only stare at the blank sides of the box and wonder what happened in there that night.

I was pretty sure I had the answers when I sat in the courtroom for the final days of the first trial, not far from Janice Morse (now Janice Hisle), who covered every day of those three long, dramatic, tortuous trials.

"A 911 dispatcher thought Ryan was too calm," I reported in an April 2009 column for the *The Cincinnati Enquirer*. "Police arrived in minutes but found Sarah's body dry, with only her hair damp. The floor was dry, although Ryan claimed that he had just pulled her from the tub. His story changed from finding her face-up to face-down. The tub had been wiped clean except for two hand prints, palms out, sliding down the inside of the tub as if Sarah was trying to push back while being held under."

It was elementary, Watson: "I think Ryan is lying. I think the handprints are chilling testimony that Sarah was murdered. But prosecutors don't know why he would have killed her or even how. It's a real murder mystery."

Ten years later it's still a real murder mystery that can't be solved by the magic of *CSI* or the sleuthing of Philip Marlowe, Travis Magee or Sam Spade. We don't get off the hook that easy. We can't close the book and pat ourselves on the back for figuring out whodunit.

Anyone who has been drawn into the vortex of a murder—witnesses, jurors, lawyers, detectives, reporters, neighbors, friends, family—becomes a member of an exclusive club that understands how murders are like lampreys on the soul that latch on and won't let go. They are fascinating and abhorrent, a slide show of images and feelings you never wanted and can't erase.

Many in the Widmer Club are still haunted by doubts and nagging questions: How did Sarah die? Was Ryan innocent?

Janice was there for the *Enquirer* from start to unfinished. She has stayed with the story long after others have drifted away. She has interviewed Ryan in prison, and combed through thousands of pages of testimony, evidence and court records. The most relentless Columbo could not be more tenacious.

When she asked me to help her edit and publish her book for the tenth anniversary of the Widmer mystery, I was still sure that Ryan was guilty. But after seeing her fresh reporting, new evidence and vivid descriptions of the trials, I am no longer so certain.

Submerged brings new doubts and questions bubbling to the surface of the "Bathtub Murder." This book compels us to take a deeper look at the Widmer case.

—Peter Bronson

CHAPTER 1
"I Think She's Dead"

"9-1-1, what is your emergency?"

"My wife fell asleep in the bathtub and I think she's dead."

With a few frightening words, Ryan Widmer's quiet suburban world went haywire.

Those words, which Ryan breathlessly blurted into his lifeless bride's cellphone on August 11, 2008, would be replayed countless times in a criminal case that would captivate—and frustrate—people in and around Cincinnati, Ohio, for years to come.

Those words launched a nationally publicized case that forever changed the course of many lives and had a lasting impact on virtually every person it touched, even from a distance.

Minutes after Ryan called 911, an ambulance's red lights flashed across the sea of brick-and-vinyl-siding houses in the Hopewell Valley subdivision, joining a police cruiser that was already parked nearby.

A bedroom community about 25 miles north of Cincinnati, Hopewell Valley was an affordable, safe, pleasant new neighborhood for young families.

Newlyweds Ryan and Sarah Widmer had hoped to fill their four-bedroom home on Crested Owl Court with children someday. They bought a newly built two-story in early 2007, a year before they were married, next-door to another young couple, Mandy Antonczak, and her husband, Ashley, known as "Ash."

The foursome related well to each other. They were 20-somethings, still figuring out how to adjust to life as couples—juggling household responsibilities, daily work commutes and time to just have fun.

They played cornhole, an outdoor bean-bag-tossing game that is wildly popular in Cincinnati, especially on the blue-collar west side where Ryan grew up.

Ryan and Ash enjoyed an occasional golf outing together; Sarah and Mandy laughed when their dogs barked at each other during neighborhood walks.

But late on a humid Monday night, Mandy's dogs started barking for another reason.

The dogs had bolted toward their home's front window and were making a ruckus, interrupting the TV show she was watching. Mandy went to investigate. Right away, she saw the red glow of the ambulance's lights. Her heart began to pound. Her mind began to race.

At first, Mandy had no idea whose house was the focus of attention.

Then she saw a medic run into the Widmer home.

Mandy rushed to tell her husband: "Something happened at Ryan and Sarah's!"

While other neighbors filed out of their homes, milling around and wondering aloud about the scene that was unfolding at the Widmers', the Antonczaks stayed inside.

They didn't want to be blatantly nosy about their closest neighbors' business. At the same time, they felt a need to know. "We were curious, confused and worried; I think everyone else was just curious," Mandy said.

So, the Antonczaks hunkered down on the floor of their guest bedroom, sitting in stunned silence as they stared out the window at the pulsing emergency lights.

It felt like forever, but within minutes, the Antonczaks witnessed a terrible, unforgettable sight: Sarah Widmer's motionless body being wheeled out of the house on a stretcher while a rescue squad worked feverishly to revive her.

The Antonczaks watched Ryan walk out of the house. He appeared to be talking on a cellphone. Then one of the medics led Ryan to the front seat of the ambulance and the Antonczaks saw his head drop into his hands.

That's when this realization hit: "We knew something awful had happened. We knew this wasn't something mild and minor, like we were originally thinking," Mandy said later.

Within two days, the Antonczaks learned the stark, stunning reality of what happened that night: 24-year-old Sarah was dead—and her 27-year-old husband was accused of killing her.

Later, Mandy would find herself pulled into the case. She would be subpoenaed to testify about what she saw and heard that night, when a crime allegedly happened right next door—while she was watching *CSI: Crime Scene Investigation* on TV.

"My wife fell asleep in the bathtub and I think she's dead."

Practically everything about the Widmer case was an anomaly.

It was big news in peaceful, conservative Warren County. Large family farms still dot the landscape, reminders of what the county looked like before developers scooped up land and built subdivisions such as Hopewell Valley in Hamilton Township.

The county, home to 207,000 people, could go multiple consecutive years without a single slaying. In Hamilton Township, then a community of about 20,000 people, there had been no "fresh" homicide for a decade before Ryan Widmer was accused of killing his wife.

And the couple were nothing like the usual homicide suspects and victims on the TV news. They were a smiling young pair of newlyweds from the suburbs. Ryan and Sarah somehow seemed more "real" to most people. Audiences were mesmerized.

It was easy for average people to imagine themselves cast in this real-life drama. They could identify with Ryan, a college-educated sports marketer who loved the hometown professional sports teams. Or they might imagine taking the role of his wife, the former Sarah Steward, a dental hygienist with a dazzling smile and a vibrant personality.

And the way Sarah died—drowned in her own bathtub, allegedly at the hands of her husband—also positioned the case among the rarest of the rare.

Most people can remember occasionally hearing about a child or an infant being forcibly drowned in a bathtub. But one adult being accused of drowning another adult in a bathtub? That was almost unheard-of. If there had ever been such a case in Warren County history, it was long ago; no one could remember anything like this.

In 2008, the year Sarah died, there were 109,689 deaths in Ohio, including 597 homicides, 16 accidental bathtub drownings and just one bathtub-drowning that was declared a homicide: Sarah's.

The brew of unusual ingredients made the Widmer case one of the most sensational to hit Greater Cincinnati in years.

Initially, authorities kept a tight lid on information.

As a news reporter for *The Cincinnati Enquirer* daily newspaper and its website, Cincinnati.com, I had heard rumors that something strange had happened in Warren County on the night of Monday, August 11. It was my job to stay on top of the news, especially on my "beat," which included Warren County.

Other reporters had gotten tips about the incident, too; one TV station posted a five-sentence "blurb" on Tuesday, August 12, saying that the county coroner was going to autopsy a drowning victim but it was unclear whether drugs or alcohol may have been factors. Reporters were unable to confirm further details.

The next day, Wednesday, August 13, the county prosecutor sent out a news release: "HAMILTON TOWNSHIP HOMICIDE," it said, announcing a news conference at six o'clock that evening—prime time for the local TV news stations to go "live."

No additional details were provided in the news release, and no information would be given by phone until afterward. So, if we reporters wanted info right away, we had to show up.

Talking among ourselves before the news conference, we wondered: Was this situation being overblown because it happened in a small township? Or was this truly a big deal? Little did we know how big the story would become.

The Warren County prosecutor, Rachel Hutzel, entered the crowded room with Lieutenant Jeff Braley, stepping into the glare of TV spotlights. Hutzel told us that a suspect named Ryan Widmer was jailed on a murder charge alleging that he had drowned his wife, Sarah. There had been no prior reports of domestic violence at the home; the couple had been married only four months.

Hutzel also told us that the county coroner had found "trauma to the body" that was not consistent with a fall or any other accidental cause. But she and Braley, the lead investigator on the case, would not describe the injuries further. But they did say that the evidence wasn't obvious at the scene of Sarah's drowning—it was discovered during the autopsy, something that required the coroner's skills to find.

Intriguing. Sounded like they had evidence that was rock-solid, dramatic and severe—virtually unassailable proof of murder. That must be why they acted so so quickly and so decisively to charge the suspect with murder, I thought.

Braley and Hutzel were accustomed to talking to reporters, but the cases they commented on generally didn't lead the evening news on TV, and only occasionally hit the front pages of newspapers. This one, however, was an attention-grabber—and it surfaced at a pivotal time for Hutzel and Braley.

A local farm girl from a big family, Hutzel had broken through the "good-old-boy network" to become the first woman prosecutor in Warren County. Lots of people liked and respected her because she was smart and hard-working. But Hutzel could sometimes come across as aloof because she chose her words so carefully; she often sounded clinical and detached when she spoke.

Some denounced her as ridiculously tough for prosecuting teenagers for offenses such as "sexting" nude photos of each other on cellphones and waging a "food fight" in a school cafeteria. But in many voters' eyes, Hutzel was the female embodiment of the county's law-and-order culture—and that suited them just fine.

Before the Widmer case broke, Hutzel was poised to become a judge on the Ohio 12th District Court of Appeals—a position she later won after running unopposed. Hutzel again was a pioneer, becoming the first woman to ascend to that position.

As for Braley, he seemed to be on track to become Hamilton Township's next police chief. He had been promoted quickly and had made some friends in powerful positions. And he made a good spokesman for the department.

While some conspiracy theorists alleged that Hutzel and Braley turned up the heat on Ryan to gain more publicity for themselves, I never saw any proof of that.

On the other side was Ryan's attorney, Charlie H. Rittgers, a criminal defense lawyer with three decades of experience. He was known for being media-savvy but usually gave limited remarks to the press. But when reporters sought comment from Rittgers about the Widmer case, Rittgers said he did not merely deny the charges on behalf of his client—he said the accusations mystified him.

He said Ryan had no history of fighting with his wife, was college-educated and had no prior record. Rittgers was skeptical about the evidence that prosecutors were keeping hidden. Friends of the couple were equally critical of the authorities' alleged rush to judgment and about their vague description of "trauma" to Sarah Widmer's body.

The "mystery evidence" would remain secret until the case went to trial.

In the meantime, speculation ran rampant in social conversations and in online comments.

Questions swirled around and around:

When Ryan told the 911 dispatcher that his wife "fell asleep," was he making a desperate, half-baked attempt to conceal that he had drowned her?

Or did an innocent Ryan find Sarah unresponsive, and just blurt out his first assumption, that she had fallen asleep?

That "falling asleep" assumption might seem nonsensical. But to Ryan's friends and family, it made perfect sense. They knew that Ryan's wife had often nodded off in unusual settings—in bars, at movie theaters and at tailgate parties.

People teased her about this so much that Sarah earned the nickname, "Sleeper," worn on a nametag at a friend's baby shower. After she drowned, there was nothing funny about it. Some began to wonder if she had a serious, undetected medical condition that incapacitated her, causing her to drown in the bathtub.

Sarah's brother, Mike Steward, publicly stated that his sister had a history of falling asleep in the tub before she met Ryan. Some of Sarah's friends knew about it, too. That's why they thought there was nothing odd about Ryan telling the 911 dispatcher: "She falls asleep in the tub all the time."

To investigators, however, that remark seemed extraneous, like Ryan was trying to deflect suspicion away from himself. Why else would he find it important to offer that comment, rather than staying focused on getting help for Sarah?

Bloggers sliced-and-diced Ryan's comments on the 911 call as though they were being put through a Cuisinart food processor. Virtually every word, every stutter was pointed out as a sign of guilt.

But people who knew Ryan say they heard a terrified, stunned person who didn't know what to say or what to do after finding the love of his life unresponsive in the bathtub.

And, at the outset, Sarah's closest relatives were adamant: Ryan was innocent.

As news spread about the case, people across Greater Cincinnati and beyond wondered: Is it even possible to just fall asleep in a bathtub and drown? Wouldn't a person wake up? Might it be possible for a person to doze off, inhale some water, choke, then drown while unable to call for help? Or was a seizure or some other disorder a possibility?

Dueling theories filled the radio airwaves, Facebook and internet news sites such as Cincinnati.com. Sometimes, discussions became so heated that webmasters disabled the "make-a-comment" function on news stories, blocking people from viciously attacking each other.

The debates polarized the community.

The "Ryan-is-guilty" crowd accused his supporters of being stupid for believing that Sarah had somehow fallen asleep in the tub and drowned. Their attitude was: "Are you freakin' kidding me? Keep the lying bastard locked up."

Ryan's defenders would fire back that the prosecution's case seemed short on evidence and long on speculation. Some even suggested that the local police suffered from the same sort of small-town ineptitude that plagued Deputy Barney Fife in the 1960s TV sitcom, *The Andy Griffith Show*.

And some people, stuck between warring factions, didn't know what to think. They were waiting to learn more.

"My wife fell asleep in the bathtub and I think she's dead."

Dramatic 911 calls such as Ryan Widmer's can make TV ratings and website traffic soar—and the Widmer story had become the next best thing to "viral" for local news outlets.

Cincinnati.com, the region's most-visited internet news site, attracted readers in droves every time a Widmer update was posted. Widmer "clicks" often numbered in the tens of thousands, usually far outpacing the second-most-popular news story.

Predictably, the news media invaded Hopewell Valley.

All four local TV stations would routinely send crews to cover the smallest tidbit of Widmer news. The mere filing of a new court document would be teased as "breaking news" or "the latest development."

Some folks seemed delighted to appear on TV, despite the morbid subject matter and despite the fact that few of them knew much about the Widmers. One TV station aired multiple interviews with a woman who didn't know the Widmers at all, yet she smiled and chuckled about the case on camera.

As the neighbors who were closest to Ryan and Sarah, the Antonczaks found the media onslaught particularly intrusive. They dodged reporters by walking out their back door and through the neighbors' backyard at times.

There was at least one positive effect: Some neighbors who had never spoken before were now talking with each other.

But the case also created rifts. At one neighborhood get-together, someone remarked to Mandy Antonczak and her husband: "Oh, you are the ones who live next door to 'the bathtub killer'"—in essence, convicting Ryan before a trial was ever held.

Mandy told the stranger that it was unfair to judge a person like that. The tension was palpable. Soon it became unbearable. Within a few minutes, the Antonczaks left the gathering.

Along their street, Crested Owl Court, it was almost as though a red line had been drawn between people who would talk to each other and those who wouldn't.

While making routine trips to the grocery store and to other local businesses, Mandy would overhear people talking about "that psycho that killed his wife in the bathtub."

Almost instantly, her neighbor, the easy-going fellow named Ryan Widmer, went from virtual anonymity to ignominy.

Images of Ryan were splashed all over TV, newspapers and the internet.

Everywhere Mandy went, she would hear people declaring opinions based almost exclusively on his appearance.

Sometimes she heard: "He looks like a nice guy. He must be innocent."

Other times: "He looks like a criminal. He must be guilty."

That's what Mandy told me when I interviewed her for a *Cincinnati Enquirer* article published in early 2009. By that time, I had already written a couple dozen Widmer articles. I would eventually write upwards of 100 stories about the case.

I remember that Mandy couldn't envision the Ryan she knew ever killing Sarah. And the Antonczaks heard no arguing next door the night Sarah died—a fact that Mandy recounted on the witness stand.

Mandy tried to keep an open mind, though. She and others who liked Ryan were anxious to see what facts would come out in court.

Regardless of the outcome for Ryan, Sarah's death had left an indelible scar on Mandy's heart—and in the neighborhood.

Sarah's personality was radiant, like the sunrise depicted on Hopewell Valley's entrance signs. But her death—and the prosecution of her husband for murder—left a dark cloud that wouldn't dissipate from Hopewell Valley anytime soon.

"My wife fell asleep in the bathtub and I think she's dead."

Almost from the get-go, alarm bells went off in investigators' heads when they responded to Ryan Widmer's 911 call.

Investigators found no sign that Sarah had taken drugs that could have contributed to her death. They also found no evidence that an intruder had broken into the Widmers' home. So suspicion centered almost immediately on the only other occupant: Ryan.

Yet, behind the scenes, some pieces of evidence weren't neatly fitting into the puzzle that authorities expected to show a murderous husband forcing his wife underwater as she bathed.

First-responding police and medics said Sarah Widmer's body felt "not overly moist," or rather dry when they touched her, but her hair was wet or damp. How was that possible if she had just been submerged in a tubful of water?

And almost everything in the bathroom seemed conspicuously dry for a drowning scene. Investigators were stumped as to why.

Besides finding no splashed water, investigators also found no wet towels—and no freshly-dried towels in the clothes dryer. Either would have been a tell-tale sign that Ryan had cleaned up a watery mess in the aftermath of a forced drowning.

And there was no other glaring sign of a struggle.

Nothing in the bathroom—or elsewhere in the house—was in disarray.

There were no defensive injuries to Sarah's French-manicured fingernails, nor on her toenails, neatly polished pink. There were no bruises or scrapes on the outsides of her elbows, her knuckles or her knees. In fact, police saw no obvious sign of injury on her at the scene—and absolutely no marks on Ryan, who was wearing only boxer briefs at the time.

Years later, precisely what happened to Sarah remained a mystery. Authorities said they never did figure out the exact scenario that ended her life. Neither did the jurors who eventually convicted Ryan.

But the case ignited controversies that shook public faith in the local criminal justice system—effects that would persist long after the jury had spoken.

"My wife fell asleep in the bathtub and I think she's dead."

I had listened to the CD recording of Ryan stating those words more times than I care to count. And even more times than that, I have replayed those words in my head.

Like many people who followed the case, I found myself noticing different things each time I listened—sometimes leaving me warier of Ryan's motives for his statements on that call. Other times, I would be left with the impression that he was just an ordinary guy who was submerged in an extraordinary situation on that night in 2008.

I eventually was able to persuade Ryan and his lawyers to allow me to interview him; I became the first Cincinnati-area reporter to interview Ryan Widmer, after *Dateline NBC* had scooped all of the local press.

As I prepared for the interview, I had hopes that all of my questions would be answered. And while Ryan did answer every question I posed, that two-and-a-half-hour interview at Warren Correctional Institution wasn't nearly long enough to explore every detail that gnawed at me.

Two years later, in 2013, the constant threat of layoffs pushed me out of the news business and into an unrelated career.

Even so, reminders of the Widmer case confronted me almost constantly as I went about my daily business.

My home is close to Hopewell Valley where Ryan and Sarah lived. Often, as I pulled my car into my subdivision, I would think about them and their neighbors, just down the road. Sometimes, I would take a detour and drive past the Widmer house and wonder about the night Sarah died.

I would think about how strange and intrusive I felt when I was the only reporter allowed to go into that house to take notes on the layout of the master suite.

I would drive past the Hamilton Township fire station and think, "I bet one of those ambulances carried Sarah, and some of the medics in there right now tried to save her."

I would drive past Bethesda Arrow Springs hospital and think, "That's where Sarah was pronounced dead. I wonder how many of the people who attended to her still work there."

Finally, as I stood in a record-breaking long line to cast my vote in the November 2016 presidential election, I felt like I had stepped into a time machine. I was standing right next to the courthouse where I covered the Widmer case—all three trials—for the *Enquirer*. Memories came flooding back.

This was where I was as astounded as everyone else when employees of the prosecutor's office hauled the entire bathtub into Judge Bronson's courtroom and plunked it down in front of the jury box for the first time.

This was where I endlessly bugged the kind ladies in the Clerk of Courts office for dozens of public records about the case, and where I interviewed spectators and legal experts.

This was where a cauldron of human emotion boiled over, with an intensity unlike anything I had ever witnessed.

Almost a decade later, many people still wondered whether justice was served for the family of a beautiful young bride who died—or whether a gross injustice was committed against the man she dearly loved.

The case never stopped hurting people's hearts and confounding their minds—mine included.

As I stood there outside that courthouse, I realized I could no longer allow the unanswered questions of the Widmer case to persist without at least trying to find answers.

After that epiphany, circumstances began lining up in just the right way. Soon, I was in touch with many people who had knowledge of the case and its aftermath... including Ohio Prison Inmate No. A599952, Ryan Widmer.

CHAPTER 2
A Love Like No Other

Ryan Widmer had the jitters.

It was the spring of 2007, and Ryan had a six-thousand-dollar engagement ring in hand, ready to ask 23-year-old Sarah Steward to marry him. They had been dating for about nine months and had recently moved into a house they bought together.

At age 26, Ryan felt it was the right time to get married; he wanted to start a family in a few years.

The ring, purchased at a custom Cincinnati-area jeweler, featured a one-carat, princess-cut diamond mounted on a platinum band.

Ryan bought the ring with money he inherited from his grandmother, Ethel Parker, who died of cancer in December 2005. That was nine months before Ryan met Sarah. If Grandma Ethel and Sarah had been able to meet, Ryan was convinced they would have loved each other. He also knew his grandma would have approved of his engagement to Sarah.

Ryan's mom, Jill, adored Sarah and was thrilled with the notion that Sarah might become her daughter-in-law. Sarah already seemed like part of the family. She liked spending weekends with Ryan and his family at their vacation home on Herrington Lake in Kentucky, just south of Lexington. There, they rode jet skis. They splashed in the water with the family dogs. They enjoyed summer holiday parties and cookouts.

So Ryan's mom went with him to pick out Sarah's engagement ring.

Jill thought it was appropriate that Ryan's inheritance from her mother's death was going toward something special. Before she died, Grandma Ethel had specifically requested that her money not be squandered on anything frivolous.

Jill was so excited about the impending proposal, she seemed ready to burst. Ryan was afraid she would slip up, say something about the ring and spoil the surprise for Sarah.

That's why, as soon as Ryan picked up the ring, he felt an urgency to give it to Sarah. With no time to plan an elaborate proposal, he improvised.

Ryan got an idea: He would tie the ring onto the collar of their French bulldog, C.J., named after Cincinnati Bengals wide receiver Chad Johnson.

At first, Sarah didn't much care for the dog, which belonged to Ryan before he and Sarah became a couple. The dog seemed standoffish, was extremely protective of Ryan and barked incessantly. But Sarah had grown to love C.J.

That's why Ryan decided to include him in their pivotal moment.

It was a Friday night. Sarah had just gotten home. She was taking a shower. Ryan grabbed the only thing he could find to tie the ring to the dog's collar, a piece of thick white string.

After Ryan heard the water shut off, he led C.J. upstairs. "He played the part perfect and ran right up to her," Ryan said.

Sarah had just stepped out of the shower and walked past the adjacent bathtub. It took a few seconds for her to notice the string—and the bling—on C.J.'s collar. Sarah's face lit up with a big smile, as she stood there, dripping wet, wrapped in a towel.

Ryan got down on one knee, and—drumroll, please—he asked:

"Will you?"

Nothing more came out of his mouth.

He never completed his Big Question with the traditional words, "…marry me?"

Sarah didn't mind. To her, Ryan's tendency to interrupt himself and to speak in incomplete sentences was part of his charm. He made her giggle.

Ryan admitted he "froze up" a little, even though he knew with all of his heart that he wanted to marry Sarah—and he was pretty certain that she would accept his proposal. When Ryan and Sarah signed the mortgage for their house a few months earlier, it was their intention to spend the rest of their lives together.

So, as Ryan had expected, Sarah said yes to his question.

They got dressed, made some phone calls to relatives and friends to share the happy news, then went out to celebrate.

Their first stop was at Ryan's mom's house, where Jill took a photo of the just-engaged couple on her back deck. It was just before sunset. The Tiki Torches were lit. And Sarah flashed a radiant smile, wearing a white halter-top dress, reminiscent of the one that movie star Marilyn Monroe made iconic in *The Seven-Year Itch.*

Ryan was all-smiles, too. Wearing a turquoise-blue polo shirt, Ryan cradled C.J. in his arms. Sarah placed her left hand on the dog's paw and Ryan's arm, proudly showing off her new engagement ring. They left C.J. behind with Jill, then went out to dinner.

Ryan took Sarah to Antonio's Ristorante Italiano, a classy Italian restaurant in West Chester, Ohio, about a thirty-minute drive from Ryan and Sarah's home.

After Ryan and Sarah left Jill's house, Jill called the restaurant and ordered a congratulatory bottle of champagne to be delivered to the young couple's table.

They were touched by the surprise, thoughtful gesture.

"They had a love like no other," Jill would say later.

Sarah's dad had died a few months earlier, before Ryan had a chance to ask for her hand in marriage. So weeks before the proposal, Ryan had told Sarah's mother, Ruth Ann Steward, about his intentions; she tacitly approved.

After dinner, Ryan and Sarah met Ruth Ann at the Houston Inn, a Mason-area hangout that started in 1953, long before Mason became a mecca for the upper-middle-class.

Ruth Ann, recently widowed, brought a male companion she had known since high school, Mike Grimes, a Butler County Sheriff's deputy.

The four of them—Ruth Ann, Mike, Sarah and Ryan—celebrated.

"It was a great night," Ryan said.

After that memorable evening, Sarah got a kick out of teasing Ryan about the mildly awkward, incomplete wording of his marriage proposal, in such an unlikely spot: the bathroom doorway.

A little more than a year later, Sarah took her last breath in that bathroom; rescuers performed CPR on her *in the same spot where Ryan had knelt down and proposed*—turning a joyful memory of a quirky engagement into an ironic tragedy.

'I love you most'

By all appearances, Ryan and Sarah had one of those coveted relationships. Just by the way they looked at each other, anyone could see that they were in love.

When Sarah talked, Ryan listened intently. Friends said he "hung on her every word," and a love-struck grin would spread across his face.

They would exchange text messages, "I love you more" and "I love you most," in a playful attempt to one-up each other. That little tit-for-tat also popped up in their conversations, handwritten love notes and greeting cards. Their close friends, Dana and Chris Kist, would hear Ryan and Sarah end phone conversations with each other that way.

Yet in some ways, the pair seemed an unlikely match.

Ryan was a big sports fan, a lifelong supporter of his hometown professional teams, Cincinnati Reds baseball and Bengals football.

A Bengals season ticket holder, Ryan weathered the team's string of disappointing losses, remaining steadfast in his support. That type of loyalty was one trait that his buddies and his two brothers admired most about Ryan.

He had a laid-back attitude; he didn't get rattled easily and rarely revealed his emotions. He was quiet around strangers but was sociable after he warmed up to people.

Ryan seemed like the quintessential "nice guy." He was known to walk away from fights, yet he stood up for what he thought was right. He implored bullies to stop picking on other kids at his alma mater, Colerain High School, a suburban Cincinnati football powerhouse.

Ryan was a dedicated athlete, playing as an outfielder for Colerain's baseball team and as a small forward for Colerain's basketball team. He worked hard to get good grades so he would remain eligible to play. Ryan didn't win many awards as an athlete. Although he did play to win, Ryan was driven mostly by his sheer love of sports.

Maybe that's why a favorite high-school athletics memory involves a near-victory, not a win.

The Colerain Cardinals basketball team was playing the Lima Senior High School Spartans, on the Spartans' home court. "They were really good and were ranked high in the state," Ryan said. "We weren't supposed to beat them—and we didn't." Still, he remembers the thrill of the game and the roar of the crowd as the game went down to the wire.

After graduating from Colerain in 1999, Ryan earned a partial athletic scholarship to play baseball at a college with an atmosphere that is the polar opposite of gritty, semi-urban Colerain: Miami University.

Located in the small town of Oxford, Ohio, forty miles northwest of Cincinnati, Miami is marketed as "Ohio's Public Ivy." The school has a reputation for academic excellence, delivered on a picturesque campus of historic red brick buildings and manicured landscapes.

Ryan spent two years at the college's satellite branch in Hamilton, Ohio, before transferring to the main campus. During college, he worked at Enterprise Rent-A-Car in Hamilton. He drove a trusty old purple Toyota Tacoma pickup truck— not exactly a chick magnet. He hung onto it even though some friends laughed about the color. His mom earned a good living, but Ryan didn't want to ask her for money for a new set of wheels. He preferred to be self-reliant, and he wanted to spend his money wisely.

In 2004, Ryan graduated from Miami with a bachelor's degree in sports studies.

That same year, he was hired in the facilities and operations department of the

Western & Southern Open, "the nation's oldest professional tennis tournament played in its city of origin." As a result of connections Ryan made there, he was hired at the Warren County Convention & Visitors Bureau. He began working for its sports marketing department in November 2004.

In contrast, his future wife, Sarah Steward, wasn't a big fan of professional sports. She gave them only passing notice for the most part, until Ryan came along.

Sarah grew up in Butler County, just outside the small city of Trenton, Ohio, along with her brother, Michael Steward Jr. Trenton is about twenty-five miles north of Colerain. With only 10,000 residents, Trenton was about one-sixth Colerain's population.

Yet Trenton and its people have a decidedly blue-collar feel, somewhat like Colerain's. Trenton's largest employer is the Miller beer brewery, a few miles from the AK Steel plant in Middletown, where Sarah's dad, Mike Steward Sr., worked in production planning.

The family lived in the same house on Hope Drive ever since the 1,334-square-foot ranch was built in 1978, shortly after Ruth Ann and Michael Steward were married.

Sarah, born in 1984, was an active child. She was into volleyball, softball, soccer and cheerleading.

Before Sarah graduated from Trenton's Edgewood High School in 2002, she held a part-time photography job at a Sears portrait studio in the Middletown area. She enjoyed coaxing people to smile for the camera. The extra cash came in handy because Sarah loved shopping—something frugal Ryan didn't do much.

Sarah was a lot more high-strung than Ryan was. She had no qualms about letting people know if she was irked. Even though she stood only an inch above five feet tall, Sarah made a commanding presence. That's why Jill Widmer affectionately referred to her as "The Little General," and a childhood friend's mom called her "Sassy Sue." But mostly Sarah was bubbly and beaming. She liked joking around and had an unmistakable high-pitched laugh.

Sarah was ultra-organized and very attentive to detail—attributes that meshed well with her chosen profession as a dental hygienist.

In fact, that was Sarah's dream job. As a child, she loved getting her teeth cleaned so much that she would beg to go back to the dentist's office and have the procedure done again. And that was when she was just 3 years old.

After finishing the dental hygiene program at Raymond Walters College in 2006, Sarah was hired by Dr. John Becker, a dentist in Fort Thomas, Kentucky, five miles from Cincinnati.

Patients loved her engaging personality and the way her bright, white smile welcomed them and set them at ease; they were pleased with the meticulous care she gave to their teeth. Sarah made their experience in the dreaded dentist's chair a lot more pleasant. Sarah particularly charmed little children. Some actually got excited when they knew it was time to go see her at the dentist's office—just like Sarah had been during her own childhood.

Despite the apparent differences between somewhat-reserved Ryan and outgoing, outspoken Sarah, both of them had a playful sense of humor. Both were crazy about dogs. And their married friends, Dana and Chris Kist, sensed that Ryan and Sarah might be good, even great, together.

Dana's husband, Chris, had been Ryan's college baseball teammate at Miami, and they also became roommates. Chris and Ryan also lived together after college for a while.

And Dana, who met Sarah through a mutual friend who was attending dental hygiene school with Sarah, helped Sarah get hired at Dr. Becker's office.

Both Dana and Sarah were energetic, articulate and fun-loving. So they became fast friends.

Dana and Chris equally enjoyed Ryan's company. When the Kists would go out socially, Dana said she was less inclined to chat with groups of women and instead favored talking to Ryan. She enjoyed his down-to-earth personality.

Ryan was a groomsman for Dana and Chris' wedding in 2005 at the House of Deliverance Church in Newport, Kentucky, where Dana's dad was pastor. The couple's wedding guests signed a rectangular piece of photo matting as a keepsake.

Ryan simply signed: "Congrats! Ryan W." Typical Ryan communication—short and to-the-point.

After the Kists were married, Ryan continued to spend a lot of time with them. "He was our 'third wheel' a lot," Dana said with a chuckle.

Ryan disliked striking up conversations with total strangers. So he wasn't overly eager to approach women and ask for dates, Dana said. She couldn't imagine him strolling into a nightclub, sidling up to a cute girl at the bar and unleashing a clever pickup line. Even though Ryan might not like to admit it, "He didn't have 'game,'" Dana said.

Throughout high school and college, Ryan had only a few serious girlfriends. "I didn't want to invest my time in something that wasn't worth it," he said.

After the Kists' wedding, Ryan had reached his mid-20s, and he was hoping to meet the right girl to marry so he could become a father by the time he reached age 30. That was his general plan, anyhow.

Meanwhile, Sarah was spending a lot of time with Dana, and she often crashed at the Kists' home in Anderson Township, on Cincinnati's east side.

Soon, the Kists figured that, because their own relationship was working well, it seemed logical that Sarah, who was a lot like Dana, would be a good fit for Ryan, whose personality was so similar to Chris'.

So the Kists set up a double date at Brazenhead Irish Pub. It was a trendy hangout that had opened the year before in the upscale Cincinnati suburb of Mason, Ohio, where Ryan's mom lived. Touted as "the largest Irish pub in North America," Brazenhead could hold 650 people. The décor was authentically Irish, including three handcrafted wooden bar tops that were shipped from Ireland.

Ryan had never been on a blind date before. He wasn't even sure why he agreed to meet Sarah, other than the fact that he trusted Dana and Chris. Dana had told him that Sarah was smart, small and cute. And she joked about the fact that Sarah was busty. Ryan laughed about that; he agreed to meet her.

He didn't dress up for the occasion. That wasn't Ryan's style anyhow. So, Ryan showed up in a polo shirt, blue jeans and a ball cap, fitting with Brazenhead's casual vibe.

On that August 2006 night, Ryan first went to the home of his brother, Kyle, for a fantasy football draft. Then he went to Brazenhead. When Ryan arrived, the Kists and Sarah were already there. As soon as he laid eyes on Sarah, a blue-eyed blonde, Ryan thought, "Wow, she's attractive." And it felt natural for him to be with her. There were no uncomfortable silences. Just pleasant chatter over appetizers and drinks.

Immediately, Ryan and Sarah seemed to "click," the Kists would later say.

Ryan was intrigued by this young lady who was as fun as she was beautiful. At one point, "I got the nod from Ryan, that this was going good," Chris said.

As the night went on, Ryan decided he liked Sarah a lot. He wanted to get to know her better. Especially because the pub was loud and crowded, making it difficult to have a meaningful conversation.

At the end of the night, Ryan walked Sarah to the Kists' car. She had caught a ride to Brazenhead with them.

Ryan gave Sarah a hug and asked if she wanted to set a time to get together again—just the two of them. She pulled out a little black calendar book and perused it thoughtfully, as though she were having a hard time squeezing in their next date. Then she told Ryan: "I'll pencil you in."

Ryan was afraid that Sarah wasn't interested. But she was. And the pair went on their first solo date at Joe's Crab Shack near Sarah's apartment in Bellevue, Kentucky. Ryan was thrilled that Sarah seemed to really like him—even though his crab-leg-eating skills were subpar and he smoked cigarettes, a habit that she, as a dental hygienist, detested because it affects oral hygiene.

As the couple continued to date, Ryan spotted Sarah's calendar book at her apartment, and he got curious about how full her calendar seemed to be when they first met. So Ryan asked Sarah if he could take a peek at the calendar. She didn't mind.

Ryan turned the page to the week after the double date with the Kists—and found completely blank pages. He thought it was cute that Sarah had pretended to be busy, so she wouldn't seem "too available" or overly eager to see him again.

Ryan, Sarah and the Kists enjoyed quite a few chuckles about Sarah's blank calendar pages.

It didn't take long for Ryan and Sarah to start getting serious about each other.

That fall, Ryan and Sarah went to a Halloween event at Paramount's Kings Island amusement park in Mason, down the road from Brazenhead. Ryan had a work-related appearance to make there that night, so he decided to bring Sarah with him—and she won his heart even more when she showed up wearing a Bengals shirt.

That shirt was brand-new, purchased especially to please him. Sarah had been so smitten with Ryan, she had told Dana, "I guess I need to update my wardrobe and get some Bengals gear because he is such a big Bengals fan."

Sarah was so eager to impress Ryan, she asked Chris to help her understand football. "We spent a whole day with Chris, with him trying to explain football to her," Dana said, laughing. "She still didn't quite 'get' it."

Regardless, Ryan and Sarah soon started spending every day together after work, and they would have long phone conversations when they weren't together.

Sarah's take-charge personality meshed well with Ryan's "go-with-the-flow" style. The Kists say neither Ryan nor Sarah ever told them about any sort of argument. There was no need to argue because Sarah would say what she wanted—and Ryan would acquiesce. "He's not going to waste the energy on a confrontation. He does not like confrontation," Chris said.

After getting together with Sarah, Ryan parted ways with his old purple Toyota Tacoma and replaced it with a newer white Toyota pickup. Maybe that was partly because the vehicle needed replacing and maybe it was partly because Sarah insisted that Ryan get rid of it, Chris said.

Dana said: "He was happy to do whatever she wanted because he was so in love with her and he just wanted to see her happy."

During Ryan's criminal court trials, some incidents that prosecutors portrayed as arguments were actually nothing more than playful banter, taken out of context, the Kists said. The Kists laughed as they recounted an exchange that they would consider typical of Ryan and Sarah:

Sarah took control—as usual—over the décor of their new home. She put her foot down about Ryan not moving his old furniture into their house and instead picked out new furnishings.

Sarah also chose every color of paint that they were using, except she told Ryan he could pick the color for one room.

"But as soon as he brought the paint can back from the store, she took one look at it and said, 'Oh no, that's terrible,'" Dana said. "You're going to have to add some other color to that, or something, because it's awful.' And he was like, 'C'mon, I can't have one color?' And he was joking when he said that." That type of playful teasing was common between Ryan and Sarah.

The Kists say the nature of the couple's relationship was among the many things that were presented unfairly during Ryan's case, casting their friend in a false and unflattering light.

Prosecutors said that sometimes even a couple's closest friends might be unaware of the private turmoil plaguing a relationship.

The Kists remained adamantly skeptical of any claims that Ryan and Sarah had serious issues. The Kists insisted they were close enough to Sarah and Ryan that they would have surely noticed if something had gone terribly wrong in their marriage. Especially because Sarah wasn't the type to hold back how she felt about anything. She was vivacious and could be fiery.

As far as the Kists could see, Ryan and Sarah were deeply in love—and having a ton of fun together, both before and after they were married.

They watched movies with the Kists. They went to Bengals tailgate parties and games. A few times, they returned to Brazenhead for gatherings with the Kists and other friends.

Worries about Sarah

But at many of those places, something unusual would happen with Sarah: She'd fall asleep—right in the middle of the festivities. Friends mostly dismissed it as "just how Sarah was," and laughed it off.

Dana's reaction was different. She harbored real concerns about her friend's well-being, and she told Sarah about them.

Dana, who had been a receptionist at the dental office, was studying to become a registered nurse. Because of her medical knowledge, Dana worried about Sarah's sleepiness more than most people did. Dana also was concerned about Sarah's migraine headaches. And her stomachaches.

Once, Dana said, Sarah complained of a severe headache that made her "see spots." Sarah also described having blurry vision.

But the prevailing problem was her sleepiness.

Sarah's sleepiness was so frequent, it interfered with her social life. "We couldn't watch a movie with her because she'd never get through the whole thing," Dana said. "We'd sit there and try to figure out: What could we do, where could we go, so that Sarah wouldn't end up asleep?"

Dana had seen videos and pictures of Sarah snoozing during noisy parties and family gatherings. "It might be normal for something like that to happen once in a while, if a person's been sick or didn't sleep well or something. But it's just not normal for that to happen *all the time*," Dana said. "Especially not for a young person."

Even Bengals fan Debbie Cupp, whose season-ticket seats had been in front of Ryan's seats for years, noticed something amiss with Sarah.

Shortly after Ryan and Sarah were engaged, Ryan brought Sarah to a Bengals game and introduced her to Debbie.

It was a daytime game and the Paul Brown Stadium crowd was loud. Debbie turned around to say something to Ryan and was startled to see that Sarah had conked out. "That's odd," Debbie thought. But she had just met Sarah and therefore just assumed, "Wow, she must be really tired."

Dana said she witnessed such episodes regularly. That's why she bugged Sarah to ask her doctor about her symptoms; she half-joked that Sarah had narcolepsy, a neurological disorder that causes excessive daytime sleepiness and "sleep attacks." Sarah responded that Dana was worrying needlessly. She would say: "I'm just tired. This is just who I am. I've always been this way."

Ryan was troubled about Sarah's sleepiness, too. He was especially taken aback when Sarah once fell asleep in mid-sentence as she was lying on the couch with her head in his lap.

He believed this was a sign that "something was wrong with her," so he implored Sarah to consult with her doctor.

So, to appease Ryan and Dana, Sarah had a talk with her physician in June 2008, two months before she died, Ryan said. According to Ryan, Sarah said the doctor brushed aside concerns about her sleepiness, telling her that some people just naturally sleep more than others.

Ryan's lawyers raised questions about this reported conversation between Sarah and her physician. Although her doctor was not called to testify, his file on Sarah was subpoenaed for use in court. The file had no notation about a conversation on sleepiness. And Sarah's mom testified she didn't know anything about it, either.

So, as far as prosecutors were concerned, the sleepiness discussion between Sarah and her doctor may have never happened at all.

Or maybe the doctor didn't take note of the conversation because Sarah downplayed the seriousness of her problems. Dana thinks that's probably what happened.

Dana said she could envision Sarah half-heartedly mentioning Ryan's concerns to the doctor. "I could see her totally blowing it off," Dana said. "That's what she did when I tried to talk to her about it."

Sarah had found ways to cope. Before work and during her lunch hour, she would go out to her car to take naps. Or Sarah would go into a dark, window-less room at the dentist's office, and curl up with a blanket. She had learned that avoiding light and other visual stimuli helped to ease her migraine head-aches.

Sarah would take Excedrin pain reliever and ibuprofen tablets for her head-aches.

And she would take long, hot baths, a habit well-known to Ryan, to her family and to her close friends.

Thus, Sarah's physical discomforts caused only minor annoyances in an other-wise seemingly idyllic life that was unfolding for the young couple.

'The kind of young man he was'

Ryan's career was on the upswing at the Convention & Visitors Bureau. He had started as a sports marketing assistant and was promoted to sports marketing manager in February 2006, a few months before he met Sarah. By the time that they were married in 2008, he had been promoted to sales manager.

Ryan looked forward to going to work every day. He loved his co-workers. They loved him, too. He was pleasant and hard-working.

With only nine employees, the office was close-knit. Ryan endeared himself to the crew of mostly older women by his gentlemanly gestures, such as lifting boxes laden with marketing materials—even before anyone asked him to lend a hand.

Generally, the group would order lunch to be brought in and they'd eat together. But Ryan began leaving on his lunch hours in 2005. They later learned why: He was going home to take care of Grandma Ethel while she was dying of cancer.

Once, in a poignant moment, Jill Widmer came home and saw Ryan lying alongside his grandmother, comforting her on her deathbed. Those are the types of stories that Ryan's friends would tell about him, calling him a gentle soul who wouldn't hurt anyone.

Ryan and his colleagues worked to promote Warren County as a destination for tourists and major events. Thanks largely to Paramount's Kings Island amusement park and The Beach waterpark, both in Mason, Warren County's top industry was tourism. That's why the Visitors Bureau labeled the county "Ohio's Largest Playground" in its marketing materials. And Ryan was doing a good job of lining up major sporting events, including a national gymnastics championship, a junior golf qualifier and a regional jump-rope contest.

Ryan's success in his job was somewhat surprising because he was not a naturally gifted verbal communicator. He was known to interrupt himself, to misspeak and to speak in incomplete sentences—just as he did during his marriage proposal.

His dad, Gary, admits to similar communication snafus and said he has been told that he writes much more clearly than he speaks. He thought Ryan probably inherited those traits from him.

But Ryan was intelligent and he worked hard to hone his verbal skills. He took constructive criticism to heart. He took advantage of workshops that his employer offered. And those efforts were paying off.

Likewise, Sarah was doing well in her job as a dental hygienist. More patients were requesting her to clean their teeth and made positive comments about her as they came and went.

And both Ryan and Sarah excitedly shared snippets of their blossoming love story with friends and co-workers.

Dana said Sarah gushed about Ryan and how sweet he was. "Soon after they got together, she told me, 'He's 'The One,'" Dana said.

Before Sarah came into his life, Ryan seemed a bit down-in-the-dumps in the wake of his grandmother's death. "He used to come into work on Mondays and not have much to say about his weekends. His weekends weren't very meaningful," said Ryan's co-worker, Lori Worley. "Then he met Sarah, and it was 'Sarah, Sarah, Sarah.' And I was like, 'Wow, he really likes this girl.'"

Soon it became obvious that "he absolutely, positively loved this girl," Lori said.

Yet amid Ryan's joy about his new relationship, he was not self-absorbed like most young folks, Lori said.

Knowing that Lori was going through a difficult divorce, there were times when Ryan would sense that Lori was having a tough day. Without her even saying a word, Ryan would tell her: "I'll cover the phones for you. Go take a break," Lori recalled. "That's the kind of young man he was."

Lori met Sarah a few times at outings with other bureau employees and also attended the couple's wedding.

Lori's impression of Sarah: "She was beautiful, smart and spunky—and she wasn't going to take shit from anyone. I remember telling Ryan, 'You've got a live wire here!'"

The only extraordinary stressor that Ryan and Sarah endured during their courtship was the terminal illness and death of Sarah's dad, Michael Steward Sr. He was suffering from malignant melanoma when Ryan and Sarah met; he died at age 53 on March 2, 2007.

That was just after Ryan and Sarah bought their home in Warren County, and less than six months after Ryan and Sarah first met. So, Ryan had little chance to get to know Sarah's dad before he passed away. But Ryan thought he was fascinating.

Michael Steward Sr. was a brilliant man who held a Ph.D. in martial arts sciences and philosophy. He self-published two books related to those subjects. He was an acclaimed international expert who performed martial arts demonstrations in eleven foreign countries. His family sometimes went along on those trips. And when they did, Sarah would let out her trademark squeal to cheer for her dad—and the family's friends would smile about her sweet, unbridled enthusiasm.

Sarah's dad was also acclaimed for training four national martial-arts champions and copyrighting a self-defense program. Although Sarah didn't practice martial arts, friends described her as a "Daddy's girl" who may have gleaned some self-defense or martial-arts knowledge from her dad.

Considering that background and Sarah's feisty personality, it's doubtful that Sarah would have allowed anyone, including Ryan, to get the best of her, Ryan's supporters said.

After Sarah's father passed away, Ruth Ann relied on Sarah's strength to help her cope with the loss of her husband of thirty years. Mother and daughter even somewhat reversed roles, with Sarah serving as the nurturer.

Sarah and her mom were very emotionally close, a bond that strengthened as they mourned Michael Sr.'s death. The women would get together nearly every Friday, Sarah's day off from work. They would spend the day shopping, running errands and grabbing a bite to eat.

Likewise, Ryan was very close to his mother, Jill. She and Ryan's dad, Gary, were divorced in 1990. The resulting tension drove a wedge between Gary and the three sons he had with Jill: Kyle, Ryan and his twin brother, Ayran—pronounced "Air-ran," but instead of using the conventional spelling, "Aaron," Jill came up with lettering that was similar to Ryan's.

By 2000, Gary and the boys had ceased contact.

So Gary was absent from the list of more than two hundred people who attended Ryan and Sarah's wedding in spring 2008.

Planning a wedding

After Ryan and Sarah were engaged, they divvied up the necessary tasks. Ryan agreed to take care of the reception and the honeymoon arrangements; Sarah, the wedding. And he pretty much gave Sarah carte blanche for that.

Ryan had the simpler part of the job. He reserved a limousine and booked the reception at Four Bridges Country Club in Liberty Township, where his mom had some connections.

Ryan arranged for airline flights that would take them to their honeymoon destination, a resort in Costa Rica, the Central American country that beckons tourists with beaches, jungles and hot springs.

He also reserved a nice room at the Hyatt Place hotel near Mason, where they would spend their wedding night. Earlier in the day, Chris Kist went to the hotel with Ryan so they could sprinkle red rose petals onto the king-size bed in a sentimental, romantic gesture.

Like many brides, Sarah had been envisioning The Big Day for years. She set the date for April 19, 2008.

In preparation for their first dance as husband and wife, Ryan and Sarah took ballroom-dancing lessons for about eight weeks prior to the wedding. Jill was surprised that her son, who didn't feel particularly comfortable on the dance floor, had agreed to do that. He wasn't the kind of guy to "bust a move."

But Ryan went all-in with the "whatever-you-want-honey" mindset. He learned how to waltz to a Tim McGraw country tune, even though he didn't like country music. He just wanted to please Sarah.

Managing the flurry of wedding details had turned Sarah into "a little bit of a 'Bridezilla,'" Dana joked, a reference to the *Bridezillas* TV program about stressed-out brides behaving like Godzilla, the monster in cheesy Japanese movies.

Sarah wrote a love note to Ryan, apologizing for being snippy and exclaiming how happy she felt about their wedding day: "I can't believe it's finally here!"

She had selected a half-dozen bridesmaids: Dana, three other friends and two cousins. And Sarah cracked the whip to make sure *everything* met her specifications, from head to toe: hairstyles, makeup palettes, jewelry, French manicures, dresses and shoes.

Lined up next to Sarah, the bridesmaids' periwinkle dresses highlighted Sarah's blue eyes.

Their bouquets reflected Sarah's personality—mostly bright and dramatic, with Gerbera daisies and calla lilies in rich yellow, orange, magenta and red hues—but accented with sweetness in periwinkle and purple.

Sarah had gone on a sensible but focused diet-and-exercise regimen to slim down, shedding twenty pounds so that her strapless gown, with a sweetheart neckline, tight bodice and billowing tulle skirt, would look even more flattering on her.

The white gown contrasted with her sun-kissed skin and bounced light onto her perfectly coiffed, shiny blond up-do, held in place with a thin white headband. A sheer white veil trailed elegantly down her back.

Ryan said he will never forget how stunningly beautiful Sarah looked. In his eyes, she always looked amazing. But on this day, he considered her to be flawless. He told Sarah's mom that he felt blessed to be marrying her beautiful daughter.

Before the wedding, Ryan joined his groomsmen—his two brothers, two cousins, matchmaker Chris Kist and Sarah's brother, Mike Steward Jr.—for a few beers in the church basement. Hanging out with them was one of his fondest memories of that day.

Ryan worried that the wedding officiant, a Catholic priest, might notice the smell of alcohol on their breaths. But he felt no anxiety about getting married.

"I wasn't nervous at all. I remember that with certainty," Ryan said. "I knew I was in the perfect place with the perfect girl. I just remember thinking how beautiful she looked and how lucky I felt to be marrying her."

Sarah chose the historic Holy Trinity Church, the first Roman Catholic church built in Middletown, Ohio, as the wedding venue. The couple smiled radiantly as they posed for a photo in front of the church's century-old rock-faced limestone façade and large oak doors.

Although Sarah attended the modern St. Susanna Catholic Church in Mason, she wanted to get married at Holy Trinity, partly because she fell in love with its appearance. Stained-glass windows soar two stories tall on three sides of the Romanesque Revival building, built in 1898.

Sadly, the church also had been the venue for the funeral Mass for Sarah's dad in the winter of 2007. Perhaps having the wedding there helped Sarah to feel her dad's presence.

After Sarah made her way down the aisle to the "Trumpet Voluntary" wedding march, Sarah's mom stood in place of Sarah's dad, and "gave her away" in marriage.

The platinum wedding bands that Ryan and Sarah exchanged were both inscribed with their wedding date inside. As an added touch, the inscription included their favorite lovey-dovey saying. Sarah's read, "I love you more." The one Sarah gave to Ryan read, "I love you most," symbolizing that Sarah wanted to have the last word about that.

Ryan's co-worker, Lori Worley, was struck by how great Ryan and Sarah looked at their wedding. She felt a strong positive "vibe" about their relationship: "You could just tell they were so 'into' each other, and that made the wedding all the more beautiful." They exuded an air of comfort and confidence that made Lori think this was a marriage that was meant to last.

St. Susanna's priest, Father John Tonkin, came to Holy Trinity to preside over the nuptials at the couple's request. He pronounced them husband and wife until death would part them.

That day would come just 114 days later. Then, the same priest who had united the couple in marriage would conduct Sarah's memorial service before a shell-shocked congregation at his home church.

CHAPTER 3
Subtle Signs of Murder

Criminal defense lawyers are accustomed to late-night phone calls from pan-icked people.

So, when attorney Charlie H. Rittgers answered his telephone around midnight on August 12, 2008, about twenty-four hours after Sarah Widmer died, he thought it was just another run-of-the-mill case.

On the other end of the phone was Kathy Clark. She worked with Jill Wid-mer at Luxottica, an Italian eyewear company that employed more than seven hundred people at its North American headquarters near Jill's home in Mason, Ohio.

Kathy was concerned that Jill's son, Ryan, had agreed to meet a detective the next morning—and he was planning to go alone, without a lawyer's counsel. Kathy and other friends doubted that was a good idea.

So Kathy contacted an attorney whom she knew through her job. He suggested that Kathy call Rittgers, saying he was probably the best-qualified local lawyer to handle it.

Suspicious deaths—and serious crimes of any sort—are pretty rare in Warren County, where Rittgers' law practice is based. So, Rittgers was among only a handful of nearby attorneys who had been involved with such cases; he had represented defendants in about a half-dozen homicides.

At the time Rittgers got that midnight call about the Widmer case, he had been practicing law for thirty years. And he was well-respected, having served as president of the county bar association and the Ohio Association of Criminal Defense Lawyers.

Rittgers also was well-connected. He was on friendly terms with key players in the local criminal justice system, including the county prosecutor, Rachel Hutzel. Courtroom adversaries—defense lawyers and prosecutors—often enjoy each other's company when they're away from the heat of litigation. That's how it was with Rittgers and Hutzel.

To Rittgers, the case Kathy Clark outlined on the phone sounded sad, but not necessarily criminal. A young woman had died suddenly, and the police wanted to talk to her husband.

It would be routine for police to question the husband, Rittgers thought, even if there was no glaring sign of anything nefarious. So Rittgers doubted this situation would amount to much. He imagined that he would just "run interference" for the husband, Ryan. Rittgers would serve as a comfortable buffer between Ryan and the police in a tragic, stressful situation. And that would be the end of it.

Rittgers was wrong about that.

The late-night phone call with Ryan propelled Rittgers into the most challenging case he had ever faced. The Widmer case would burrow into his heart and soul. It would cause him stress and strain like no other case ever had. And it would leave him second-guessing himself almost a decade later.

"I didn't think there was a murder or anything like that," Rittgers said in 2017, recalling his initial thoughts as he talked to Ryan. "I just thought the police were following up because there was a death. So I said, 'Yeah, I'll talk to the guy. No problem.'"

Kathy, who was with Ryan and his mother at Jill's house, handed the phone to Ryan. Rittgers asked him what happened.

As Ryan talked and sobbed, Rittgers scrawled notes on an unlined white piece of paper: names, phone numbers and a few biographical details about Ryan.

"You always want to be cautious and get some background on the client. But this guy, he was college-educated, with no criminal history, had only been married a few months," Rittgers said. "He didn't fit any kind of criminal profile, and it didn't appear that there were going to be any charges."

Ryan seemed iffy about even getting a lawyer.

But a chorus of voices had warned Ryan that it would be foolish for him—or for anyone—to meet alone with the police.

One of those voices was his cousin Sean Cronin. Earlier in the day, Ryan had talked on the phone with Sean. As kids, Sean and his two brothers would hang out with Ryan and his two brothers.

"We were like six brothers, growing up together," Sean said.

The boys were all very athletic. They would sometimes "roughhouse," as boys often do—and Sean laughed when recounting Ryan's uninspired attempts to go along with it. "It was comical," he said.

Ryan was calm, even somewhat stoic—one of the least-confrontational people Sean had ever known.

Sean was far more aggressive than Ryan ever hoped to be. While Sean played as a defensive lineman for Georgetown College in Kentucky, his team secured national championships in 2000 and 2001. Then Sean became an acclaimed college football coach.

At the time of Ryan and Sarah's wedding in spring 2008, Sean was a graduate assistant, coaching football at the University of Florida. Sean and his future wife, Emily, traveled to Ohio for the wedding.

That summer, when Sean got word that Sarah had drowned, he was thunderstruck.

He felt awful for Ryan. Sean offered his condolences to Ryan by phone on Tuesday, August 12th, the day after Sarah's death. Ryan mentioned that he was going to meet with a detective the following morning. Sean asked Ryan if a lawyer would be going with him.

"No, I don't need a lawyer," Ryan said. "Why would I need a lawyer?"

Those responses left Sean feeling uneasy. But, then again, that was how Ryan was: naïve and trusting.

For the moment, Sean set aside his concerns about the lack of a lawyer. He didn't want to criticize his cousin at such a sensitive time. He repeated how sorry he was about Sarah's death. Then he ended the call.

Later, Sean shared the gist of that conversation with a high-powered Florida lawyer. That attorney's reaction was unforgettably visceral. He grabbed Sean by both sides of his shirt collar and jerked Sean close to his face, "just like they do in the movies," Sean said.

Then the lawyer said, "Listen to me, you dumb son of a bitch! Innocent people get locked up every day in this country. You get that kid a lawyer right now!"

That shocked Sean into realizing the gravity of the situation that his cousin might be facing.

With a lump in his throat, Sean called Ryan back and told him in no uncertain terms: Dude, you need a lawyer.

Still, Ryan was resistant.

Ryan's experience with the legal system was limited to a stint on jury duty and a single traffic ticket for turning the wrong way onto a one-way street.

Nothing alarmed him about his phone conversation with Lieutenant Jeff Braley, who said he wanted to "update" Ryan about the investigation into Sarah's death. During that call, Ryan was riding in a car with his mom, Sarah's mom and Sarah's aunt Kathy Steward. They had just left the Middletown, Ohio, funeral home that would handle Sarah's arrangements.

The three women heard Ryan's end of the conversation. None of them seemed concerned about it. Ryan offered to meet Braley at the police station right away. But Braley said, no, come to the police station at 9 the next morning.

Friends and relatives warned him: You're going to be interrogated. And they didn't think she should go alone.

Confused and concerned, Ryan called a good friend, attorney Zak Zoz, to ask his opinion. Zak agreed: Get a lawyer.

Ryan relented. That's when his mom's friend, Kathy, made some inquiries on his behalf, resulting in the late-night call to Charlie Rittgers.

After hearing Ryan share his version of the events, Rittgers thought it sounded plausible that Sarah had fallen asleep and drowned. Later, Rittgers learned that was virtually impossible. "But I didn't know that at the time; Ryan didn't know that. We're not experts," Rittgers said.

Ryan's initial "story" didn't seem suspicious to Rittgers. Not at all.

Even so, Rittgers reinforced what everyone else was telling Ryan: You need a lawyer. "Even if it's not me," Rittgers said.

By this time, Ryan was feeling queasy. "I guess I just started to sense something bad was happening," he said.

So, Ryan agreed to hire Rittgers. That was sometime in the early hours of Wednesday, August 13, 2008.

A note in Rittgers' file says Ryan would pay a one-thousand-dollar retainer for Rittgers to "hand-hold" him during the scheduled meeting with the police about nine hours later.

That meeting never happened.

Before that day ended, Ryan would be locked up on a murder charge.

Questions and contradictions

Ryan's decision to hire a lawyer probably added fuel to the fire of suspicion. Detectives often assume that a suspect who gets "lawyered up" has something to hide.

But defense lawyers argue that ordinary people, guilty or innocent, aren't equipped to go up against trained interrogators. Their tactics are designed to trip up the guilty but also might snare an innocent person into making self-incriminating statements. When cops give the Miranda Warning—"anything you say can and will be used against you in a court of law"—they mean it.

The closest thing to an interrogation of Ryan happened within a few minutes of his wife being declared dead.

After Ryan made a dozen phone calls trying to reach his mother and Sarah's mother, he did finally connect with both women as the ambulance screeched toward Bethesda Arrow Springs hospital in Lebanon, sirens wailing. In the back of the ambulance, medics were furiously working to save Sarah's life. Ryan was in the front, making calls to both moms and crying.

Ryan's mother, Jill, arrived at the hospital first because she lived closer to Bethesda than Sarah's mom did.

Escorted into a chapel-type waiting room while doctors continued working on Sarah, Jill and Ryan hoped and prayed that Sarah would be OK. They sat in the room by themselves for what seemed like a frustratingly long time.

Finally, a nurse entered and asked if she could get them anything. Jill asked: "Are you still working on Sarah?" No, the nurse replied.

A terrible feeling welled up inside of Jill; she felt compelled to ask another question, dreading the answer—but at the same time, knowing in her heart what that answer would be.

She gulped and forced out the words: "Is she gone?" Yes, the nurse replied.

Ryan fell to his knees next to a chair. He buried his face into the seat cushion. His body convulsed with sobs.

Time of death: 11:41 p.m. Monday, August 11, 2008. That was fifty-two minutes after Ryan had called 911.

"I didn't want to believe she was dead," Ryan remembers thinking at the time. "I wanted them to save her."

Jill asked the nurse if she and Ryan could go say goodbye to Sarah. "No," the nurse said, offering no explanation.

At 12:08 a.m., Sarah's mom, Ruth Ann Steward, was allowed to go see Sarah. At first, she didn't know that Sarah had already passed away. A nurse had entrusted a relative with Sarah's sole personal possession at the time of her death: A pair of white stone stud earrings.

Coroner's Investigator Doyle Burke entered the chapel.

Burke offered his condolences to Ryan and his mom, identified himself as a coroner's investigator who was working with the police, and started asking Ryan questions.

Ryan didn't know what a coroner's investigator was; he said later he was too upset to comprehend much. Jill didn't quite understand who Burke was, either, because she was still in shock, she said.

Regardless, Ryan talked to Burke. Ryan said he was willing to provide any information that would shed light on what had happened to Sarah.

Burke and Ryan met sometime after midnight on August 12th.

By 12:35 a.m., Burke had obtained Ryan's signature on a "consent-to-search" form, which gave investigators the right to probe the newlyweds' home for clues about Sarah's death. Burke had agreed to get that form signed for Braley.

Ryan said he signed the form without hesitation. "I didn't question it or think about it one bit," he said. Ryan said he had nothing to hide, so he "never gave a thought" to signing away his rights. And he certainly didn't think Burke or the police suspected him of doing anything harmful to Sarah. Ryan said he thought, "They were trying to figure out what happened to her."

Eventually, Ryan said he got a rude awakening. He became convinced that investigators never explored other possible explanations for Sarah's drowning. He settled on the firm belief that the investigators, after encountering a death they considered unusual, leapt to the conclusion that he had killed Sarah, even before much, if any, investigation had been done. "They were blaming me from the beginning," he said, "and I had no idea."

Maybe the investigators' suspicions were justified. The interview Ryan gave to Burke and the statements Ryan made during his 911 call were both riddled with inconsistencies and with comments that seemed extraneous.

Back at the scene, a whirlwind of questions picked up momentum, swirling faster as emergency crews and investigators scratched their heads, trying to make sense of Sarah's death. Several police officers gathered around and listened while a dispatcher played back a recording of Ryan's words on the 911 call. They couldn't reconcile his statements with other clues—nor with their gut instincts.

Among the most glaring immediate questions:

Why would Ryan begin the 911 call by stating his wife "fell asleep in the bathtub," immediately offering an "excuse" for why his wife would end up unresponsive in the bathtub?

Why did he assume she was dead? Did he already *know* she was dead because he had killed her?

Why was there so little moisture on and around Sarah after Ryan told the dispatcher that he had found her submerged in a tubful of water?

Police also were suspicious that Ryan felt the need to tell the 911 operator that he was downstairs watching TV, then came upstairs and found Sarah in the tub. Was he trying to establish an alibi for himself—away from the scene where his wife drowned?

Ryan also told several police officers something more specific: He was watching the Bengals preseason game vs. the Green Bay Packers.

Well, then, police wondered: Why was the downstairs TV tuned to *the wrong channel* for the Bengals game—and, instead, the *upstairs* TV was tuned to the Bengals' channel?

That type of contradiction—a suspect's assertion conflicting with factual evidence—has tripped up many a guilty defendant.

Like hawks that can spot rabbits from a mile away, detectives swoop in on inconsistencies like that one. Still, police trainers and crime-investigation experts warn that hyper-focusing on details can blind detectives to the rest of the investigative landscape if they're not careful.

No obvious trauma

At 11:30 the night Sarah died, Doyle Burke, the coroner's investigator, had received a call summoning him to the hospital to investigate a death. That was eleven minutes before a doctor officially declared Sarah deceased. But it had become clear that valiant life-saving efforts were doomed; Sarah never exhibited any flicker of life during forty-five minutes of aggressive efforts to revive her.

No breathing. No heartbeat. Nothing.

Burke spoke to the Hamilton Township paramedics who worked on Sarah. "None (of them) noted any dampness in the carpeted area where the deceased was found," he noted.

Burke examined Sarah's body and wrote: "The deceased was naked and showed no obvious sign of trauma."

Burke saw no telltale sign of murder. If there had been, Burke almost certainly would have picked up on it.

Before being hired to work as a coroner's investigator in Warren County, Burke served as a cop in Dayton, Ohio for twenty-nine years, including a long stint as a homicide detective.

The notes Burke took at the hospital continued: "Deceased's hair was wet, but her skin was not." That description was written more than an hour after Ryan had called 911—at a time when Sarah's skin would be *expected* to be dry. So why did Burke point that out? Perhaps Burke was just being detailed and thorough. Or was his notation a sign that investigators were influencing each other's perceptions?

Ryan and his lawyers thought so.

Although Ryan told the 911 dispatcher that the tub water was "draining" and was "completely drained," nearly everyone who responded to the scene commented that they had expected more wetness at a drowning.

Were first-responders unaware that Ryan had told the dispatcher that the bathwater was gone? Or had they disregarded Ryan's statement because they

41

thought he was lying about draining the bathtub—and about many other things, too?

A guilty conscience?

After Sarah was pronounced dead at the hospital, Ryan's mom, Jill, drove to Ryan's house to pick up some clothes for him. He waited as his mom went upstairs without him. He couldn't bear the thought of going back to the spot where his beautiful young bride had just taken her last breaths.

The house was deserted and eerily quiet. The crime-scene tape had been taken down, and C.J. the dog was gone; police had left him with a neighbor.

There was no sign that anything unusual had even happened, Jill thought—until she went to the master bedroom to get Ryan's clothes. She noticed squares of carpeting had been cut out and removed, leaving bare spots on the floor near the master bath.

How strange, she thought.

Then Jill stepped into the adjoining bathroom to take a look around. She spotted Sarah's wedding and engagement rings on the bathroom vanity. She grimaced as she pictured Sarah removing her jewelry before stepping into the tub and then, inexplicably, drowning.

Jill wondered: What in the world could have gone wrong with her? The thought never crossed her mind that anyone would blame Ryan for Sarah's death.

Ryan was a sweet, thoughtful son, the kind of young man who would go out of his way to help with any task before he was even asked.

And Sarah was like the daughter that Jill, a mother of three boys, never had.

Already steeped in sadness, Jill felt an even harder pang of pathos as she picked up Sarah's rings.

She flashed back to helping her son shop for Sarah's engagement ring. She remembered the couple's excitement when they came to her house to show it off. She thought about how happy Ryan and Sarah had seemed on their wedding day as they exchanged their shiny platinum rings. But now, considering Sarah's sudden death and Ryan's gut-wrenching grief, the wedding bands somehow seemed to have lost their luster.

Jill picked up the rings, went downstairs and handed them to Ryan. She hoped the jewelry might help him feel closer to Sarah. But she also knew the rings would painfully remind Ryan of the love he had lost.

He clenched the rings, his only tangible connection to Sarah. And he wept, missing her. He remembered thinking, "I still hadn't wrapped my head around what happened and why Sarah was gone."

Meanwhile, Jill's sister and brother-in-law, Jackie and Kevin Cronin—the parents of Ryan's football-coaching cousin, Sean—were waiting at Jill's house, ready to console Ryan and Jill when they arrived.

That night, the four of them sat at Jill's dining room table. They cried and talked about Sarah until about 5 o'clock that morning.

Then Ryan collapsed onto his stomach on his mom's couch, crying, "just trying to understand how Sarah could have died," he said.

He said it tormented him to know that while he was downstairs watching TV, Sarah was upstairs in the bathroom, drowning—alone. If only he had gone upstairs sooner, maybe he would have been able to save her. He wracked his brain for some insight, some revelation about what had happened to Sarah.

At least that's what Ryan said he was thinking that night.

Skeptics might counter: If Ryan felt horrible, maybe that was because he knew he had just committed murder—and he was afraid he would get caught.

Co-workers see a tragedy; coroner sees a killing

After that long, traumatic Monday night, Ryan called his workplace the next morning, Tuesday, August 12th, to say that he would be absent from work because Sarah had died.

His co-workers at the Warren County Convention & Visitors Bureau were floored.

They had happily witnessed the couple's courtship. They teased Ryan about taking pre-wedding dance lessons because they couldn't imagine Ryan being much of a dancer. They loved seeing Sarah at office outings, including the annual Cincinnati Reds' Opening Day celebration.

Nearly all of Ryan's colleagues had attended the couple's wedding in April 2008.

And now, just a few months afterward, it was unbearable to hear that Sarah, only 24 years old, was gone—and that Ryan, at age 27, instantly changed from newlywed to widower.

Ben Huffman, Ryan's boss, took the startling call from Ryan's mom, Jill. He went to see the bureau's executive director, Shirley Bonekemper, in her office. Ben shut the door and told Shirley: "I have to tell you something horrible." He was in tears as he announced what Jill had told him: "Sarah fell asleep in the bathtub and drowned."

Shirley gasped. She was practically speechless at first.

But then Shirley realized that, as the office's leader, she needed to call an emergency staff meeting. The staff huddled together and wept in the conference room—where Lieutenant Jeff Braley would later interrogate all of them.

That afternoon, Shirley called Ryan to express her condolences. "On the phone, he would sound really 'dry' to anyone else. But because I know him, I could tell he was in shock," she said.

That day, while Ryan was making funeral arrangements for Sarah, Braley and Coroner's Investigator Doyle Burke had driven north to Dayton, Ohio, so they could be present for Sarah's autopsy.

It was performed at the Miami Valley Regional Crime Laboratory. The Warren County coroner, Dr. Russell Uptegrove, worked there as a forensic pathologist—a medical doctor with years of extra training about performing autopsies and determining causes of deaths.

Uptegrove quickly issued a preliminary ruling on her cause of death: drowning. The manner of death: homicide. Critics later pointed out that Uptegrove made that ruling based on incomplete information.

Ryan's lawyers envisioned Braley possibly making influential statements to Uptegrove during Sarah's autopsy—and they speculated that Braley, who was known to enjoy the media spotlight, may have pressured Uptegrove to make a speedy decision.

But there was no recording of the autopsy-room conversations, and Uptegrove denied that he just rubber-stamped what Braley told him.

Regardless, Uptegrove's homicide declaration allowed Braley to shift into high gear against Ryan.

"This would not have been a case without Uptegrove," Rittgers said. "He came to his conclusion—and everyone ran with it."

Thus, the wheels were already in motion for Ryan to be charged with killing Sarah. But neither Ryan nor Rittgers had a clue. "The train had already left the station," Rittgers said, "and we didn't even know it at the time."

So, while Ryan made his emotional, late-night call to Rittgers the evening after Sarah's autopsy, he was unaware that Braley already had the homicide ruling in his back pocket.

First thing the following morning, Wednesday, August 13th, Rittgers called Braley on Ryan's behalf.

There are conflicting accounts about what happened next.

In a memo for his case file, Braley wrote that he received a voicemail from Rittgers, "stating he had been retained to represent Ryan Widmer and he would not be available for an interview."

But Rittgers denies he ever flat-out refused to make Ryan available to talk with Braley. Rittgers said he might have stated that Ryan was unable to meet at that specific time, but he wouldn't have "closed the door" to meeting with Braley.

At some point that day, Rittgers did speak with Braley. And, during that conversation, Braley made it clear that he had no interest in talking with Ryan, Rittgers said: "He assumed it was a murder from the beginning, and he was sticking with that."

Rittgers asked Ryan to come to his office in Lebanon, Ohio, a few miles from the hospital where Sarah had been pronounced dead.

Ryan and his mother showed up promptly.

That morning, Ryan's first statement filled three yellow legal-sized pages of notes. "He told me, in detail, everything that he remembered," Rittgers said.

Soon, Rittgers broke the news to Ryan: "They're most likely going to charge you with murder."

Ryan's whole body trembled. He rocked forward and back in his seat, his arms hugging his midsection.

"Calm down," Rittgers told him. Ryan found that impossible. He was scared and confused.

"How in the f_ck can I calm down?" Ryan responded. He said later, "It made no sense and I couldn't understand what was going on."

As new facts emerged, Ryan never tried to alter his story to fit the evidence, his attorneys said—not even when doing so would have benefited him. "That said a lot to me," Rittgers said. "Ryan never gave me a reason to disbelieve him."

But authorities found plenty of reasons to doubt almost everything Ryan had said the night Sarah died.

From funeral home to jail

After learning Ryan was going to be charged with murder, Rittgers sprang into action.

He fired off an electronic message to the state criminal defense lawyers group, seeking advice about strategy and experts for a disputed death case.

That's how Rittgers got connected with Dr. Werner Spitz, an internationally acclaimed forensic pathologist.

He testified to Congress about the assassinations of President John F. Kennedy and civil rights leader Dr. Martin Luther King Jr. And he had testified in dozens of famous court cases, including the California civil trial of O.J. Simpson, the former pro football star who was acquitted in the 1994 slaying of his ex-wife, Nicole Brown Simpson, and her friend, Ron Goldman.

Now Spitz was being recruited to offer his opinion about the death of 24-year-old newlywed Sarah Widmer in southwest Ohio.

Rittgers thought: This guy's the Grand Poohbah of Death Investigation. Why not get the best?

Rittgers began amassing as much information as possible to defend Ryan—the new client whose seemingly mundane case had suddenly become a very big deal.

After Ryan and his mother left Rittgers' office, they drove a half-hour to return to the Middletown funeral home to finalize Sarah's arrangements.

This time, Jill and Ryan also had a new request for the funeral home: keep Sarah's body intact until Spitz could come and conduct a separate, independent autopsy on her.

Because of the planned autopsy, "I was told I couldn't even touch Sarah, but I did get to see her one last time," Ryan said.

Hesitantly, Ryan walked into the room where Sarah lay on a table, dreading what he was about to see, yet feeling as though seeing Sarah, cold and lifeless, would force him to believe the unbelievable. "I was still in just so much shock that she was gone," he said.

Sarah was lying on a table, covered with a plain white sheet from shoulders to toes; her face was even more pale than Ryan had imagined it would be. His mom, Jill, kept her arm draped around Ryan's shoulders as he wept and told Sarah: "I love you most."

After confronting the horrible, undeniable reality that Sarah was gone, Ryan's thoughts shifted to his hopes for the second autopsy: Surely that would reveal why Sarah had drowned.

While Ryan was still at the funeral home, Rittgers called and informed Ryan: The police had a murder warrant with his name on it. He advised Ryan to come to his office and turn himself in to the police. Ryan agreed to do that. But he was dumbfounded.

He was a dazed, nervous wreck.

Katie Cook, who served as Sarah's Matron of Honor, was at the funeral home when she learned Ryan was being accused of murdering Sarah, her friend since childhood. "She couldn't believe it, either," Ryan said.

He was unaware that, at the very moment he was weeping over Sarah's body, police were tagging and bagging forty-three items at his home.

Hours earlier, they had rammed through the front door, splintering its frame. That happened at 9:02 a.m., two minutes after the time Ryan was supposed to have met with Braley, the detective leading the investigation into Sarah's death.

Acting on authority of a search warrant, officers scoured drawers and closets for anything that might shed light on the newlyweds' relationship: financial records, love letters, blueprints of the house.

But the search warrant request had made no mention of officers' intentions to confiscate the largest piece of evidence in the case—the entire bathtub—setting up a persistent controversy in the case.

As evening approached on August 13, 2008, police were wrapping up their search of the Widmer home; Braley and other officers arrived at the Rittgers & Rittgers law firm to arrest Ryan. He became Hamilton Township's first homicide suspect in a decade.

The officers parked their vehicles in the lot behind Rittgers' quaint office on East Warren Street, surrounded by historic homes. Ryan said Braley tried to sweet-talk him, "but I wanted nothing of it."

Ryan's twin brother, Ayran, had driven Ryan and their mom, Jill, there. Ryan handed his wedding ring to Rittgers and asked him to give it to Jill later.

As police read Ryan his rights, Ayran said it seemed almost like they all were watching a movie. *This couldn't be real, could it?*

Ayran and Ryan both shook uncontrollably. Ayran felt helpless as he watched his twin brother's life change forever. He tried to comfort their mom, but his efforts failed. Sobs wracked her body.

"I couldn't believe what happened," Ryan said. "They cuffed me, put me in a cruiser and took me to get booked in."

Braley drove separately while another cop drove Ryan to the county jail.

The drive from Rittgers' office to the jail took four minutes— a long, silent four minutes. "I didn't say much of anything. I almost couldn't," Ryan said. "I was scared, shocked, horrified, confused."

Shortly, Braley was standing alongside Prosecutor Rachel Hutzel, giving their much-anticipated news conference in her office.

That was 350 yards away from the jail where the "Newlywed Accused Killer" was being locked up.

The story exploded online, over the radio and TV airwaves. But Ryan had no idea about any of that. He was shell-shocked as he sat in a jail cell for the first time in his life.

That was how the first forty-eight hours following Sarah's death came to a close.

But for Ryan, his family, Sarah's family and for everyone connected to the case, it was just the beginning of their descent into a hellish alternate reality.

CHAPTER 4
Sinking into the Abyss

Gary Widmer sat motionless, wide-eyed and unable to comprehend what he had just seen.

It was Wednesday evening, August 13, 2008, and Gary and his wife, Kim, had been sitting at the dinner table of their home on Cincinnati's west side. Both were relaxing, each reading a book. Suddenly, Kim's son called out for her from his bedroom upstairs.

Kim went to find out what her son wanted. Seconds later, with urgency in her voice, she yelled, "Gary, you need to come up here!"

As Gary walked toward Kim and her son they were gesturing toward a glowing computer screen. He sensed they were about to show him something important. What he learned in those next few seconds would force him to make one of the most pivotal decisions of his life.

A headline jumped off the screen and sucker-punched Gary in the face: **"Husband charged in tub death."** A jail mugshot of his son, Ryan, stared back at him.

"In that instant, I just went blank," he said later. He was too numb to even finish reading the article I had written for Cincinnati.com, the *Cincinnati Enquirer's* website.

Gary slumped onto the bed. He turned pale.

Thousands of strangers had read the article online, just as Gary had. And Gary was almost a stranger to his own son.

Unlike the other readers, Gary was connected—yet disconnected—from Ryan and from the real-life drama that was enveloping his son.

The ties that bound father and son had frayed, then snapped, in the wake of a contentious divorce from Ryan's mother, Jill.

Gary hadn't even laid eyes on Ryan since 2000. That was when Ryan's youngest brother, Kyle, graduated from Colerain High School, Ryan's alma mater on Cincinnati's west side.

Eight years had elapsed since that time.

Gary didn't even know that Ryan had gotten married. So, he was especially shocked to see that Ryan was accused of killing his newlywed wife, Sarah, a woman Gary didn't even know existed in his son's life.

Now Gary stared blankly at the computer screen. Just about the only thing he could think was: "I can't believe this."

He retreated to the couch and stared at the ceiling, trying to collect his thoughts.

Among the three sons Gary had with Jill, Ryan was the one with the sweetest disposition, Gary said. There was something endearing about his calm demeanor, his offbeat sense of humor, his naiveté and his passion for sports.

Because of that particular blend of qualities, Ryan had admittedly been Gary's favorite son—and, by all accounts, he was Jill's favorite, too.

"I'm not quite sure what it is that creates that sort of bond you have with someone," Gary said, "but it is what Jill and I both had with Ryan."

Gary wondered: In what sort of twisted universe could mild-mannered Ryan have mutated into a killer? And if he had, what could have altered him so drastically? If circumstances hadn't driven a wedge between him and Ryan, would things have turned out differently?

Forcing himself to consider the chance that Ryan actually had committed murder, Gary told his wife: "If he did it, he's going to have to pay the price." Gary had no way to foretell how costly the case would become for everyone involved.

Try as he might, Gary couldn't turn off his thoughts that Wednesday night.

He didn't sleep at all.

He didn't cry, either.

That was partly because weeping was not his nature. And it also was because Gary had hardened his heart to his children. That was the only way he could cope with being separated from them. "The boys, they were everything to me," he said.

All three were talented athletes—abilities that he knew they didn't inherit from him; he wasn't athletically inclined *at all,* he said, with a laugh.

After he and Jill divorced in 1990, Gary got along fine with her for a couple years. But then Gary says Jill cut off contact with him; he was unsure why.

For years after that, without his sons' knowledge, Gary would sort of "stalk" them. He would find out when and where they were playing basketball or baseball games. And Gary would show up to watch Ryan, Ayran and Kyle from the bleachers.

Gary was an anonymous observer from a distance, just another face in the crowd. Yet he was still their Dad. And that's why Gary couldn't help but smile with pride, masking the persistent pain he felt inside—a heartache unique to parents who are estranged from their children.

At his home, which Gary's sons had never visited, Gary kept a picture of the boys hanging on the wall of a spare bedroom. Gary rarely entered that room. And when Gary did go in, he would instinctively avert his eyes from that picture.

Every so often, Gary let his guard down. The photo would magnetize his gaze toward it when he wasn't careful. And the mere sight of those three smiling, innocent young faces would dissolve Gary into tears. He would wonder where all the love and where all the years had gone.

Now he was facing the grim prospect that one of those boys, Ryan, might have taken a shocking turn and killed someone. The thought sickened and possessed Gary.

He didn't know what to do. He told a few confidantes about Ryan's predicament; some had already learned about the case from media reports.

The night before Gary learned the news about Ryan being accused of murder, Ryan had heeded the unanimous advice of friends and relatives who told him he needed a lawyer.

Now Gary was hearing admonitions about his own dilemma: Stay away from this mess. You don't want to get involved with that. Why would you?

Gary debated with himself for several days.

That weekend, no longer under pressure of the work week, his mind snapped into clear focus. He realized what he had to do. With a knot in his stomach, he braced himself to take a step he dreaded. He went outside to his home's back deck. He took a deep breath. And he dialed the phone number of his ex-wife, Jill.

Gary wasn't even sure if her number was still in service. But it was. And she answered his call.

As soon as Jill answered the phone, Gary asked: "Do you think he did it?"

Jill's response: "No, of course he didn't do it!"

Gary and Jill talked about Ryan's character; Jill said Ryan had not changed. He was still the same goofy, lovable Ryan.

She briefed Gary on the situation. Jill described how intensely Ryan had loved Sarah. She told Gary that Ryan plunged deeply into grief over her death and was struggling to comprehend why he was accused of killing her.

Jill told Gary that she was sure there had been a horrible mix-up, that the local police had jumped to the wrong conclusion about Sarah's death—and about Ryan.

Gary's heart began to melt. He wanted to band together with Ryan's mom to fight for their son. They could set aside their differences for this common purpose, couldn't they?

During the conversation, Gary's wife, Kim, was standing by his side. And Gary surprised Kim when she heard his direct, confident and insistent tone during his talk with Jill. That's because Gary wouldn't usually invite a confrontation with anyone. Especially not with headstrong Jill.

Gary and Kim had known each other for sixteen years. And she had never heard such determination in his voice until Gary told Jill: "I don't care what you say. I'm going to see my son."

Jill apparently didn't put up a fight. "I could tell they were having a conversation where they were civil to each other—for the first time in all the years I had been with Gary," Kim said.

Gary listened for more than an hour as Jill emphasized they needed to amass money—lots of it—to pay for Ryan's bail bond, for lawyers and for experts who could find out what had really happened to Sarah. She mentioned it might cost $90,000 to cover attorneys' fees alone.

Whoa.

That's a lot of money to people like the Widmers, who were middle- or upper-middle class but not wealthy. Some folks erroneously assumed that Ryan and his family were connected to Widmer's Cleaners, a local dry-cleaning empire with more than a dozen Cincinnati-area outlets. No such luck; these Widmers were ordinary folks who worked hard for everything they owned.

Jill had started as a secretary at Luxottica, the Italian eyewear company in Mason, Ohio. During the next quarter-century, she climbed the corporate ladder to a six-figure salary and an impressive position: Vice President of Marketing.

That was Jill's title when she retired from Luxottica in early 2008. Shortly thereafter, Sarah was dead—and, as a result, Jill never got to enjoy the retirement she had anticipated during her entire adult life.

Instead, Sarah's death and the charges against Ryan pulled Jill into a vortex that sucked every ounce of money, energy and sanity away from her.

For his part, Gary earned a decent living, but not as much as Jill. If he got involved with Ryan's case, it would be a stretch to come up with the big dollar figures that Jill was throwing around.

"I'll do what I can," he told Jill. Then Gary hung up the phone.

Still numb, still shell-shocked, Gary still didn't cry.

To settle his mind, he needed to see Ryan, face-to-face, man-to-man.

Working with Jill, Gary arranged to visit his son in the Warren County Jail a few days later.

Because inmates must approve their visitors, Gary wrote to Ryan. "First of all, let me say how sorry I am to hear of your troubles…You are my son, and when you are hurting, I am hurting."

Gary said he regretted that so many years had passed since they last saw each other, but "I am asking that you put me on your visitation list…I thank and ask God every day to put you back in my life. I pray that I see you and we can engage in a relationship again. I don't know how you feel, especially with everything on your mind, but I would be truly honored, as your father, to come and show you this father's love."

Jail policy limited Ryan's visitation time to fifteen minutes, split among several visitors. Gary took his turn. He felt uncomfortable as he stared at Ryan through a clear, thick plastic barrier that separated father and son, just as surely as they had been apart for the past eight years.

Gary picked up a telephone handset; Ryan held an identical one to his ear on the other side of the partition. Gary asked how Ryan was doing. Then he realized how ridiculous that must have sounded, considering the situation.

So, Gary cut to the chase and asked: "Did you do it?" His son looked him squarely in the eyes and replied unflinchingly: "No, I didn't."

That was good enough for Gary. He went all-in. And he knew there would be no turning back.

Sarah's family defended Ryan—at first

Around the same time that Gary was staring at the headline about his son, Sarah's family was across town in the northern suburbs, mourning Sarah's death and discussing Ryan's predicament. They were figuring out what to say and what to do during Ryan's first court hearing, set for the following day, Thursday, August 14, 2008.

That was three days after Sarah died.

Because so much had happened in that brief span, everyone close to Ryan and Sarah was in a tailspin.

Sarah's closest relatives initially agreed with Jill Widmer: Authorities made a colossal blunder when they charged Ryan with killing Sarah. The Ryan they knew was flat-out incapable of violence, let alone murder. At least that's what Sarah's relatives said in the immediate aftermath of her death.

Family spokesman Mike Steward, Sarah's brother, publicly acknowledged that Sarah was known to spend hours in the bathtub. She would even study schoolwork while bathing, he said.

So, Mike said, it was not far-fetched for Ryan to think that Sarah might have fallen asleep in the tub. And Mike was sure—initially—that Ryan had played no part in Sarah's death. That was what he told me in an interview. It's also what he told two different judges within days of Sarah's death.

But Mike retreated to the background after those first days—and pretty much remained there afterward.

If Ryan had anything to hide from Sarah's relatives, he didn't show it. He had frequent contact with the Stewards in the aftermath of Sarah's drowning.

The night she died, Monday, August 11th, Ryan talked with her mom at the hospital.

On Tuesday morning, the 12th, Ryan went to the funeral home with Sarah's mother and her aunt.

And on Wednesday the 13th, just before Ryan surrendered to the police, he had confided in Sarah's brother, "Mike, I'm so scared, I can't even cry."

Amid those interactions, the Stewards were telling Ryan they believed he would never hurt Sarah. But later, they cut off contact with Ryan for reasons that they never divulged to news reporters—nor to Ryan.

Sarah's mother, Ruth Ann Steward, maintained a public silence throughout the case, perhaps partly because a judge's order prevented witnesses from making statements to the press for much of the case.

When called to testify in all three trials, Ruth Ann came across as somewhat shy and soft-spoken. But Ryan said Ruth Ann seemed outgoing to him; he said he enjoyed his relationship with her, while it lasted.

Ruth Ann and Mike both said they considered Ryan part of their family.

During a phone interview with Mike, I mentioned something about Ryan "turning himself in," and I clearly recall Mike saying that term sounded unfair because it implied Ryan was guilty.

Ryan's first court appearance would be via "video arraignment," which had become standard for many criminal suspects in Warren County and in other communities to save time, hassle and risk of escape.

Before court began, I heard Ruth Ann coaxing Jill Widmer and others to sit near a center aisle in hopes that Ryan could see all of them there, sitting in solidarity to support him.

Ruth Ann had mistakenly believed that Ryan would be able to see images of the courtroom. But that wasn't the case.

Ryan could only *hear* what was happening while he sat in the county jail and his image was projected onto a video monitor in Warren County Court, a cave-like, no-frills courtroom where sounds echoed against concrete walls.

On a typical day, the docket would be filled with people busted for minor offenses: petty theft, traffic citations, drunken brawls, drug abuse.

On a rare occasion, a serious, high-profile defendant would appear in County Court before the case was transferred to Common Pleas Court, where all felony cases are handled.

Both courts, the jail, the prosecutor's office and other government offices sit along a gently curving road in Lebanon, Ohio. Officials named it Justice Drive, emblematic of Warren County's law-and-order, God-and-country values.

Thursday, August 14, 2008, was one of those rare days when a huge case—Ryan's case—overshadowed the mundane misery of the other cases.

Sarah's brother, Mike Steward, stood up and addressed the judge, Joseph Kirby, saying that the Steward family believed there was no way that Ryan had committed murder.

Mike called Ryan a "hero" for trying to save Sarah. Mike implored the judge to set Ryan's bond as low as possible, saying the Steward family was putting Sarah's funeral on hold until Ryan could get out of jail and attend.

But after prosecutors stressed the seriousness of the charge, the judge set Ryan's bond at $1 million. "Oh my God," someone said.

The enormity of that number astounded Ryan, too. All it meant to him was this: He wasn't getting out of jail anytime soon.

After the court appearance, a county sheriff's detective who was working with Lieutenant Jeff Braley was scheduled to meet with the Stewards at Ruth Ann's home. Instead, Mike Steward asked to meet near the court where Ryan's video arraignment was held. Right after leaving the court hearing, Mike Steward said the family was "being harassed by reporters," so the family agreed to meet with the police at Prosecutor Rachel Hutzel's office nearby.

Hutzel introduced herself to Mike Steward, his wife and his mother. Hutzel, some of her staffers and detectives met with the family in private.

When investigators asked whether Ryan had told the Stewards any details about what happened to Sarah, Mike said no. He also said the Stewards "did not want to press the issue and make Ryan 'relive the experience,'" an investigator noted.

Even as friends and family were publicly advocating for Ryan, a grand jury was meeting in secret to consider Ryan's case. That's the way it's always done.

On Friday, August 15th, a day after Ryan's first court appearance, the grand jury handed up an indictment with a more severe charge: aggravated murder.

If convicted, Ryan would be sentenced to twenty years to life in prison—five years longer than the minimum sentence for "straight" murder, as it's called in legal circles.

The aggravated murder charge alleged that Ryan had planned the crime to some extent—or at least had time to think about what he was doing but didn't stop himself from continuing to attack Sarah.

Sarah died during "a violent struggle," the prosecutor's office said in a news release, citing "physical and circumstantial evidence" that led investigators to conclude: "This was no accident."

The news release also stated that Widmer had been arrested Monday night at his home—the same night Sarah drowned. But that was inaccurate. Ryan had turned himself in at his lawyer's office on Wednesday, two days after Sarah's death.

Was the prosecutor's incorrect statement about the timing and circumstances of Ryan's arrest an honest mistake? Or was it an early attempt to "spin" the story, creating an impression that the evidence was so obvious and so overwhelming that an immediate, on-scene arrest was justified?

Either way, most court watchers agreed that Ryan was charged very quickly considering the circumstances. Many homicide suspects are charged after much lengthier investigation. A former prosecutor in nearby, more urban Hamilton County, Mike Allen said he couldn't remember seeing a murder suspect indicted during the same week that the victim had died—but that's what happened in Ryan's case.

Suspects who roll on a fast track to prosecution typically are those caught in the act, captured on video or snared after a hot pursuit that began at the crime scene—none of which applied to Ryan.

Police and prosecutors never publicly revealed specific reasons for moving ahead so swiftly against Ryan. In court, prosecutors said they considered him a "flight risk." They surmised that Ryan's work-related contacts across the United States might come in handy if he decided to run from the law.

Ryan insisted that fleeing never crossed his mind.

For months after he was charged, Ryan thought that, somehow, the authorities would come to their senses and would see that he had done nothing to hurt his wife.

Ryan and his supporters say investigators prematurely slammed several doors shut, cutting off pathways that could have led to the truth.

But the authorities asserted that the truth had quickly come into plain view. Murder seemed to be the only sensible explanation for Sarah Widmer's drowning in her own bathtub. For them, any other possibility must have seemed as imaginary as a Walt Disney cartoon.

A bad first impression

When news broke about the strange and sensational Widmer case, people devoured it like piranhas ripping into goldfish.

In the first wave of publicity, Ryan's mugshot didn't look too bad, as mugshots go. He was pictured wearing a poppy-red T-shirt, with a blank, solemn look on his face. But that was before Ryan spent his first night in jail.

The next morning, after a nearly sleepless night, Ryan looked shockingly bad, even to those who knew him well.

In an image that photojournalists "grabbed" from the County Court video-arraignment screen, Ryan's nearly shaved head is lowered; his long fingers are interlaced just below his lower lip.

His reddened eyes peer upward into the camera lens, beneath slanted, pointy eyebrows that look like a Hollywood makeup artist had air-brushed them a la *Star Trek*'s Dr. Spock.

Ryan is wearing a black sleeveless top, revealing menacing-looking tattoos: an abstract tribal design that looks like a spider is etched into his right upper arm; on the left, a skull, wearing a top hat, laughs about the "lucky sevens" roll of a pair of dice.

Ryan had chosen that tattoo years earlier, only because he thought it looked cool—and, he says, he was "young and stupid." He used to joke that it was his lucky tattoo; he later concluded it was *unlucky*, because that image helped brand him as "Scary Ryan" in the early media coverage of his case.

Unbeknownst to the public, the black sleeveless garment Ryan wore that day was a "suicide-prevention safety smock." At the time, other reporters and I were told that it was a "suicide vest," and that it had been issued solely because of the seriousness of the charge that Ryan faced. I remember specifically asking the authorities whether he was suicidal; I was told that he wasn't. Yet his jail booking record says "YES," under both "potential danger" and "suicidal risk."

Because inmates sometimes use jail-issued clothing to hang themselves in their cells, a California jailer invented a smock with thick, strong nylon fabric that prevents a suicidal inmate from fashioning it into a noose.

As soon as Ryan was booked, he was required to remove his T-shirt and shorts and to change into that black sleeveless smock. It covered him from shoulders to calves.

Underneath, Ryan was forbidden from wearing underwear. For him, that added to the indignity of the whole process. He felt humiliated. But he didn't question being ordered to wear it at the time. He was in self-preservation mode. His thoughts swirled in a maelstrom.

Ryan didn't consider that the blackness of the vest, the macabre motifs of his tattoos and his weary, sleep-deprived face combined to produce a sinister picture. The effect was greater than the sum of its parts.

That depiction of Ryan was almost unrecognizable to people who knew him. They were used to seeing him in polo shirts and khakis, business suits, and Bengals jerseys. They were used to seeing him with a wry, a gap-toothed grin, a chiefly European feature he inherited from his Polish-German mother.

They couldn't imagine that Ryan, a guy who seemed too innocuous to ever hurt anyone, could be accused of killing someone—especially not the woman he loved.

But Ryan indeed was accused of being a creepy killer—and now, in that awful photograph, he looked the part.

After Ryan's employer, Shirley Bonekemper, got a phone call telling her that Ryan had been arrested, she was astounded—and angered—by his courtroom image on TV. "I was just livid," she said, "because that was not the picture of the Ryan that I knew."

Staring at the picture of the Ryan she *didn't* know, Shirley wanted to break down and cry. She thought the authorities were trying to present the worst possible image of Ryan, to influence public opinion from the start.

A lot of people told her: "Oh my God, he had to have done it. He looks diabolical!"

Ryan's co-worker, Lori Worley, said Ryan "wasn't a show-off person," so many people didn't even know he had the tattoos that were now on display.

The Scary Ryan picture made him seem unsavory, Lori said: "That image plants a little seed in everyone's mind, right off the bat. Had we put Ryan in a nice suit, like he was known to be in, it wouldn't have left that impression."

When Ryan's lawyer, Charlie Rittgers, saw the disturbing image of his client pop up on the video monitor in court, Rittgers' eyes widened, then narrowed in disgust. "I'll never forget it," Rittgers said. "I thought that was intentionally done to prejudice a future jury pool. I was really pissed."

He asked someone in authority why Ryan was wearing the suicide vest instead of the standard jail-issue uniform, which would have concealed his tattoos. Rittgers remembers being told: "It was protocol."

Rittgers was surprised to see the suicide vest because Ryan had exhibited no suicidal tendencies. "There was nothing wrong with him mentally—not one damn bit," Rittgers said.

But Rittgers accepted the authorities' response: The seriousness of the charge called for the suicide vest.

I had seen other murder defendants without the suicide vest in Warren County, so I did momentarily wonder why Ryan was wearing it. But I also reasoned that the county was being extra-cautious after another high-profile murder suspect, a French-Canadian named Michel Veillette, hanged himself in his Warren County Jail cell.

Veillette was accused in a headline-grabbing crime: He allegedly stabbed his wife to death then set a fire that killed all four of their children. The blaze left their high-end Mason home in ruins and stunned the region in January 2008.

Four months later, without warning, Veillette, who was still locked up in the county jail awaiting trial, wrapped a bed sheet onto a towel rack attached to the end of a desk. He wrapped the wadded-up fabric around his neck, then slumped onto the floor until the ligature blocked airflow from his windpipe.

Jailers found Veillette with his neck grotesquely bent and suspended from the towel rack.

That was in April 2008, four months before the Widmer case broke.

So perhaps the county authorities wanted to ensure that this big fish—Ryan—wouldn't wriggle off the hook as Veillette had done; maybe Ryan unwittingly said or did something that made jailers worry about that potential.

Regardless of behind-the-scenes rationale, the Scary Ryan photo triggered an immediate, visceral response from lots of folks. One *Cincinnati Enquirer* reader posted her verdict, based on his appearance alone: "He is guilty," she wrote in comments at the bottom of my story.

That reader argued that Sarah's relatives must have been supportive of Ryan only because they were in denial, unable to believe they could love this guy and that he could kill their beloved Sarah.

The commenter envisioned Sarah being miserable, stuck in an abusive relationship that she was afraid to end. "She probably did everything she could to make public opinions of their marriage positive. Then, when the door closed at home, the devil came out and wanted to play," the reader wrote. "She probably fell asleep in the bathtub to get away from him."

That type of speculation saturated local news websites. But people who knew Sarah could never see her as a pushover. They said she was a take-charge kind of gal who would never tolerate abuse. And Ryan, friends said, was as henpecked as they come.

Seven months before Scary Ryan hit the news outlets, a picture of "Friendly Ryan" had been published in *The Enquirer.*

In that photo, a grin pushes against Ryan's round cheeks; he's wearing a suit and tie, beneath the headline, "Allen Howard's Good Neighbor." Friendly Ryan was featured in the newspaper's good-news column for his successes with the Convention & Visitors Bureau.

In retrospect, the little article packed a double dose of irony: Ryan, the "good neighbor," allegedly had turned into a murderous husband. And Ryan, described as one of the county's biggest boosters, later would publicly assail the county's criminal justice system.

For some people, the conflicting impressions of Ryan Widmer were indelible. Peter Bronson, the editor of this book (who is unrelated to the Widmer case judge, Neal Bronson), was so struck by Ryan's images that he wrote an article for *Cincy* magazine nearly two years after the case broke:

"Who is the real Ryan Widmer? ... Is it the one in a suit and tie? Or the one with creepy tattoos...? Is it the distraught newlywed who dialed 911 or the calculating caller who tripped on his own tangled stories and 911 tapes?"

Nearly a decade later, Peter and I would still be debating those questions as I worked on ferreting out the truth.

Same 911 call, differing opinions

It's strange how a group of people can witness the same event, or listen to the same thing, yet perceive those experiences so differently.

That was what happened with Ryan's call to 911.

On the morning of August 13, 2008, about thirty-six hours after Sarah had drowned, a couple tipsters finally provided a time frame and an address for the "weird incident" I had been hearing about in Warren County.

Those details enabled me to put together a public-records request for Ryan's 911 recording; I was the first news reporter to get one.

Hoping to break some news, I hurried back to my office at the *Enquirer's* North Newsroom in West Chester, a thirty-five-minute drive from Ryan and Sarah's home.

I had listened to hundreds of 911 calls during my time as a reporter. I had listened to people who babbled hysterically and to people who sounded strangely calm. I had learned that innocent people can react in either of those ways. And I had listened to people who lied, lied, lied about what really happened—sometimes convincingly, sometimes not.

Wondering which variety of caller this one would be, I put on my headphones, connected to my laptop computer. I slid the CD in and hit "play." I closed my eyes. And I listened.

I didn't hear a hysterical caller. Nor did I hear one who seemed way too calm. Instead, I heard a caller who seemed to be suffering from a verbal version of "deer-in-headlights" paralysis. I thought I heard a person so stunned, he could hardly say anything at times. That was my initial interpretation of the caller's demeanor. It also occurred to me that a guilty conscience could be causing his hesitation.

Either way, I was confident that the facts would eventually surface. Everything would become clear, just as they had in so many other cases I had covered over the years.

By itself, the 911 call didn't give me enough "meat" to write a story yet.

That would come after Prosecutor Rachel Hutzel and Lieutenant Jeff Braley held their news conference later that day. That's when I wrote the story that floored Ryan's dad. And that's when my editors and I posted Ryan's 911 recording to the *Enquirer's* website, Cincinnati.com.

Soon, comments were buzzing around town, and all over the internet.

The consensus: This Widmer Guy must have done it because he didn't sound upset enough during that 911 call—and because his "fell asleep in the bathtub" explanation seemed ludicrous.

And that was the mindset of many people even *before* the Scary Ryan photo debuted.

At the Convention & Visitors Bureau in Lebanon, Ryan's colleagues were shocked. "We were all stunned, walking around like zombies—just trying to function, trying to figure out what we could do," said Lori Worley.

She remembers several co-workers clustering around a TV to hear part of Ryan's 911 call. "When we listened to that, we cried for Ryan," Lori said, "because we heard his hurt and his anguish and his desperation. That's what *we* heard."

She couldn't comprehend what other people "heard" on that same recording: a cold-blooded killer who was making a bungled attempt to hide his crime.

"It was like all these people were listening to another 911 call," Lori said. "What we were hearing was *our Ryan,* terrified. And everyone else was taking what he said and twisting it. I couldn't even wrap my head around it. I felt like I was in the Twilight Zone."

Ryan's co-workers, friends and neighbors were scrutinized like bugs under a microscope—sometimes by the public, sometimes by the police. Everyone who worked with Ryan was interrogated—multiple times.

The office's executive director, Shirley Bonekemper, was petite, impeccably dressed, soft-spoken yet assertive. She epitomized the term, "lady;" and wasn't the type of person who would go around bad-mouthing anyone.

Yet Shirley, who retired from her position in 2010, was blunt when she expressed her opinion of Lieutenant Jeff Braley vis-à-vis other people who talked to her about Ryan's case.

"Most people were kind. They knew it was our loss, too," Shirley said. "The only person that was a sleazebag was Braley."

At first, Braley was saying all the right things: "Oh, I'm so sorry," and "We'll get to the bottom of this." But Shirley sensed insincerity; Braley made her B.S.-detector go off.

"He was too effusive, and not genuine," Shirley said. "He was digging, and he wanted to 'get' something on Ryan so badly. But we were all like, 'You've got the wrong guy.'"

Braley repeatedly asked whether Ryan was cheating on Sarah. "They were trying to set it up like one of them was having an affair," Shirley said.

Ryan had worked at the Visitors Bureau for four years, and everyone there thought he only had eyes for Sarah. They saw how his demeanor changed after Sarah came into his life. Ryan was animated, happier, googly-eyed.

Shirley reminisced about the times she had seen Sarah and Ryan at office get-togethers. As a couple, Sarah and Ryan charmed Shirley. Sarah glowed when she was around Ryan. And as for Ryan, "He was adorable," Shirley said, "You could see he was smitten with her. He would just smile all the time."

Shirley remembers the couple being excited to make improvements to their house; they chatted happily about working together to build a deck and install landscaping. They appeared blissful, contented.

On Saturday, August 9, 2008, two days before Sarah's death, Ryan was at a sports-marketing event with his direct supervisor, Ben Huffman. While there, Ryan told Ben that he and Sarah were excited to be adopting a puppy—a date already had been set to pick up the dog. They hoped the puppy would be a good playmate for C.J. Sarah and Ryan were jokingly referring to the puppy as "our first kid." Because sometime after that, Ryan and Sarah were planning to add a baby to their little family, Ryan had said.

Ryan and Ben also talked about a sports-marketing conference they were planning to attend in Cancun, Mexico, in a few weeks; Ryan had already purchased a ticket for Sarah to go along, too.

Those were all indications that Ryan was planning for the future—a future with Sarah in it.

"So what possibly could have happened that would have made him want to kill her?" Shirley wondered. "To me, there's nothing."

Co-worker Lori Worley was similarly perplexed. And, like Shirley, Lori disliked Braley's attitude: "He tried to come in and convince me, with his actions and his words, that a crime had been committed, and that Ryan had done it. He hiked up his pants and said, 'There's a crime here.' He was cocky."

From the first time she saw Braley, Lori got the feeling that Braley was trying to intimidate her. But she saw his brash, know-it-all attitude as "comical." His demeanor told her: "I know that you know something, and I'm going to get it out of you."

She said Braley asked her the same question several different ways—a common interrogation tactic.

You've never met Ryan outside of work?

You've never been to his house?

You didn't hang out with him?

No, no, no, she answered.

Lori started to sense that Braley was insinuating that she and Ryan were having an affair.

That notion was preposterous to her. Although she and virtually everyone in the small, close-knit office adored Ryan, there was a big age disparity between him and his co-workers. They were mostly females over the age of 40. Ryan, at the time Sarah died, was 27. Lori, about a decade older than Ryan, was happily engaged to be married. Her fiancé had a jealous streak; if he had caught any hint of an affair, he wouldn't have tolerated it, Lori said.

In Lori's view, she and many of Ryan's female co-workers were like surrogate moms for him.

She racked her brain to figure out what could have made Braley so insistent that she could somehow be romantically tied to Ryan.

Lori knew that Braley had confiscated the office's computerized records. So, she thought maybe something in the office emails triggered this line of questioning.

Lori and Ryan held jobs that rarely intersected, so the two of them exchanged few emails. Then it dawned on Lori: Braley was probably misinterpreting an email that had followed an anti-smoking conversation between her and Ryan.

Ryan told Lori he was trying to quit smoking cigarettes. Sarah was concerned that unhealthy habit would ruin Ryan's teeth—top-of-mind for Sarah, given her job as a dental hygienist and her obsession with clean, white teeth.

Lori confided that she, too, was trying to quit smoking. She told Ryan that she was thinking about getting a prescription for the smoking-cessation drug, Chantix, which was relatively new at that time.

Ryan said he thought about trying it, too. He later followed up with an email asking Lori, "Did you start taking that pill yet?"

When that email message flashed into her mind, Lori realized that Braley must have seen Ryan's reference to "that pill," and had assumed that Ryan was referring to a birth-control pill, not Chantix. Braley never specifically mentioned the email to Lori.

Regardless of what fueled Braley's suspicions, Lori finally got fed up with Braley and told him: "Look, I love Ryan as a co-worker and a friend." Nothing that Braley said or did would change her opinion of Ryan or change what she was telling him about their relationship, Lori said.

Lori also told Braley that if she knew her own son had committed a crime, she would tell the truth about it. Likewise, Lori told Braley she would have admitted if she had any reason to believe that Ryan had done anything wrong— and she had no reason to doubt his innocence.

Finally, Braley backed down. He told Lori he had heard similar opinions from other co-workers.

The theory that Ryan Widmer was a killer and that Lori was his mistress was unthinkable and surreal, Lori said.

The office's executive director, Shirley Bonekemper, said Braley tried to pull out all the stops with her, too. Braley grilled her relentlessly, as though he were going to extract a deep, dark secret that Shirley was hiding about Ryan.

She vividly recalled how Braley behaved when he questioned her.

"He was getting nowhere, and you could see visibly he was getting frustrated. He paused and he looked down. And then he looked up, real dramatic-like, and said, 'I don't know if this will help, but I'm also a minister,'" Shirley said.

Wow, Shirley thought, Braley was suggesting it was safe to "come clean" with him because he was a man of the cloth. Braley, was, in fact, serving as a minister at a church in nearby Loveland, Ohio.

Regardless, Shirley said, "I was offended that he would think that somehow this would change what we were saying."

Then Braley told her: "You know, we're not trying to convict Ryan here. We're just trying to get to the truth."

Shirley and other Visitors Bureau employees stared back at Braley and replied, "We still think he's innocent."

Braley retorted, "Something terrible happened in the house that night. I can't reveal it to you now, but it's going to come out—and you'll see what we're talking about."

Those words left Shirley feeling uneasy. "I thought, 'Oh my God, what happened?'"

Her stalwart confidence in Ryan's innocence was shaken, ever so slightly.

Braley's words frightened Shirley because, "He said it in such a convincing way," she said.

Shirley's gut still told her that Ryan was incapable of murder. But Shirley was also smart enough to know that she needed to keep her mind open to the facts. As Ryan's case moved toward trial, Braley's words echoed in her head. She still believed in Ryan, but she also felt anxiety over Braley's assertion.

She wondered: What damning evidence might prove that Ryan was a killer?

Shirley would have to wait and see, along with everyone else who was interested in the case.

Nothing made sense

Ryan's mind was a jumbled mess.

Everything about the life he had once known was topsy-turvy.

For two years—a long time when you're in your 20s—Ryan's life went something like this: Sarah, sports, sports-marketing; Sarah, sports, sports-marketing; lather, rinse and repeat.

Suddenly, Ryan was thrust into a hostile, unfamiliar arena: no Sarah, no sports, no sports-marketing.

He had landed on a chessboard where cops, coroners, jailers, lawyers and medical experts played by a set of rules that made little sense to him. He felt like he was nothing but an expendable pawn.

Being accused, then arrested, then booked, then appearing in court—none of it made sense, he said: "I couldn't understand why it was continuing to go on."

Ryan had no access to the Widmer case news reports that saturated the airwaves and cyberspace. At the time, he was unaware of the negative public perceptions that were forming, thanks to the Scary Ryan pic and his own words on the 911 call.

Among the Cincinnati region's 2.1 million citizens, most adults probably knew more about Ryan's case than he did.

But few of them knew much about Ryan. And no one understood what was going on inside his head. *He* didn't even understand it.

His every attempt to be logical ended in failure.

Under the jail's suicide protocol, Ryan had more restrictions than the average Warren County Jail inmate. Besides being issued no bed sheets, he couldn't be trusted with pens, pencils, paper or books. He wasn't allowed out of his cell except for one hour around midnight, probably to keep him away from the general inmate population.

When he was allowed out of his cell, Ryan would shower and watch TV. And he would call his mom. That's about all he could do.

The jail cell was cold, hard and spartan—just the way many "lock-'em-up" crusaders think it should be.

He occupied himself by pacing the floor of his cell, which was about nine feet long. He did sit-ups and push-ups to exhaustion.

When Ryan wept, his sobs reverberated against the cinder-block walls, concrete floor and metal furnishings. There was a platform-bed with a hard mat on top, bolted to the wall, along with a metal desk and an attached round stool. A sink and toilet, both stainless steel.

A steel door separated Ryan from the world as he had known it.

He was by himself, except for two unwelcome cellmates: his meal tray and his thoughts.

Three times a day, a guard would deliver the plastic, sectioned-off tray of food. The guard would place the tray on the desk, hardly speaking a word, then clank the door shut as he exited.

Ryan would just pick at the food.

His lack of appetite wasn't solely because jail chow is unappealing. It was mostly because his mind was too preoccupied to divert energy to his digestive system.

Reflecting on Sarah's drowning, Ryan realized that it was his misfortune to be at home alone with her on that particular night.

More often than not, he watched football games on TV with his buddies. If he had done that as usual, either at his house or at a friend's house, Ryan believed he never would have been accused of killing Sarah.

And he had turned down a second opportunity that would have kept him away from home that evening. He had declined an invitation to go on a guys' golfing trip. He could have been 148 miles away, in Bright Leaf, Kentucky.

Ryan's friend who played matchmaker, Chris Kist, regrets going on the golf trip. "If I hadn't gone, I probably would have been watching that game with him," Chris said. "Either way, she still would have been dead in that tub. The only difference would be that Ryan wouldn't be blamed for it."

Ryan's supporters make a stand

After a week in the county jail, a new, Not-So-Scary Ryan appeared in Warren County Common Pleas Court for arraignment—in the same courtroom where he had served as a juror in 2005.

He was too preoccupied to recognize the irony of being a defendant in the same room where he once decided another man's fate.

"I was still trying to figure out why this was all happening," Ryan said, "and I just wanted it to go away."

He flashed back to his service as a juror—the first time he had set foot in a courtroom.

Ryan and his fellow jurors had listened to prosecutors and to a guy who defended himself *pro se,* without a lawyer. The defendant's name didn't stick in Ryan's head. But Ryan remembered how much responsibility he felt when he and his fellow jurors considered whether to convict that man.

Ryan also remembered the defendant's reaction to the split verdict. Although the jury found the defendant guilty of a drug-paraphernalia charge, the man jumped for joy after learning that he was acquitted of the more serious drug-possession charge. The evidence prosecutors presented did not support the charge, Ryan and his fellow jurors decided.

Now, as Ryan the former juror stood in that same courtroom as a defendant accused of aggravated murder, he thought the truth surely would come out. That's what's supposed to happen in the justice system, he thought.

Or maybe something would convince the authorities that they had made a huge mistake, and they would dismiss the charges.

That was Ryan's hope.

It also was the hope of about two dozen supporters who took time off from their jobs late on a hot Wednesday afternoon, August 20, 2008. They came and sat in court to show Ryan that he was not alone.

The battle lines were drawn. And it seemed that the police and prosecutors were squared off against everyone else: Ryan, attorney Charlie Rittgers, friends of Ryan and Sarah, and even Sarah's relatives.

News photographers huddled in the darkened Media Room that overlooks the courtroom, aiming cameras at Ryan through a rectangular window. The red lights on TV video cameras glowed as they recorded the first in-person images of the newlywed who was accused of killing his bride in an especially cruel way. Newspaper photographers click, click, clicked their cameras' shutters, trying to capture the essence of who this guy was.

News reporters, including me, scribbled down our first impressions of Ryan Widmer in notebooks and typed them into laptop computers.

We had all been trying to get an interview with him. Predictably, his lawyer had advised him to keep his mouth shut.

For now, the only thing we reporters could do was observe Ryan from a distance.

As soon as Ryan entered the courtroom, escorted by deputies, several of his friends began to weep. They couldn't stand seeing Ryan this way, even though he looked considerably less menacing than the Scary Ryan photo broadcast several days earlier.

Jailers had relaxed the restrictions on Ryan. They gave him a flexible ink pen that would be nearly impossible to use as a weapon against himself or against anyone else. And they allowed him to get out of the suicide vest. He changed into the standard-issue jail uniform: an orange V-neck shirt and matching pants, along with brown rubber slide-on shoes.

That was what Ryan wore when he came into the Common Pleas courtroom where he would later stand trial. He also wore handcuffs attached to a chain on a belt that encircled his waist; shackles clanked between his ankles, an extra precaution to ensure he wouldn't try to run away.

Ryan looked far less threatening this way. His face looked wan. Ryan felt embarrassed and belittled, being led around in chains in front of his friends, co-workers and family. Yet he appreciated having them there for support.

He grew emotional when Sarah's brother, Mike Steward, again stood up in court to profess his belief in Ryan's innocence—for the second time in less than a week.

Ryan cried when he heard Mike ask the magistrate to reduce Ryan's $1 million bond so he could come to Sarah's funeral. I quoted Mike in my *Enquirer* article: "In our heart of hearts, we don't believe Ryan did this."

A victim's advocate from the prosecutor's office sat next to Sarah's brother and mother to provide insights and comfort—although the Stewards were opposed to the prosecution of Ryan at that time.

On Ryan's behalf, Rittgers entered a not-guilty plea to the upgraded aggravated murder charge.

A magistrate, who was filling in for the usual judge, Neal Bronson, refused to reduce his $1 million bond. He suggested that Rittgers could ask Judge Bronson to reconsider the bond amount later.

Two days later, on Friday, August 22, 2008, Rittgers persuaded Judge Bronson to drop Ryan's bond to $400,000.

That was the same day that Sarah's memorial Mass was celebrated at St. Susanna Catholic Church in Mason, where Sarah had worshipped, sometimes going there with her mom, but not with Ryan; he wasn't Catholic.

The Widmer family tried to get Ryan released in time for him to attend the service.

His dad, Gary, posted the required 10 percent of Ryan's bond amount—$40,000—with a bondsman. Most people don't know, his dad Gary said, "forty thousand dollars is what they charge you; you get nothing back" from the bondsman.

Unbeknownst to Ryan, Gary covered the entire $40K with a withdrawal from his retirement fund.

"That's a big chunk of change to put down just to get somebody out of jail temporarily," Gary said. But it was something he felt compelled to do; this was his son and he loved him, despite all of the years that had elapsed without contact.

Gary wrote to Ryan shortly after his arrest: "I've missed so much of your life but I feel like I've not missed one beating of your heart... I have never stopped loving you."

Getting a person out of jail takes time and is more complicated than it seems—just like every other procedure in the justice system, Gary would learn.

Ryan was released from jail two hours too late to attend Sarah's memorial service.

At the request of Sarah's family, the church had sent out a notice, asking news reporters to stay off church property.

I was among the reporters who watched mourners file into the church from a distance. We stood outside a car-repair shop, baking in the summer sun and hoping that someone would come over and talk to us. No one did.

The couple who introduced Ryan and Sarah to each other, Dana and Chris Kist, noticed the news crews. But the Kists thought little about us as they pulled into the church parking lot that afternoon. ,

Dana, in particular, was almost paralyzed with dread.

"I need a minute," she told Chris as he opened the door for her to step out of the car.

Dana didn't want to face the reality: Sarah was really dead. Going inside that church for the memorial service would force Dana to confront that painful fact head-on.

As Father John Tonkin—the same priest who had married Ryan and Sarah—performed the service, Dana flashed back to Ryan and Sarah's wedding day. How could that happy union now be severed by death, a scant four months later? It didn't seem possible.

But there Dana sat, listening as Father Tonkin did his best to infuse some small measure of comfort into the intense heartache filling the air.

Dana cried for both of her dear friends.

Dana wept for Sarah, missing her smile, her sweet enthusiasm, her feisty attitude—everything about her. Dana also wept for Ryan, her Bengals buddy. He had been hit doubly hard: Unable to come to the service to mourn and to honor Sarah—while facing an unthinkably horrid accusation: that he had snuffed out his wife's life.

Dana couldn't imagine how difficult it had been for Ryan to know that Sarah had undergone two autopsies—and then Ryan had to make the difficult decision about final disposition of her remains.

Sarah's family wanted Ryan to make that call because he was her husband.

Ryan didn't know what to do. He and Sarah had never discussed what funeral arrangements each might prefer. They were so young, had been married such a short time, and, presumably, were so far from death.

Upon reflection, Ryan decided that, if he had died, he would have preferred to be cremated.

So that was partly why he chose cremation for Sarah.

Another reason: Cremation was less expensive than burial. Sarah had no life insurance policy to cover her final expenses.

Later, the topics of life insurance and cremation would affect Ryan in ways he couldn't have imagined.

At the memorial service, an urn containing Sarah's cremated ashes sat along-side a photograph of her at the altar.

The priest who had married Ryan and Sarah, Father John Tonkin, delivered a message about love: "Sarah's family showed her how to love, and Sarah showered her love on those around her. And it was this love that brought Sarah and Ryan together. Those of us gathered here today have no need to doubt the love that Sarah has for Ryan—and Ryan has for Sarah."

Even though Ryan was unable to attend the service, Ryan's words, read aloud during the service, rang in mourners' ears and stuck in their heads.

Scrawled on a piece of notebook paper, Ryan had written a eulogy. But it read more like a love letter to his dead wife—the one he was accused of killing.

> Sarah:
>
> You were truly a special one of a kind person. Even though we only knew each other two years it felt like a lifetime. Those two years were the best two years of my life and I could not have chosen a better person to marry. Words cannot describe how much you meant to me but I am going to give it a try. You are beautiful, kind, honest, trustworthy, funny, sweet, thoughtful, unique, practical, reasonable, witty, and even though I already mentioned it truly thoughtful.
>
> You had a special gift to put one's thoughts and feelings before yours. But that is just the type of person you are. You had a way of making someone feel very special and important, which is only a part of why I fell so deeply in love with you!
>
> This world definitely has lost one of the best people it will ever see and I will never forget those two great years we had together. I will remember that smile and that oh so special look you could give.
>
> Sarah, I love you so much and I am going to live my life knowing you are still right here with me and watching. Even though I don't quite know what I am going to do without you. I am honored you chose to marry me and I will

never disappoint you. You were the best thing
to ever happen to me and I will never forget
you! I could go on forever, but everybody who
knew you already knows how great you are.

I LOVE U MOST!

Ryan

People at Sarah's memorial service were touched.

Many were moved to tears, thinking these were the sweet, poignant words of a grieving, wrongfully accused widower.

Instead, could those have been the words of a calculating criminal, trying to generate sympathy he didn't deserve?

That was one of many questions that would persist long after Sarah was gone.

CHAPTER 5

How? And Why?

Lieutenant Jeff Braley was rapidly accumulating seemingly damning documents in a fat three-ring binder labeled "WIDMER HOMICIDE Case #08-005768."

The big, black capital letters on the white front cover emphasized the Widmer case's significance. Braley had investigated one other slaying, a "cold" case that registered a few mentions in the news.

In contrast, the public's appetite for all things Widmer was voracious. News reporters went into a feeding frenzy.

Such a sensational case, drawing off-the-charts public interest, might come along once in a career for a detective in an obscure community such as Hamilton Township. It could be a career-maker—or a career-breaker.

Previously, the case that probably drew the most notoriety for Braley happened in the fall of 2007. Braley had posed as a teenage girl online and chatted with a man who wanted to meet "the girl." So Braley lured the man to a meeting in the Ohio Statehouse on October 31, 2007; it was Halloween Day and the chat-room suspect was tricked when he came looking for his twisted idea of a "treat." Police arrested the duped man just after Braley finished testimony urging state lawmakers to enhance penalties against internet sex predators.

At the time, Braley denied setting up the sting to maximize publicity about his Statehouse testimony. Braley's critics, however, cited the Statehouse incident as an example of his orchestrating circumstances to draw more attention to himself.

Regardless of the debate over Braley's motivations, the internet sex-sting touched off a few small tremors—nothing comparable to the seismic effect of the Widmer case.

And the morning after Sarah died, Braley snagged a linchpin: The county coroner made a preliminary ruling that Sarah was the victim of a homicidal drowning in her own home.

The unofficial ruling, issued within twelve hours of Sarah's death, supercharged the investigation.

And this was no "whodunit" murder mystery. There was only one obvious suspect: Ryan.

Ryan admitted he and Sarah were home alone the night she drowned, and there was no sign of a break-in.

Therefore, Braley concluded, if Sarah was the victim of a homicide, the only person who could have killed her was Ryan. Plain and simple.

For Braley, the case was as black-and-white as the cover of his case-file binder.

This guy's 911 call just didn't sound right—the lame explanation that she "fell asleep" in the tub, and that she was "face-down" at the faucet end of the tub, opposite of where she should have been bathing. Then there were contradictions about what TV channel he was watching and whether Sarah was face-up or face-down in the tub. Perhaps most troubling of all: the drowning scene and Sarah were both strangely dry—and there were two mysterious, diluted-looking bloodstains on the carpet where she had lain.

None of it made sense. All of it seemed suspicious.

Braley had lots of work to do before he could mentally stamp the file "case closed."

He'd have to cover the "Five W's and one H:" who, what, where, when, why and how. The first four elements came into focus in a flash. The last two—why and how—proved to be more elusive. Braley was hunting for anything that would prove *how* Ryan had drowned Sarah—and *why*.

Marks found on Sarah helped point to *how*.

During Sarah's autopsy, Braley watched the coroner and scrawled on a legal pad: "...two cuts on lip...three bruises on scalp...hemorrhage on chest...consistent with holding over tub." The final note on the page reads: "...no way an accidental drowning."

Still, Braley knew he needed to explore questions that would puzzle a jury.

What caused the virtual absence of wetness in and around the drowning scene?

What caused the two bloodstains on the carpet under Sarah's body?

Was there any physical evidence linking Ryan to Sarah's body? Or to the bathtub?

Was there any proof that Sarah was knocked out? If so, maybe that would explain why Sarah suffered no "defensive" injuries—no scratches, scrapes or bruises on her elbows, knuckles and knees. Maybe that was how Ryan managed to walk away unscathed as Sarah fought for her life.

Could anything at the scene help show that Sarah was pushed underwater?

A possible answer to that last question materialized before Braley's eyes, almost magically.

It was Wednesday, August 13, 2008, two days after Sarah's drowning. Ryan was with his mom, talking to his lawyer and making Sarah's funeral arrangements, when Braley and other officers executed a search warrant at the Widmer home.

Braley went upstairs and, with the swirling motion he was taught in crime-scene training, he applied fingerprint-dusting powder onto the bathtub. Suddenly, the black powder on the white tub revealed "two sets of what appeared to be fingerprints on the back side of the tub ... a full set of both hands in a scraping motion down the side of the tub," Braley wrote in a memo.

Braley, Coroner's Investigator Doyle Burke, and another officer hurried downstairs and revealed their discovery to other officers.

Ohmigosh, Braley must have thought. Braley most likely envisioned the scenario that prosecutors later described: *Scary Ryan manhandled his sweet little wife as she desperately clawed for the tub's edge, leaving the hand streaks on the tub. Sarah couldn't get a grip, so she succumbed under the water.*

When Braley tried to figure out how to cut out the section of tub that contained those marks, a fellow officer suggested: Why not take *the entire bathtub?*

Good idea, Braley concluded. He got a workman to remove the tub from the Widmer home.

Ryan's lawyer, Charlie Rittgers, thought that seizing the tub was probably illegal. Police are required to specify what types of evidence they are seeking during a search. That preserves the U.S. Constitution's Fourth Amendment protections against unreasonable searches and seizures. But the tub was conspicuously absent from the Widmer home search warrants.

Nevertheless, Rittgers let it ride. He didn't want the public—and potential jurors—to think he was playing games, trying to hide evidence. He wasn't worried about the tub, anyway. He didn't think it contained any damning evidence. He didn't anticipate that The Bathtub and its finger streaks would soon become the star of The Widmer Show.

Tiny red flags

The Widmer case "to-do" list was growing—and Braley was the only detective then working for the twenty-five-member Hamilton Township Police Department. So Braley accepted reinforcements from the Warren County Sheriff's Office, a much larger police agency with more experience handling big cases.

As the investigation continued, Braley slid a version of the Scary Ryan photo into his case file. It must have served as a silent yet powerful reminder of Braley's mission: *Make sure this killer pays for his crime.*

The investigative team eventually interviewed more than a dozen people who knew Ryan and Sarah.

Computer experts scoured the couple's home computer, Ryan's work laptop and the server from Ryan's workplace. The cops combed bank records and phone records.

Through it all, they had trouble finding any reason for Ryan to kill Sarah.

Even though prosecutors aren't required to prove motive to get a murder conviction, juries *want* to know why one person would kill another. A case is simply stronger with a persuasive motive than without one.

During their investigation, Braley and other officers stumbled upon repeated references to Sarah's headaches and her unusual sleepiness. But Braley's file revealed no sign that anyone followed up on those concerns. Perhaps this was their mindset: Why wander down rabbit holes about headaches and sleepiness when you're searching for a murder motive?

There *had* to be *something* in Ryan's background that would put Sarah's slaying into context, the cops figured. But no big red flags popped up during interviews—only a few Tiny Red Flags, hints of possible motives.

Investigators were asking these types of questions—and they got these types of answers:

Had Ryan been cheating on Sarah?

No sign of that, said virtually everyone who had contact with the couple.

A woman who was more than twice Ryan's age came under suspicion as an alleged paramour. She was aghast.

Were Ryan and Sarah fighting?

Not that anyone noticed.

In fact, quite the opposite. One interviewee told the police that it was "neat to see" the way Ryan and Sarah interacted.

But police had taken a picture of something that raised questions: Sarah's clothes packed inside a pink suitcase. It was on the laundry room floor, near the door used to enter and exit the house through the garage. Had Sarah packed that bag with the intention of leaving her new husband?

Cops mentally labeled the packed suitcase Tiny Red Flag No. 1—but not for long.

Because they learned an innocuous reason for the packed clothes: Sarah and her mom had just returned from a road trip to St. Louis the day before she died; Sarah apparently hadn't unpacked yet.

The packed suitcase barely earned a passing mention or two when Ryan's case went to trial.

Nevertheless, that suitcase became almost legendary, a piece of Widmer lore. Years later, some police officers would talk about it in hushed tones, offering this "inside information:" Ryan killed Sarah in a rage because he found out she was going to grab that suitcase and leave him!

That would have been a fine motive for murder—if investigators found evidence to support it. They never did.

Were Ryan and Sarah having money problems?

There was no sign of that. Sarah earned about $60,000 a year, about $10,000 more than Ryan. Together, they made about $110,000—very comfortable for a young couple just starting out in southwest Ohio, where the cost of living is low.

But investigators learned that Ryan would comment about Sarah's inability to spend less than a hundred bucks during a trip to Target, and he seemed to track her expenses, according to her mom.

Prosecutors decided to offer testimony about that, considering it Tiny Red Flag No. 2. This testimony was used to portray Ryan as "controlling," a hallmark trait of an abusive husband.

Did Ryan kill Sarah to claim a fat life insurance check?

Sarah had applied for a life-insurance policy at work two weeks before her death. But it wasn't in force yet, so no one could benefit financially from Sarah's demise.

Still, the timing of that application set off suspicions, especially because Ryan reportedly had tried pressuring Sarah into getting life insurance. Prosecutors decided that was definitely worth bringing up at trial. Wave Tiny Red Flag No. 3.

Was Ryan a drunk? Maybe even a mean drunk?

Police were suspicious about Ryan's drinking habits because of some things they saw in the Widmer house: several beer cans, a kegerator (a small refrigerator that dispenses beer), and empty cartons of Bud Light and Miller Light inside the red recycling bin at the Widmer home.

No one reported seeing Ryan mean or belligerent after he drank beer, although Ryan did tell police he had drunk four beers the night Sarah drowned. Drinking beer became Tiny Red Flag No. 4.

Did Ryan have a bad temper?

Detectives searched exhaustively for any indication that Ryan ever got mad at anyone or anything. They came up empty-handed except for a childhood friend, who claimed that Ryan would get riled up about sports because he was so competitive—when he was 10 years old.

Authorities apparently decided that was a "reach." So they yanked that potential Tiny Red Flag and tossed it aside.

But detectives did discover a clue that seemed to suggest the Widmer marriage wasn't as rosy as everyone thought: a pair of envelopes, found in the couple's nightstands, marked, "In Case of a Marriage Emergency."

When I saw those envelopes on a list of property seized from the Widmer home, I wondered: Why would a pair of newlyweds have envelopes labeled like that? The answer would be revealed when the case went to trial.

The envelopes became Tiny Red Flag No. 5.

Other Tiny Red Flags popped up, and prosecutors used many of them at trial, too. When there's no clear-cut motive, each Tiny Red Flag really counts. Without even a glimmer of a motive, some jurors might feel uneasy about convicting a guy who had been nothing but law-abiding before that fateful, allegedly hateful night.

Defense team kept secrets too

While police were digging for the *how* and the *why* of the case, Ryan's defense team was figuring out how to neutralize suspicions.

Attorney Charlie Rittgers had gathered some information about the lead investigator, Lieutenant Jeff Braley, and some of it was unflattering.

But Rittgers was reluctant to use that dossier. He knew that the average juror dislikes seeing a defense lawyer bullying a cop on the witness stand. Jurors generally think of cops as "the good guys," public servants who put their lives on the line every day.

Besides, Rittgers knew a lot of officers and liked many of them.

That mindset, plus the belief that there was plenty of evidence on Ryan's side, led Rittgers to decide against assailing Braley on the witness stand, except as a last resort.

Rittgers' assessment of the case went something like this:

Jury might be sympathetic to guy like Ryan: College-educated, clean-cut, no criminal or violent past, married only four months. Wife suffered weird bouts of sleepiness and headaches. Wife told several people she didn't feel well hours before she died. No scratches, scrapes, other defensive wounds on wife. No injuries of any kind on husband. No history of violence or arguments. No motive.

All of that is undisputed.

Reasonable to believe that undiagnosed medical disorder took hold while wife happened to be in bathtub. Inaccurate coroner's ruling, based on incomplete info, led to unfair charges, hastily filed, against husband. Experts with superior qualifications disagree with coroner's homicide ruling.

Based on all of that, the jurors should have "reasonable doubt" about Ryan's guilt—and would be compelled to acquit him.

Rittgers and his old friend, Warren County Prosecutor Rachel Hutzel, dug in their heels for an epic tug-of-war over the Widmer case.

Amid a flurry of legal skirmishes during the fall of 2008, Rittgers knocked Hutzel off-balance.

Rittgers kept trying to get Hutzel to reveal what evidence the county coroner used to conclude that Sarah's death was violent. Rittgers noted that reports—from emergency medical crews, the hospital and the coroner's investigator—all explicitly noted no obvious sign of trauma to Sarah's body.

Rittgers said he couldn't prepare an adequate defense without knowing what physical evidence the coroner found and the rationale behind his ruling.

Hutzel stood her ground. She refused to disclose what the coroner had discovered. She fought Rittgers' attempt to get his hands on the coroner's secret grand jury testimony. Rittgers was taking a long shot; he knew that courts rarely order disclosure of grand jury testimony.

Finally, in late October 2008, Rittgers did manage to get the coroner to talk privately with him about the autopsy on Sarah.

Six days after that meeting, Rittgers revealed that Dr. Werner Spitz had conducted a second autopsy—and that the renowned forensic pathologist was slated to testify on behalf of the defense. Rittgers said the delay wasn't the result of any strategizing. Rather, Rittgers had been waiting for Spitz to finish his report.

The revelation that Spitz had done a second autopsy on Sarah left Hutzel and her staff unpleasantly surprised—putting it mildly.

While Rittgers had publicly complained about the prosecution holding back vital information, Hutzel and her staff had supplied more than five hundred pages of documents and dozens of photographs to Rittgers. Hutzel counter-accused Rittgers of springing Spitz and another medical expert on the prosecution at the last minute. Rittgers provided the Spitz autopsy report to prosecutors on October 30, 2008, eighteen days before the trial's planned start date on November 17.

After a hearing about the prosecution's beef with Rittgers, the judge ordered the trial delayed until March 23, 2009—the next date open on his docket for a two-week trial.

Ryan didn't like the postponement one bit.

He vented his frustrations in an email sent to Rittgers' secretary, Kathy Edwards: "I know I am probably barking up the wrong tree, but how is this fair? ...They indicted me so quickly without even doing a true investigation and oh, are still 'investigating.' I'm sorry but this whole system is so unfair...I just want my life back."

Ryan had not waived his right to a "speedy trial." Under Ohio law, authorities have 270 days to try a defendant who is free on bond, as Ryan was. The deadline for trying Ryan would have been just 90 days if he had remained locked up. If a speedy-trial deadline is missed, the consequence is severe: charges are thrown out permanently.

That wasn't going to happen in Ryan's case because the new trial date in spring 2009 was well within the 270-day limit. Yet prosecutors now had more time to load up ammunition to fire at Spitz—and more chances to fill in some gaps, including the lack of motive.

At the time of the November 2008 postponement, Ryan had already waited three months to go on trial. Now he would have to wait another four months. He was frustrated. He felt like he was hit with the murder charge with lightning speed, just two days after Sarah died, then a dark cloud hovered over him for seven long, dreary months while he waited for the trial.

Ryan believed that the sooner the trial would come, the sooner he would be exonerated—if there was any such thing as justice. Then he could truly grieve for Sarah. Maybe that dark cloud would drift away. Then Ryan could try to get on with his life, while still trying to honor his memories of Sarah. He wanted to contribute to a dental-hygiene scholarship that had been set up in her name. He also wanted to help Hutzel's critics throw her out of office. He believed she was more interested in impressing potential voters than in securing justice—an accusation that gained traction among Ryan's supporters but rankled people who respected Hutzel.

While the trial date was still months away, all Ryan could do was mark time.

It was almost as if he were in Purgatory. He was trapped somewhere between Heaven—where Ryan felt like he had briefly lived with his angel, Sarah—and Hell, where some people thought Ryan should be headed if he had killed her.

Ryan's lawyer tested him

While Ryan was glad to be out of jail, he wasn't really "living," as his mother, Jill, put it. He was just "existing." So was she. The weight of the case took its toll on both of them, and on everyone close to them.

Ryan didn't eat much. He had trouble sleeping. And he was nervous about going anywhere. Ryan was afraid that, if people recognized him, he would be ridiculed, possibly hounded by news reporters or, worse, he might inadvertently violate a rule and be thrown back in jail.

Ryan, like his dad, usually kept his emotions to himself. But whenever he thought about the night Sarah died, his face would contort. And tears, which never flowed freely for Ryan before, gushed nonstop when he was alone.

His thoughts would flash back to the happy times he and Sarah had shared for a year and a half inside their home on Crested Owl Court, and during their six-month courtship before that. The memories left Ryan feeling an acute ache in his heart for his lost love—the woman he was accused of murdering.

If Ryan actually killed Sarah, his torture was of his own making, and it was only the beginning of his just desserts.

But Ryan maintained that he was completely innocent. And because Sarah died and he was accused of killing her, he said he was cheated and robbed. Her death cheated Ryan out of the chance to experience more joyful times with Sarah; being prosecuted robbed Ryan of the ability to hold onto those treasured memories.

Just as a computer hard drive can only hold so much data, Ryan's mind seemed to have little remaining storage space to devote to the pleasant pictures of the past. Those memories were supplanted by the *right here, right now* of his court case. It was all-consuming; his brain short-circuited trying to compute what was happening and to chart a course through it all.

Ryan hesitated to go back to the house filled with memories of Sarah. But it was sometimes necessary because nearly everything he owned was still inside.

Once, when Ryan tried to go retrieve some belongings, his electronic-monitoring ankle bracelet, issued to keep track of defendants on bond or probation, sounded an alarm. Then a deputy called Ryan and declared he was forbidden from the premises. The house was still considered a crime scene, he told Ryan.

Rittgers wrote a letter to the deputy, pointing out that nearly a month had elapsed after officers finished scouring the Widmer home for evidence.

Ryan eventually was able to get his possessions.

Because of such experiences, Ryan started feeling paranoid.

Heck, Ryan said, he wouldn't be surprised if the authorities would try to drum up something else to "pin" on him. As if the murder accusations weren't enough.

Ryan knew that if he violated any condition of his release on bond, he would be jailed until he went to trial. And even though that would force prosecutors to put him on trial much faster under speedy-trial limits, Ryan yearned to remain free. So he was extra careful about following the rules.

He was ordered to live at his mom's house in Mason, Ohio, and he was under a curfew. He had to remain inside the house between 9 p.m. and 7 a.m. daily.

Besides wearing the electronic-tracking ankle bracelet, Ryan believed he was being tailed everywhere he went. His brothers also noticed people following them when they were with Ryan.

Ryan was required to undergo urine tests to make sure he wasn't doing drugs. When a friend offered an energy drink, Ryan turned it down. He had heard rumors about herbal ingredients in such drinks causing "false positive" drug-test results. Ryan refused to consume beverages other than coffee, tea or milk.

He was taking no chances.

He tried to help his defense team, although he often felt powerless to do so.

At one point, early in the trial-preparation process, Attorney Rittgers and Ryan returned to the Widmer home to review, step by step, what had happened the night Sarah died.

As they approached the house, Rittgers knew there was a crucial question he had to ask Ryan. It would test Ryan's honesty. And the way Ryan answered it could change the way Rittgers defended Ryan.

It was about the two bloodstains on the carpet: One near Sarah's head; the other, near her pelvis. When Ryan first met with Rittgers on August 13, 2008, Ryan had said something that "fit" with the two bloodstains, Rittgers thought.

At the time, Ryan almost certainly was unaware that the bloodstains even existed. When Ryan last saw Sarah, her body was on top of the bloodstains, covering them. Police escorted Ryan out of the room while medics worked on Sarah, so he had little or no opportunity to see the two bloodstains.

Notes from Ryan's first meeting with Rittgers said: "He pulled her out, half in br (bathroom), half in bedroom ... cop pulled with (Ryan) out on floor."

After learning about the two bloodstains, Rittgers realized that the movement of Sarah's body provided a simple explanation: Bloody froth had gushed from her mouth and nose, creating Bloodstain No. 1. After Sarah's body was moved a few feet further into the bedroom, her pelvis was positioned above Bloodstain No. 1—then more bloody froth created Bloodstain No. 2, the one near her head.

Voila. The mystery of the bloodstains was solved, Rittgers thought.

Also, he reasoned, if Sarah was lying in the doorway as Ryan had described— the lower half of her body in the bathroom and the upper half in the bedroom— medics would have needed more room to work on her. An experienced police officer would have realized that.

Yes, Rittgers figured, this version of events fits the evidence. And it makes sense.

So Rittgers thought Ryan was most likely being truthful about the officer helping him move Sarah.

But Rittgers hit a snag with this key aspect of Ryan's story.

Rittgers was acquainted with the first-arriving police officer, Deputy Steve Bishop. And Rittgers always thought of Bishop as "one of the good guys," an officer who went into law enforcement for the right reasons. One who behaved with integrity. One who told the truth. One who tried his best to serve and protect, even if that meant jeopardizing his own life or safety.

So Rittgers had every reason to believe Bishop would accurately describe his actions on the night Sarah drowned.

But when Rittgers asked Bishop whether he helped Ryan to reposition Sarah, so that her whole body was on the bedroom carpet, Bishop gave an answer that knocked the wind out of Rittgers. The officer said he "didn't remember" that happening, Rittgers told me.

Rittgers was taken aback. Bishop's failure to corroborate Ryan's account created a dilemma for Rittgers: Should he believe Ryan?

Rittgers set out to test Ryan's truthfulness.

When Rittgers and Ryan arrived at the Widmer home to review the events surrounding Sarah's death, Rittgers let Ryan tell his story once again.

As Ryan got to the part where he stated that the first-arriving officer helped him to move Sarah, Rittgers confronted his client: "Would it surprise you if I told you that he doesn't remember moving her body?"

Ryan got a puzzled look on his face, then exclaimed: "He should remember that, 'cause he's the one that told me to move her!"

Rittgers looked for any sign of deception in Ryan. He saw none.

Over the years, Rittgers had caught quite a few of his clients in lies. But he says that never happened with Ryan.

Rittgers thought Ryan was being truthful about all the circumstances, including his insistence that the first officer helped move Sarah. Even so, Rittgers didn't want to cast aspersions on Bishop.

Confronted with this glaring contradiction between his client's statement and the deputy's, Rittgers wondered: What should I do about this? Should I question Bishop further? Or leave this alone?

That was one of hundreds of decisions that Rittgers would need to make before the case went to trial—or during the trial. As every trial lawyer knows, each judgment has potential to change the course of the entire case.

Sarah's family drifts away

Ryan had been confident that he could count on the support of his wife's family. They knew the kind of guy he was. They knew how much he loved Sarah. They knew he would never harm her.

He believed that Sarah's family didn't see her death as a crime. He believed that Sarah's family saw her death as a horrible tragedy, a consequence of her weird drowsiness and other symptoms. He believed Sarah's family thought he was unfairly accused—and they would stand by him.

Ryan remembered a poignant visit with Sarah's mom, Ruth Ann Steward, while he was still locked up in the county jail. "She was asking for my approval to do Sarah's (funeral) Mass and told me we would do a private burial when I was out," Ryan said. "We were both crying and I remember her telling me she knew I had nothing to do with this (Sarah's death)."

Ryan said yes, of course, go ahead with the memorial service, even if he couldn't get out of jail in time to be there.

Soon, however, Ryan began sensing that the Stewards' support for him was fragile.

In late August 2008, shortly after Ryan was released on bond, a conversation with Sarah's brother, Mike Steward, left Ryan dismayed.

The two men were at the home of Ryan's mom, Jill, on the back deck, talking about Sarah's tragic death—and about the charges against Ryan. As Ryan recalled it, the conversation went something like this:

"We're ninety-five percent sure that you didn't have anything to do with this," Mike said.

Ryan responded, "Well, I don't see how you're even giving a five percent chance, because I would never hurt her. Never."

Then Mike stated that Lieutenant Jeff Braley "seemed like a nice guy," and Mike encouraged Ryan to just let the detective do his investigation and see what turned up.

Ryan could hardly believe his ears. How could Mike call Braley "a nice guy," considering that Braley was instrumental in getting Ryan charged and locked up?

Ryan's jaw dropped open. He was too stunned to give Mike much push-back. But it left him feeling that Mike might be drifting away from his corner, and he couldn't figure out why.

Ryan believed he could at least rely on Sarah's mom and grandmothers. They seemed to really like him.

Ryan fondly recalled that, shortly after Sarah's death, Sarah's maternal grandma made a home-cooked meal of liver and onions for Ryan and his mom, Jill. Ryan loved that type of hearty, simple meal. It was the same type of comfort food that Ryan's grandma Ethel used to make for him before she died of cancer.

As Ryan, Jill and Sarah's grandma ate together, they reminisced about Sarah.

Ryan went by himself to visit Sarah's paternal grandmother and had an equally pleasant visit with her.

Ryan also thought he had a solid relationship with Sarah's mom, Ruth Ann. After all, she had given Ryan her blessing to marry Sarah. But Ryan didn't know what Sarah's mom had told police: she had harbored reservations about Sarah marrying Ryan in the first place.

Ruth Ann didn't know details of the couple's finances, but she told a detective that, "Sarah made considerably more (money) than Ryan." This troubled Ruth Ann "because she believed the man of the house should be the primary provider and maybe Sarah should reconsider her marriage to Ryan," the detective wrote. "Sarah said she loved him and Ruth Ann said okay to the marriage."

No other statements from the Stewards were included in the Widmer case file that Braley kept. Not unless you count statements in the *Enquirer* article I wrote about her family publicly voicing support for Ryan—the only news article Braley found significant enough to keep in the Widmer file.

On October 11, 2008, exactly two months after Sarah died, her family held a private burial for her cremains. Once again, Father John Tonkin, the same priest who married Ryan and Sarah and conducted the public memorial Mass, was there to comfort Ryan and other loved ones on that cool Saturday morning.

Sarah's ashes were interred in Butler County Memorial Park, at the foot of her dad's gravesite. The family plot sits in a section called, "Garden of Eternal Love," between a wooded area and an access road. Later, a brass grave marker was added to Sarah's final resting place: "SARAH ANN," no last name, with her dates of birth and death; an angel sits in the bottom left corner.

During the burial, Ryan thought that Sarah's family seemed strangely distant to him.

Two days afterward, a "family meeting" was listed in Braley's notes, with no further details. Was that meeting pivotal in Sarah's family turning against Ryan?

Possibly. Because shortly thereafter, Ryan stopped hearing from the Stewards.

Crime suspects routinely are court-ordered to have no contact with relatives of the purported crime victim. No such order was in place when Ryan was released from jail; that order was added months later, without comment.

In early November 2008, nothing would have forbidden Sarah's family from contacting Ryan. He emailed Rittgers and told him that Mike hadn't returned his phone call, so Rittgers could go ahead and make one last try to reach the Stewards. "If this is going to go on any longer, they need to know the truth and not get persuaded with lies any more than they might (have been) already," Ryan wrote in an email to Rittgers' secretary.

Noting that Sarah's mom and brother were both listed as trial witnesses for the prosecution, Rittgers wrote a letter to Ruth Ann on November 11, 2008.

"I can only assume due to the lack of communication with Ryan and me that the prosecutor has somehow tainted your impression of Ryan," Rittgers wrote. "Until a couple of weeks ago, I truly did not have an understanding as to the prosecutor's conclusions. As of the drafting of this letter, my opinion of Ryan's innocence has not changed."

Rittgers wanted to know what the Stewards' potential testimony might be. "I would also like to take that same opportunity to share with you what I know about Sarah's death and why your impressions of Ryan's innocence when I first met you were well-founded ... and why the state's coroner came to an incorrect conclusion."

He never got a reply. Rittgers knew what that meant: Ryan could no longer count on the Stewards' support.

"I was stunned by their reversal," Rittgers said.

Lots of people were.

As of early 2018, when the case was approaching its ten-year anniversary, the Stewards still had not publicly disclosed what caused their apparent change of heart.

Ryan, lawyers, police keep probing

In the months prior to trial, Ryan and the legal teams who were working for him and against him all pressed forward, trying to answer the most important *how's* and *why's,* as they perceived them.

Police and prosecutors were trying to figure out: *How* exactly did Ryan kill Sarah, and *how* can we show that to a jury? *Why* did Ryan kill Sarah?

Ryan's lawyers were trying to figure out: *How* did the coroner conclude that Sarah's death was a homicide? And *how* can we convince a jury that his conclusion was incorrect? *Why* did the coroner rule so quickly?

Ryan was trying to figure out: *How* can I make them see that I didn't do this? *Why* is this happening to me? *Why* won't they try to find out what really happened to Sarah?

All of them found more frustration than answers.

After investigators re-interviewed Ryan and Sarah's neighbors, one of the neighbors posted a comment on Cincinnati.com, saying that a detective had admitted, "They really didn't have anything. His words. Not mine."

The neighbor continued: "I have no idea of Ryan Widmer's innocence or guilt. But I am going to call a spade a spade and say that everything that has been presented SO FAR has been extremely underwhelming." That comment was made in November 2008, when news broke about the trial being reset for the following March.

The neighbor also said it was doubtful that the county prosecutor "has a barrelful of secret evidence she is waiting to spring at trial."

In the weeks leading up to the trial, Ryan started filling a white, three-ring binder with paperwork. It resembled the one that Braley filled. But there were no big, bold letters on the cover. Instead the cover was completely blank.

To those who believed Ryan killed Sarah, maybe the blank cover could be symbolic of Ryan's refusal to admit his wrongdoing. To those who think Ryan was wrongfully accused, the blank cover could reflect Ryan's utter inability to put any kind of label on what he was going through.

Either way, Ryan had no idea which papers were important and which weren't. This was all new to him. So he saved even perfunctory one-line notes from his lawyer, notifying him that certain documents had been provided to prosecutors. Ryan inserted those records into the binder under a divider tab marked, "TRIAL STUFF."

Another of Ryan's documents showed how desperate he was to find any shred of evidence to support his version of events.

After learning about the fuss over Ryan's downstairs TV being tuned to the wrong channel for the Bengals game—despite Ryan's statement to police about his TV-watching—Ryan decided to write to his satellite TV provider, DIRECTV, for help.

Ryan thought DIRECTV might have records that would demonstrate that he indeed was watching the Bengals game the night that Sarah died, just as he had claimed, and that he had just switched channels to check on the Olympic Games.

If Ryan could prove that he was telling the truth about watching the Bengals game, he naively believed that some of the suspicion about him might evaporate.

In November 2008, Ryan emailed DIRECTV: "I am in need to find out if you can show what I watched at a specific time and date? I need this to prove something in a court of law. Can you show what I was watching on the date of August 11, 2008 from 6 p.m. to 11 p.m.? I know that my account is suspended now, but if there is any way to show this I would greatly appreciate it."

DIRECTV responded that the company kept no record of a customer's TV-channel-switching.

Although crestfallen that he couldn't even prove this small point, Ryan was still clinging to the hope that *something* would surface that would make the prosecution realize that they were wrong to accuse him. Then they'd drop the charges. Or, if the case went to trial, surely the jurors would see he was innocent—wouldn't they?

Even if Ryan had succeeded in proving he was truthful about his TV-watching, that wouldn't have proven he was telling the truth about playing no part in Sarah's death. The prosecution still had plenty more reasons to make a jury suspicious of him.

Meanwhile, Ryan's legal team continued interviewing people who knew Ryan and Sarah. Common themes emerged, reconfirming what Rittgers already believed about the case:

Sarah was too headstrong to allow herself to be mistreated, said her best friend Katie Cook and others. In fact, most friends said Sarah was the dominant partner in the Ryan-Sarah relationship.

Ryan was patient, thoughtful and had little or no temper, Katie and others said; he certainly didn't seem capable of launching into a murderous rage. "Ryan was not the type of person that ever really got angry about anything," Katie told one of Ryan's lawyers. In fact, Katie, who helped Ryan and Sarah build their back-porch deck, gave this description: Ryan could be re-drilling a screw into the deck for the eleventh time and he still didn't get upset.

Katie said she was "floored and flabbergasted" when she found out Sarah was dead, and that Ryan was accused of killing her, because nobody could think of any reason why Ryan would kill Sarah.

It seemed that everyone who knew Ryan and Sarah believed the couple was soaring on a cloud of wedded bliss.

The day before Sarah died, a longtime family friend, Greg M., golfed with Ryan on a public West Chester, Ohio golf course. He said Ryan was more animated than usual that day, as he chatted happily about his young bride.

Greg, his son, and Ryan usually golfed together several Sundays a month. But the trio hadn't been together for a while because of scheduling conflicts. In fact, this outing was the first time the three men had gotten together since Ryan and Sarah had honeymooned in Costa Rica that April.

So, on August 10, 2008, while Sarah was driving back from St. Louis with her mother, Ryan spent nearly the whole golf outing beaming and recounting how much fun he and Sarah had during their honeymoon. The most memorable adventure: a zip-lining excursion through the rainforest.

"He was a happy young man, as happy as a young man could be," Greg M. told one of Ryan's lawyers.

There was no outward sign of trouble brewing in the newlyweds' marriage that day. Nor was there any tension apparent that evening when Ryan and Sarah went to a cookout at Ryan's mom's house, relatives said.

But the following night, Sarah would be dead, allegedly at the hands of her doting husband.

Marking time

Ryan and his twin brother, Ayran, marked their 28th birthdays on November 3, 2008. They got together with a few other relatives at their mom's house, even though no one felt much like celebrating. There was a somber undercurrent because Sarah and her high-pitched giggle were noticeably absent—and everyone felt the weight of the criminal charges on Ryan's shoulders.

Oddly, though, there also was a feeling of anticipation. The Widmer family was looking forward to the November 17 trial date, because they believed that would be the start of some good things for all of them. The truth would come out, Ryan would be acquitted and he would be set free, his relatives thought.

But nine days after the Widmer twins' birthday, Ryan's trial was reset for March—dashing hopes that their ordeal would be over soon.

One small consolation to Ryan's family: Along with the trial-postponement order, the judge ordered Ryan's electronic-monitoring device to be removed, eliminating the $400-per-month fee that had to be paid while he was wearing it.

The Thanksgiving and Christmas holidays passed with no notable developments in the case.

Christmas was especially hard for everyone who knew Sarah, because she absolutely loved that holiday. She would get very excited about decorating the house and making everything look festive. And she would squeal with delight when she picked out just the right gift to make each recipient happy. Her absence was particularly acute at Christmas. Ryan daydreamed about what it would be like to have her back with him again.

One can only imagine how bleak the Stewards' holidays were without Sarah. She had lit up their lives for all of her 24 years; Ryan had known Sarah for only about one-tenth of her life.

Her relatives kept their grief to themselves; they didn't return the phone messages I left seeking comment for news stories several times while the case was pending.

Occasionally, I'd reach Mike, Sarah's brother. But he would always decline comment very politely. I wasn't used to that type of treatment from people I contacted about criminal cases. Understandably, hearing from a reporter was often the last thing that stressed-out relatives of victims and suspects would want. They'd frequently hang up on me.

But that wasn't the case with Mike. I thought that said something about his character and his upbringing. And I respected the Stewards' decision to stay private. Still, my editors insisted that we try to get the Stewards to comment at key junctures. And it did seem fundamentally unfair to the Stewards that so much was being reported on Ryan's behalf, while so little was being said about Sarah. But that was partly because her family was so tight-lipped—and because the prosecutors weren't saying much, either.

Their part of the story was being kept under wraps, and we reporters could do nothing other than wait to see what the Stewards and the prosecution would say at trial.

In the meantime, several people urged Ryan to start keeping a journal. It would help him to organize his thoughts. It would allow him to vent his frustrations. And it would help pass the time until the trial started.

Ryan resisted at first. He didn't think writing down his thoughts would make him feel any better. But he decided it couldn't hurt.

Finally, on New Year's Eve of 2008, nearly five months after Sarah died, Ryan sat down with the high-quality journal that a relative had given to him for Christmas.

Ryan opened the soft, chestnut-brown leather cover, embossed with a fleur-de-lis design. And he began to write.

Kim & Josh's house. Yet another terrible day and night without Sarah. Spending the evening as the ball drops to a new year all alone watching TV in the basement.

That was it. Those three sentences were all that flowed out of his pen that night.

Ryan slid the brown satin bookmark along the crease of that first entry. He looped a leather cord around the journal and pulled its metal fastener tight. A sense of futility overtook him. It seemed pointless to spill his guts in a journal.

But in the coming days and weeks, that journal would become his confidante. Ryan would eventually fill fifty-nine pages with his innermost thoughts and feelings, sprinkled with details of routine daily activities. Ryan recorded how he and his family members occupied themselves and stayed out of public sight by playing games such as ping-pong, *Monopoly*, *Axis & Allies* and *Life*.

The contents of Ryan's journal, however, would remain secret for many months.

For now, it was just Ryan writing solely for himself, expressing what was in his heart and what was in his head, as best he could, as his trial date approached.

The final entry in Ryan's journal was dated March 17, 2009—six days before Trial One began. In that entry, Ryan reported that he was happy with the way his lawyer, Charlie Rittgers, handled a motion hearing. Ryan also noted that a TV station was reporting that Prosecutor Rachel Hutzel had backed out of the case.

Hutzel had promised to personally prosecute Ryan, which was unusual.

In general, elected county prosecutors rarely take a case to trial themselves; they let assistant prosecutors do most of the trench work. If the chief elected prosecutor does decide to directly try a case, that usually would happen only when the case is well-publicized—and when it is perceived to be a "slam-dunk," a clear-cut win.

I had noticed that Hutzel's name was suddenly absent from court filings for the Widmer case. Previously, her signature had appeared along with those of two assistant prosecutors whom she had assigned to it.

I asked Hutzel why her name disappeared from the Widmer filings; her response in a *Cincinnati Enquirer* article just before Trial One in March 2009: "There were already three of us on it," Hutzel said. "Our general feeling was that it was too many people to have on a case ... while this one is important, it is one of many, many important cases."

Big cases hardly ever happened in Warren County; everyone knew that. So I wondered whether Hutzel had other reasons to distance herself from the Widmer case. Had she lost confidence in the evidence because of the Spitz autopsy? And Hutzel was pursuing a judgeship. If she lost a high-profile case such as Widmer's, that almost certainly would not play well with voters.

When I was able to confront Hutzel face-to-face, I asked her whether she doubted the strength of the Widmer evidence. She responded that she would never let her assistant prosecutors go to trial on a case that she didn't believe in. That was her ethical obligation as a prosecutor: to seek justice, not just a conviction.

With that, I strapped in tight and waited to see what would be revealed in court.

Finally, the Friday before trial arrived.

Nervously, Ryan picked out a suit, shirt and tie to wear. In fact, he selected three different options. He knew he had to make a good impression with what he wore. He drove to Attorney Charlie Rittgers' house to get approval on his wardrobe choices.

Rittgers vetoed one of the shirts, a peach one, Ryan said, because the hue was "too bold." Rittgers settled on a black suit with faint blue pinstripes for his client to wear for the first day of the trial.

Rittgers thought the suit looked fine, even though it wasn't the best-fitting. It looked baggy on Ryan because he had lost so much weight. While awaiting trial, Ryan seemed to be withering away. His once-robust 190 pounds had shrunk to 155 pounds painfully clinging to his six-feet, two-inch frame.

Besides talking about Ryan's apparel choices, Rittgers reminded Ryan about the proper way to behave in court while sitting in the defendant's chair. Sit up straight. Don't grimace. Don't fidget. And avoid showing emotion, no matter what happens. If you cry, it might seem like you're faking being upset. If you let a nervous grin creep across your face, it might seem like you're not taking the situation seriously enough.

Bottom line: Any reaction can and will be held against you. The jurors will be staring at you, trying to read your mind, trying to picture whether you committed the crime as alleged.

Rittgers gave Ryan one final admonishment: "You realize that there will be people who think you're guilty just because you're sitting in that chair, don't you?"

Ryan's eyes widened and he swallowed hard. He didn't think that was how the legal system was supposed to work.

CHAPTER 6
Trial One, Strike One

It was a sunny spring morning outside, but inside Judge Neal Bronson's courtroom in Lebanon, Ohio, the air felt electrically charged, as if a thunderstorm
were brewing.

It was the first day of the much-anticipated Ryan Widmer trial.

More than seven months had passed after Ryan made his now-infamous 911
call and reported: "My wife fell asleep in the bathtub and I think she's dead."

The initial wave of publicity lasted several weeks after Sarah Widmer drowned
in August 2008. A few legal skirmishes grabbed headlines in the ensuing
months.

And now it was showtime.

A throng of media had descended upon the courthouse, along with dozens of
prospective jurors and spectators. News reporters tried to find a strategic van-
tagepoint amid the sea of hunter-green chairs. The national TV show, *Dateline
NBC,* had concealed cameras in a tall black box. Then *Dateline* would share
video footage with local TV outlets, which, in turn, would feed national TV
networks.

TV crews could watch the live video feed on monitors in a room down the
hallway. But the judge had forbidden live TV broadcasts. Widmer Watchers
could get the next best thing: a "live blog," courtesy of Cincinnati's WLWT-TV,
Channel 5.

The WLWT blogger, Travis Gettys, would type direct quotes and testimony
into his computer, along with his own observations. His words would then pop
onto blog-watchers' computer screens.

This was a novel phenomenon for Cincinnatians, and folks got addicted to it
quickly. They hung on Travis' every word. They chimed in with comments and
questions, some of which Travis would post alongside his responses. Some
people even corrected Travis' mistakes and provided extra insights based on
their personal knowledge; one commenter said he was a lawyer.

I staked out my spot, then fired off a couple emails to let my editors at *The Cincinnati Enquirer* know that I would soon be filing updates for Cincinnati.com. Then I went into the hallway to do some snooping, just in time to see Ryan arrive. As he entered the courthouse, spotlights atop TV cameras lit up; photojournalists' cameras whirred and clicked as Ryan walked toward the courtroom.

He remembers his mind being filled with fear and disbelief. Fear, he said, of being convicted of a crime he didn't commit—and disbelief that all of this was happening. It was as if he had been tossed into a whitewater-rafting trip without a raft.

Then Ryan sat down in the defendant's chair—the one that his lawyer warned him about, the one that would cloak Ryan with an aura of guilt in many people's eyes.

As the trial was about to begin, a conversation with a fellow journalist surprised me. After seeing Ryan in person for the first time, a photographer nudged me and whispered, hesitantly: "I kinda think he might be innocent."

Wow, I thought, that's unusual for a photographer to express such an opinion, particularly so early in a case. I was intrigued.

"What makes you think that?" I asked.

"Just the way he looked at us," said the photographer. "It was really different from the way other accused guys usually look at us."

Some criminal defendants exude "swagger," a cocky attitude; they relish the photographers' attention. It's as if these suspects fancy themselves as stars, eager to feed the insatiable paparazzi.

Other crime suspects get defensive or belligerent when they see news cameras. A few try to hide their faces in shame.

Ryan did none of those things.

He was pretty much a blank slate, the photographer said. Except for his eyes. They looked sad. And tired.

Ryan's lack of overt reaction seemed to suggest he wasn't trying to hide anything. Nor was he trying to put on an act. At least that was the photographer's sense about him. To a degree, that was my sense, too.

Maybe Ryan would turn out to be a "what-you-see-is-what-you-get" guy, the photographer told me. The "vibe" the photographer got was that Ryan was an ordinary fellow who didn't know what to think of the chaos that was enveloping him. He froze up; he seemed overwhelmed and numb.

Other people had a very different interpretation of Ryan's stoicism: Maybe his lack of emotional response emanated from a cold, hard heart—the heart of a killer.

As for my opinion of Ryan, it was hanging in limbo.

I hadn't spoken to Ryan yet, but I had talked to people who knew him. They were adamant: No way, no how could Ryan *ever* kill anyone, especially not his wife Sarah. He was too nice, too sweet, too in love with Sarah.

Yet, I reminded myself: We've all heard about people who were well-liked and well-respected—role models, even—until it became shockingly obvious that they had committed disturbing crimes.

But if Ryan had killed his wife, *why* would he do it? This real-life mystery involved a young couple who, as a blogger named "BengalBeotch" bluntly put it, "had the world by the ass." Both were college-educated, working good jobs with newer cars and a nice house. They were "still honeymooning, still playing house," BengalBeotch wrote. Besides being a loyal Bengals fan like Ryan, BengalBeotch was also a close friend of Ryan and his family.

BengalBeotch wrote that, after Ryan and Sarah's promising future screeched to a halt, the depths of Ryan's grief were obvious to anyone who observed him.

"I don't even know how to explain it, but he was broken," the blogger-friend wrote. "I've never seen a grown man so lost and devastated."

BengalBeotch was convinced Ryan was innocent. She was hoping the jury would see it that way, too.

Opinions, theories, evidence

Ryan's detractors theorized that he must have "snapped" and forcibly drowned his bride. Sarah died before she was able to see the photo album their wedding photographer had compiled.

The primary evidence against Ryan appeared to be subject to interpretation: the coroner's ruling—his *opinion*—that Sarah's injuries showed she had been killed.

And the defense seemed prepared to effectively counter-punch against the coroner's ruling with Dr. Werner Spitz's testimony. During my two decades of covering court cases, including quite a few murder trials, I'd never seen a case with a second autopsy done by an outside expert. Until Widmer.

I wondered: What were Spitz's findings? And would jurors be impressed with

Spitz's credentials? And what might he say about Sarah's strange sleepiness?

In advance of the trial, I did a little research on conditions that might have plagued Sarah. I learned that a large percentage of people with excessive daytime sleepiness, or narcolepsy, also suffer from cataplexy, sudden loss of muscular control or paralysis while remaining conscious. If that happened in the bathtub, drowning could result.

I tucked an internet printout into my file and waited to see whether Spitz or someone else would raise the possibility of such a disorder.

If even one credible expert said that Sarah's purported sleepiness could have been a sign of some underlying medical problem, that might equate to "reasonable doubt" and an acquittal—unless the prosecution rolled out some blockbuster evidence to shore up their case.

But we knew little about that evidence.

From the search warrant, we knew dozens of items had been seized.

And from Prosecutor Rachel Hutzel's statement, we knew that the county coroner had ruled Sarah's death a homicide because he saw evidence of a "violent struggle."

That description piqued my curiosity. Ditto for the evidence list.

What, precisely, was the evidence of a violent struggle?

What caused the bloodstains first-responders noted near Sarah's head and pelvis?

What clues had the bathtub yielded?

What did investigators learn from the Widmers' computers and phone records?

And what was the deal with the envelopes labeled, "In Case of a Marriage Emergency?"

Once a trial starts, seemingly disjointed factoids can come together in unexpected configurations—or a case can fall apart because there's no glue to join the jigsaw pieces into a cohesive picture.

Which direction would the Widmer case go? That was anyone's guess.

But the stage was set. The actors were ready. And the curtain lifted as the Widmer murder mystery began to play out on the "stage" in Lebanon. Such high courtroom drama had rarely been seen since the charming little city was founded in 1802.

DAY ONE

MONDAY, MARCH 23, 2009

Despite his lawyer's warnings to hold back his emotions, Ryan was unable to stop teardrops from escaping several times as jury selection began.

He pressed his fingers to his eyes, as if he could force the tears back inside.

The first time I noticed Ryan crying that day was when Judge Neal Bronson emphasized "the presumption of innocence" to the prospective jurors.

Years later, when I asked Ryan what was going through his head at that time, he replied: "I still couldn't comprehend how and why this was going on. My stomach had butterflies the whole time."

More than eighty people, culled from the county's voter registration rolls, showed up as potential jurors, more than twice the number usually summoned for cases in this county.

Before driving with his mom to the courthouse, Ryan had slept little and had eaten nothing. He ignored his growling, churning stomach. He put his trust in God, in his lawyer, Charlie Rittgers—and in the jurors who began filling the twelve seats in the jury box, adjacent to the witness stand and Judge Bronson's bench.

Rittgers was almost as much on edge as his client was.

He believed Ryan was innocent, and it was his job to try to expose the prosecution's case as deficient. If Rittgers failed to get the jury to see the evidence his way, Ryan could go to prison for the rest of his life.

Adding to the pressure, the trial was getting national attention and was expected to be packed with spectators. Even so, Rittgers felt confident about his preparation and his evidence. He felt ready.

But he worried that feeling pressure would make his voice crack. When he began talking, however, the words came out steadily and clearly. He breathed a sigh of relief; he now could lay out his case and project the confidence he felt despite his raw nerves.

He also spoke confidently outside the courtroom as he passionately defended Ryan in response to reporters' questions.

If the two assistant prosecutors, Travis Vieux and John Arnold, were anxious, they managed to hide it.

They came across every bit as self-assured as Rittgers did. But there was one major difference: They weren't talking to reporters. Not even casually.

Perhaps that was because Prosecutor Rachel Hutzel wanted to be the primary spokesperson for her office on this case.

But we reporters also got the distinct feeling that neither Arnold nor Vieux liked dealing with the news media—which was odd because Hutzel's other assistant prosecutors generally were media-friendly and media-savvy.

First thing in the morning, the prosecution and defense teams went into a private conference with the judge.

Then both teams of lawyers entered the courtroom to begin jury selection. The "jury pick," as laypeople often call it, might more accurately be labeled, "juror elimination." Prosecutors and defense lawyers try to get rid of prospective jurors who seem less-receptive to their theory of the case.

The lawyers try to suss out jurors' inclinations based on their personal backgrounds, answers to questions and just a "gut feeling" about facial expressions or attitude. Some lawyers even hire jury consultants who advise what characteristics to avoid in potential jurors.

In legal parlance, jury selection is called *voir dire* (pronounced "vwarh-deer"), Old French-Latin for "to say the truth."

People with an obvious conflict of interest are usually booted off the jury right away, dismissed "for cause." People with scheduling conflicts, medical issues, family obligations and financial hardships also may ask to be excused; most of those requests are granted with minimal questioning.

Each side can kick off four potential jurors without stating why, using "peremptory challenges."

Because pretrial publicity about the Widmer case had been so pervasive, lots of people worried whether an impartial jury could be seated.

Even though I had helped create some of that publicity, I was concerned about that, too. Everywhere I went, people seemed to be talking about the Widmer case.

A potential juror with prior knowledge of the case would be disqualified only by admitting to an opinion, being unable to disregard that opinion and/or being unable to base a verdict solely on facts presented in court.

Folks were asked to raise their hands if they had read, heard or seen anything about the case of Ryan Widmer. Quite a few hands went up. Among those people, about a half-dozen admitted to deeply entrenched opinions; they were excused right away.

Then people cited a litany of reasons to be excused from jury duty: Plans for a spring-break trip. Mother diagnosed with cancer. A disruptive cough. A man's pregnant wife ready to give birth. And one that threw Judge Bronson for a loop: Reluctance to miss judo lessons.

The remaining potential jurors were asked things such as:

Would you hold it against Ryan if he doesn't testify?

Will you wait until you hear all of the evidence before you make up your mind?

Can you tolerate looking at "pretty graphic" autopsy photos of Sarah? Ryan wiped tears from his eyes as he heard that description.

Questioning went on for several hours.

Prosecutors used peremptory challenges to remove two jurors, including one who said he might have a hard time convicting someone of murder without a motive.

Rittgers also felt uncomfortable about two jurors.

One was an engineer. Many lawyers are leery of anyone who works in such an exacting, analytical role. Their thought processes might be too black-and-white. Many legal concepts, such as "reasonable doubt," are painted in shades of gray. Other lawyers think that engineers might help remove emotion from a case, which could help other jurors to see cold, hard facts.

The second juror Rittgers felt uneasy about was an older gentleman named Jon C. from Lebanon, where the courthouse is situated.

Rittgers had a "gut feeling" that Jon C. might be resistant to the defense's contentions.

Yet Rittgers decided to keep both the engineer and Jon C. on the jury. He feared that those men's potential replacements, plucked from the remaining jury pool, might be even less favorable to Ryan—like drawing bad cards in a game of poker.

As it turned out, the engineer played an important role; his fellow jurors chose him as their foreman.

And Jon C. may have been the most significant juror that Rittgers had ever encountered in his 30-plus years as a trial attorney. Jon C. would drastically change the course of the Widmer case.

Around 3:30 p.m., about six hours after jury selection began, both sides told Judge Bronson they were satisfied with the composition of the jury seated before them: six men and six women.

Prosecutors had used two of their four peremptory challenges; Rittgers, none.

Based on how they answered questions, Ryan thought the jurors who made the final cut seemed intelligent. He thought they would keep their eyes and their minds open. He thought they would see *reasonable doubt* staring them in the face by the end of the trial; they would *have* to vote "not guilty."

Prosecutors were betting, however, that the jurors would find it was *unrea-*

sonable to believe that Sarah succumbed to a medical problem in the bathtub, based on the circumstances that they were about to unveil.

Previewing the evidence

As the trial began, Ryan and Rittgers thought the police and prosecutors were sliding every miniscule thing under a microscope, trying to magnify grains of sand into mountains.

The defense team wanted the jury to see that those pieces of evidence were mere specks when scrutinized plainly, without magnification. And Rittgers was planning to use the prosecution's witnesses as *his* witnesses, to show how insufficient the evidence was.

Prosecutors, however, hammered on the notion that the only reasonable explanation for Sarah's death was: *HOMICIDE!* That word, in capitalized italics, was projected in bright red onto a blue background while prosecutor John Arnold previewed the evidence.

As Arnold spoke, another message glowed on the screen: *Proof of motive is not required.*

And then came Ryan's jail mugshot, contrasting with a photo of sweet, smiling Sarah. Her tanned skin was radiant as she wore a white turtleneck and gold hoop earrings, framed by a Christmas tree's lights and ornaments shining in the background. The snapshot had an ethereal, angelic quality. Almost haunting.

Then Arnold disclosed what authorities believed was damning evidence of a violent struggle: "hemorrhage in the deep muscles of the neck at the midline."

"I'm afraid this will not be the *CSI* of Warren County," Arnold said, referring to the popular TV show, *CSI: Crime Scene Investigation*. "This is fairly fundamental and routine stuff. There will not be any evidence of DNA snatched from the air or anybody running with little gas filters sniffing things out."

Instead of being bedazzled by forensic evidence, the jurors instead would need to use their noggins and "accept what's reasonable and reject the unreasonable," Arnold said.

"You're going to be called upon to determine what happened to Sarah Steward Widmer that night, August eleventh, to render a verdict that's fair to everybody involved," Arnold said.

He concluded by telling the jurors that he trusted them to "render a true and just verdict."

Arnold never flat-out asked for a conviction—which made me wonder: Was he unsure of the strength of his case?

Just as a confident salesman asks for the sale, attorneys generally use their opening statements to ask jurors for the verdict they want.

Why wouldn't Arnold, a former military man with a brash personality and booming voice, jump right in and tell the jurors to find Ryan guilty?

In contrast, Rittgers specifically urged the jury to acquit Ryan.

The most dramatic moment of Rittgers' opening statement: He held up a long, curved metal instrument—a laryngoscope, which medics use to guide a breathing tube into a patient's windpipe.

Rittgers told the jury that medics repeatedly used this intimidating device during "heroic" efforts to save Sarah's life—and that the injuries found on her body were all consistent with those efforts.

Rittgers admonished jurors to pay attention to the results of the "wonderful investigation," which snared Ryan and Sarah's personal records, business records, cellphone records and computers. Yet, he said, "They found nothing—nothing!"

He also advised the jury to "follow the evidence … follow the science ... and you need to listen to the *lack* of evidence." It jurors did that, he said, "You will find him not guilty."

Jurors went home for the night, mulling over the words they had heard from Arnold and Rittgers. They also surely wondered how the evidence would unfold—and how stressful it might be to decide one of the biggest local trials in their lifetimes.

Praying for "the truth to be heard"

As Ryan's trial got underway, a petite woman with studious eyeglasses and short brown hair took a seat in the courtroom gallery. She swore to herself that she would do what the jury was ordered to do: view the evidence with an "innocent-until-proven-guilty" mentality.

That woman, Kim Widmer, felt torn and tormented by her dual connections to the case: She was the wife of Ryan's father, Gary—and she was the stepmom who didn't know Ryan at all.

Because of the rift between Gary and his ex-wife, Jill, Kim had no contact with Ryan. She had only seen him in passing at baseball games.

For Gary's sake, Kim hoped that Ryan was innocent.

It made her sick to think how soul-shattering it would be for Gary to see his son convicted of murder.

Even though father and son hadn't seen each other in years, Gary accepted Ryan's unflinching denial of the accusations—and Gary was betting everything he had on Ryan's innocence. He had pledged to his son: "I'm going to do whatever I can to help you get out of this mess. I promise you that."

As a mom, Kim understood and respected Gary's commitment to his son, even though it derailed every personal goal that they were on track to achieve as a couple.

Kim and Gary were stuck with post-divorce financial hardships before they got married in 1993. To dig out of debt, he worked as a mechanic and she worked in the office of a printing company.

Finally, in August 2008, Gary and Kim were on the verge of becoming debt-free.

In just one more month, they would have all their debts paid off. They planned to celebrate with a champagne dinner at a fancy restaurant.

But then came that unforgettable moment when Gary, Kim and her son stared at the Cincinnati.com article about Ryan being accused of murder.

The zero balances on their debts remained just a dream. Because nine days after seeing that news article, Gary withdrew $90,000 from his retirement fund to help Ryan.

After paying Ryan's bondsman, Gary had $50,000 left. It evaporated rapidly as expenses for Ryan's defense mounted.

Kim had consented to cracking their retirement nest egg, and she was on board to do everything possible to help Ryan. "I agreed to it because I would do it for my son," she said. "I just couldn't tell Gary, 'No, you can't help your son.'"

Yet Kim also was a stranger to Ryan; she didn't know anything about the kind of guy he was. She didn't want to hurt her husband by confessing it, but she had a bad feeling about the case.

"It's so rare that you hear of someone drowning like that, especially at her age. I honestly thought, 'He had to have done it.' I thought it was just too weird, the way she died," Kim said.

Nevertheless, Kim tried to set aside her preconceived notions. "My mindset was, 'I'm going to go into that courtroom and decide for myself, based on the evidence.'"

She had never set foot in a courtroom before. Now she was committed to sit in Judge Neal Bronson's courtroom all day, every day, until Ryan's trial was over.

Each day, Gary and Kim would travel to Jill's house, the meeting spot for the Widmer clan. They came to court together, presenting a united front despite Jill and Gary's acrimonious split.

Jill and Gary would sit in the front row; Kim sat several rows behind Gary. And each morning, before Judge Bronson's bailiff called court into session, Kim would bow her head and silently pray: *Dear Lord, allow the Holy Spirit to be present in this courtroom. Lord, open our ears for the truth to be heard.*

Kim constantly felt sick to her stomach.

Just being in the formal, foreign environment of the courtroom was stressful enough. But it was worse knowing how severe the consequences would be for everyone involved.

No matter what happened, Sarah's family had already been torn apart; the Stewards had lost Sarah forever.

Watching the Widmer family, Kim's thoughts came at her like baseballs hurled out of a pitching machine: *What if this goes bad? What if he gets convicted? What would this do to my husband? To our relationship? To Jill and her kids? To Ryan? To so many people?*

Then she would calm down and reassure herself: *Maybe this is God's way of bringing us all together. But maybe we have to go through this hell first.*

DAY TWO

TUESDAY, MARCH 24, 2009

First impressions

The prosecution launched its case with the dispatcher who answered Ryan's 911 call.

Prosecutors played a recording of the call, allowing jurors to hear the words that so many people had already heard in nonstop news coverage: "My wife fell asleep in the bathtub and I think she's dead."

Asked about Ryan's demeanor on the call, the dispatcher said, "It seemed he was rather calm."

Yet, on the 911 call recording, the dispatcher can be heard telling Ryan: "I need you to calm down for me, I can't understand the address." And Ryan can clearly be heard crying at several points.

Ryan could see what was happening: The prosecution was attempting to portray him as a cold, unfeeling killer.

Trying to reinforce the notion that Ryan was unemotional during the 911 call, Vieux asked the dispatcher: "And how would you compare this call to one from a hospice location?"

Rittgers objected to that question and Judge Bronson sustained; the dispatcher was not allowed to answer.

Still, the implication was clear: Ryan should have been more upset during the 911 call if he had truly been surprised to find his wife drowned in the bathtub.

From the first witness, the prosecution's portrait of Scary Ryan was taking shape.

Additionally, the dispatcher said it sounded like Ryan may have been "blowing into the phone" instead of trying to do CPR rescue breathing on Sarah.

Ryan was incredulous to hear how he and his actions were being described. As the dispatcher testified, his mind flooded with retorts:

I was trying to do CPR on Sarah, just as YOU told me to do!

The breaths only sounded loud because the phone was close to my mouth. I was still trying to listen for instructions. And because of that, you think that I was faking CPR?

How can you say I was calm?! I'm not an emotional guy but I sure as heck was CRYING harder than I had ever cried in my adult life when I was talking to you.

Ryan bit his lip and kept the torrent of thoughts to himself. This was the prosecution's show; the defense would get its turn later.

Then, Ryan thought, the jury surely would see that Scary Ryan—the one in the black suicide vest, the one characterized with hospice-like "calm" on the 911 call, the one who seemed to be feigning CPR—was a distorted caricature.

Or maybe the jurors would conclude that Scary Ryan was *real*. Maybe the evidence would convince them that, just as surely as Sarah was dead, her doting husband had morphed into a murderous monster.

Chain of suspicion

Up next: Warren County Sheriff's Deputy Steve Bishop.

Ryan wondered what Bishop would say about the position of Sarah's body. Ryan knew that, according to Rittgers, Bishop had said he didn't remember moving her.

Up went Exhibit 1, the photo of Sweet Sarah with the Christmas-tree backdrop. Yes, Bishop said, that was the young woman he saw lying naked on the floor, not breathing.

Twice while prosecutor John Arnold questioned Bishop, it sounded like Bishop was on the verge of acknowledging that he had moved Sarah. Both times, Bishop used these words: "I grabbed her arm."

But Bishop testified that he only grabbed Sarah's arm to check her pulse at her wrist, and "kind of gave her a shake to see if she was going to be responsive."

Then Arnold directly asked Bishop whether Sarah's body had been repositioned. Bishop's response was unequivocal: "From the time I got there, until the time she was transported (to the hospital), she was not moved from that position."

That assertion had significant implications. Prosecutors were now free to argue that the two bloodstains on the carpet were created by Ryan moving Sarah's body to somehow "stage" the scene.

If Ryan testified, he could allege that Bishop had helped move her—as he had told Rittgers. But who would the jury be more likely to believe—a murder defendant? Or a police officer?

Even if Ryan didn't testify, Rittgers could challenge Bishop. But Rittgers decided there was nothing to be gained from that. It would be better to highlight the lack of evidence supporting the prosecution's much-vaunted "violent struggle."

Rittgers greeted Bishop by his first name, signaling a friendly familiarity. He showed Bishop more than a dozen photos, each time asking whether anything looked out-of-place. The officer repeatedly said no and finally declared: "No, I didn't see any signs of struggle."

Bishop was the first witness to bring up the TV-channel contradictions—one of the first things that made officers think they had caught Ryan in a lie.

As officers talked amongst themselves, they learned that Ryan had told Bishop he was watching the Bengals game *downstairs* while his wife was taking a bath *upstairs.* Yet the *upstairs* TV was tuned in to the game, Bishop said; the downstairs TV was off, and when cops turned it on, it was tuned to a channel that was *not* airing the Bengals game.

That didn't seem like such a big deal.

But Bishop and other prosecution witnesses piled on other observations that seemed odd for a drowning scene. Everything was strangely dry: Sarah's body, Ryan's body, the bathroom floor and the bedroom floor; only Sarah's hair was "damp" or "wet."

The "dry" body fit investigators' theory that Ryan had already removed Sarah from the tub before he dialed 911. They also thought the "dry" bathroom signaled that Ryan had cleaned up water that would have been splashed as he and Sarah struggled.

But investigators found no wet towels anywhere, and no freshly dried towels in the clothes dryer. The only possible sign of a cleanup: A used Lysol disinfectant towelette, smaller than a regular-sized letter envelope, crumpled-up on the ledge of the tub.

Another officer testified, "It looked like something had been wiped down with it; it was still a little damp." That testimony pointed to someone—Scary Ryan—using The Lysol Wipe to clean away evidence from the tub. The Lysol Wipe was admitted as Exhibit 12.

Thus, the chain of suspicion—wet hair, dry body, wrong TV channel, tub wiped down—became a recurring theme as prosecution witnesses testified.

The word, "dry," would be uttered more than a hundred times by the end of the trial. Dryness was incongruous at a drowning scene. And dryness implied that enough time—an unknown number of minutes—had elapsed for wetness to evaporate from Sarah's skin before Ryan called 911, possibly while she was already outside the tub.

Another well-used word during the trial: "pruning." There would be at least fifty references to pruning, the wrinkling of a person's fingertips and toes after being immersed in water for a while.

And Sarah's unwrinkled fingers and toes showed Sarah must not have been soaking in the bathtub very long—and Ryan must have lied when he estimated she had been bathing for about a half-hour. That should have been long enough for pruning to appear, some witnesses said.

As first-responders continued to testify, Rittgers established a small but important fact: Sarah's skin was "warm" or "hot" when a medic arrived, an indicator that Ryan hadn't waited long before he called for help. If Sarah had been dead very long, her skin would have felt cold.

Rittgers also got a medic to admit that his report said Sarah's hair was "wet" although the medic had described her hair as "damp" when he testified.

Rittgers made another point when he got a medic to step down from the witness stand and demonstrate on a mannequin how he used that long metal laryngoscope, the one Rittgers featured in his opening statement.

There were at least five failed attempts to use that device to insert a breathing tube into Sarah, and medics did manipulate her neck during that process. Rittgers was trying to support his theory: injuries to Sarah's neck might have been caused during those procedures but were instead being blamed on Ryan.

But medics denied inadvertently applying pressure harder or longer than usual in their urgency to help Sarah.

The medics described in excruciating detail every procedure they performed on Sarah. They described carefully carrying her to avoid causing injuries, even hoisting her body overhead to clear a divider wall as they maneuvered downstairs, around a precarious angle.

And the medics also reinforced the prosecution's biggest point so far: Just about everything was dry, dry, dry, including Sarah's skin.

The dryness was relevant to medics because if her skin had been wet, AED sensor pads wouldn't have adhered to the skin on her torso. The AED (Automated External Defibrillator) is a device that analyzes heart rhythm and can deliver an electric shock to restore a normal heartbeat.

After the first few witnesses were done testifying, many Widmer Watchers agreed that the prosecution had presented compelling evidence that dryness at a drowning scene was pretty peculiar—and so were some of Ryan's statements.

Questions about timing and dryness turned out to be among the biggest issues that fixated and frustrated the Widmer jury. Such questions also mystified the public, including Kim Widmer, Ryan's stepmom. She thought that the dry descriptions heightened suspicions about Ryan. But she also thought that dryness didn't prove Ryan killed Sarah.

And Kim had already seen signs that seemed to point to Ryan's innocence. When Kim saw that intimidating-looking laryngoscope, she thought: *Maybe THAT was what caused the injuries on Sarah, rather than some kind of violent behavior from Ryan.*

Even so, Kim reminded herself: The testimony had not yet revealed Sarah's injuries, so it was premature to guess whether medical procedures inflicted them.

Kim and a growing number of other Widmer Watchers—inside the courtroom and on the internet—went to bed that Tuesday night wondering whether Wednesday's testimony would make things clearer... or only more confounding.

DAY THREE

WEDNESDAY, MARCH 25, 2009

Sleepy bathers don't drown

A sleep expert from The Ohio State University, Dr. Aneesa Marie Das, spent a couple hours on the witness stand shooting down the believability of Ryan's 911 statement: "my wife fell asleep in the bathtub."

"It would be virtually impossible for somebody, without the influence of drugs or alcohol or something external, to fall asleep and not wake up" and drown while bathing, Das said. Sarah had no drugs and no alcohol in her system; only caffeine.

The survival instinct to restore oxygen is one of the human body's strongest urges—and a sleepy bather would certainly awaken if the bather's face submerged, water went into the bather's windpipe and oxygen levels decreased.

Kim Widmer's heart sank. This doctor seemed very believable. Smart. Authoritative. This didn't look good for Ryan.

However, Das did discuss the disorder that I had wondered about, cataplexy. She said 80 percent of diagnosed narcoleptics experience cataplexy—loss of muscular control while conscious. But Sarah's medical records revealed no sign that she was narcoleptic or cataplectic, nor that she should have been tested for such disorders.

When it was his turn to question Das, Rittgers confronted her with passages from the "bible of forensic science." The book is about two-and-a-half inches thick, with an impossibly long title: *Spitz and Fisher's Medicolegal Investigation of Death: Guidelines for the Application of Pathology to Crime Investigation.*

The co-author of that 1,325-page text was Dr. Werner Spitz, the internationally renowned death investigator who performed the second autopsy on Sarah.

Das was unfamiliar with the book, although it is widely used in medical schools throughout the U.S. However, Das noted that forensic pathology was outside her specialty.

Spitz's book states that epilepsy can cause "sudden and unexplained death in several different ways." Epileptic fits that cause unconsciousness or loss of muscular control can result in mishaps such as drownings and traffic accidents, his book says.

Das agreed.

Rittgers also got Das to acknowledge that a single epileptic seizure can be fatal. And Das was unable to dispute Rittgers' assertions that it was possible for people to have seizures or heart problems that would not be detectable during an autopsy.

Rittgers proposed a scenario: Sarah may have fallen asleep, suddenly woke up and gasped, breathed in a large amount of water and then became so startled that her heart malfunctioned. Then she drowned as a result.

After indicating she couldn't rule out various scenarios Rittgers described, Das concluded her testimony by stating that none of those situations seemed likely.

Das' testimony supported the prosecution's contention: Sarah did not fall asleep and drown. But that was a theory that Rittgers never advanced.

Rittgers never tried to assert that Sarah had fallen asleep and drowned. But Rittgers was stuck with his client's 911 statement: "My wife fell asleep in the bathtub and I think she's dead."

Later, Rittgers did try to put Ryan's "fell asleep" statement into context, asserting that it was reasonable for Ryan to assume Sarah had fallen asleep because of her bizarre drowsiness. But Das' testimony reinforced the notion that Ryan's 911 statement was a lie, a feeble attempt to explain away a murder.

Two witnesses who testified after Das raised another question: Did Ryan lie about Sarah's position in the bathtub?

He had said she was "face-down" during the 911 call and repeated that to police officers. But a nurse testified that Ryan told her Sarah was "face-up."

And Doyle Burke, the coroner's investigator, testified that Ryan described Sarah's position as "face-down," only a little while after the nurse spoke to Ryan.

Was Ryan flip-flopping to cover up his alleged crime? Had he innocently misspoken? Or had some listeners misunderstood him?

All possibilities still seemed open—at least for the time being.

A star is born

At mid-afternoon, Travis Vieux, the assistant prosecutor, asked Judge Neal Bronson for a recess, saying: "We need to move a piece of evidence into the courtroom."

Judge Bronson excused the jury for a few moments. Spectators and news reporters remained in place while a crew from the prosecutor's office, wearing protective synthetic gloves, carried the tub into the courtroom and put it down on the floor next to the jury box.

Usually, when a piece of evidence is that big, photographs suffice as evidence. Several reporters whispered, "What in the world are they trying to prove with this?"

The Bathtub emanated a certain eerie energy.

It felt creepy to lay eyes on that tub, where the life had ebbed from Sarah Widmer's body.

Despite the unsettling thoughts that the tub aroused, everyone in the courtroom craned their necks to see it. It became an attention magnet, much like a wrecked car on the highway.

As jurors were called back into the courtroom, they, too, seemed transfixed by it.

The tub looked filthy, as if a coal miner had bathed in it and had left behind a week's worth of underground grime. But the black streaks were not coal dust. They came from fingerprint-dusting powder that adhered to markings on the tub's surface. An expert was called to testify about his interpretations of those marks.

The Bathtub became a star witness.

Even prosecutors may not have anticipated how viscerally the public—and the jurors—would react to The Bathtub.

It would be an understatement to say that the tub's presence helped jurors and spectators envision Sweet Sarah in that tub, fighting for her life. It practically *compelled* those horrifying thoughts—especially after criminalist William Hillard testified.

A 35-year veteran of the Cincinnati Police Division, Hillard had worked on hundreds of homicides before he was asked to examine the Widmer bathtub at the Hamilton Township police station.

Hillard—and the jury—were unaware that Lieutenant Jeff Braley had consulted with two other experts in unsuccessful attempts to find useful evidence in the tub. Then, almost three months after Sarah drowned, Braley contacted Hillard and asked him to take a look.

Hillard explained that no one, not even Ryan, would have been able to see "latent prints" on the tub until the dusting powder was applied. Such impressions can be left by hands and other human body parts after natural oils and sweat come into contact with surfaces.

Hillard found no fingerprints that could be linked to any specific person; they were all too smudged to yield the fine "ridge details" needed to identify an individual's unique fingerprint characteristics.

But Hillard did find:

1. A forearm print, "probably from a male," based on its size and hair-follicle impressions; that print was an "overlay" on top of some semicircular impressions.

2. The semicircular markings appeared to roughly correspond with bottles of toiletries that were lined up along the bathtub's ledge; some photos show a couple bottles lying on the bottom of the tub. But the number of circular marks exceeded the number of bottles, so either more bottles were present at some point, or the existing bottles may have occupied

different spots at different times.

3. Fingertip streaks, which appeared to have been made by a pair of hands in a downward motion. The streaks were found on the tub's back wall, at the faucet end of the tub, and Hillard said they appeared to have been made by a smaller person, possibly a female.

4. Marks that left swaths where the bathtub apparently had been wiped clean.

5. Partial palm prints all over the tub.

However, Hillard acknowledged there was no way to tell specifically *who* made any of the marks nor under what circumstances. And he couldn't estimate *when* they were made, either.

Hillard said there was nothing unusual about palm prints or wipe marks on a bathtub, considering that most people clean their bathtubs.

Based on the markings, "There's no way to reconstruct any murder scene here?" asked Attorney Rob Dziech, who was assisting with Ryan's defense.

"No, sir," Hillard responded.

Assistant Prosecutor Travis Vieux capped Hillard's testimony by asking what was important to conclude about the tub markings.

Hillard's response: "There was somebody in that tub, or some person placed those impressions there."

The consensus of several people in court: Oh geez, *somebody* was in the bathtub *at some time*? What a nothingburger.

Regardless of the inconclusive findings, images of the bathtub, coupled with Hillard's observations and opinions, animated a nightmarish virtual video, playing in a continuous loop through some people's minds:

Scary Ryan forces Sweet Sarah under water, face-down, as she tries to push herself out of the tub, her hands slipping down the tub's wall. Toiletry bottles tumble into the tub. Sarah stops moving.

Scary Ryan replaces bottles on the tub's ledge, staging the scene to look normal. Carelessly, he leaves the forearm mark, betraying what he had done. Then he removes Sarah from the tub and uses that Lysol Wipe to remove traces of his crime—but he misses the spot with the finger streaks!

Finally, he calls 911 and tells a bunch of lies.

Tapping into that collective subconscious, Peter Bronson wrote a column for the *Enquirer,* concluding: "I think the handprints are chilling testimony that Sarah was murdered."

Little things that could mean a lot

The bathtub was removed from the courtroom because prosecutors expected to call a witness who had nothing to say about the tub.

But after a bit of scrambling, prosecutor John Arnold apologized to the judge and announced the prosecution was calling Lieutenant Jeff Braley to the witness stand; The Bathtub needed to be brought right back into court.

"You got your crew ready?" Judge Neal Bronson asked, wryly. So, once more, the gloved bathtub brigade was pressed into service.

With the tub back in place, Braley started to testify.

Prosecutors were trying to make at least two main points with Braley's testimony: More confirmation of the dry conditions, and a description of how the bathtub markings were discovered and preserved.

The night Sarah drowned, Braley got down on his hands and knees and crawled around the carpeted area, feeling with an ungloved hand. He detected no moisture where Sarah had lain.

Braley also said he looked for wetness in the bathtub and saw only "droplets" clinging to the shiny metal stopper. Items on the floor next to the tub—magazines, a bath towel, a rug and clothing—were all dry, Braley said.

But two significant factors cast doubt on whether the scene was as bone-dry as the prosecution was contending.

First, under questioning by Rittgers, Braley admitted he did his kneeling and feeling *roughly two-and-a-half hours after Ryan called 911*. That may have been enough time for the carpet's top surface to dry, especially with the air-conditioner turned on in the Widmer home that night.

Second, a forensic scientist displayed evidence that showed the carpet was wet. Bloodstained carpet samples, cut from the flooring where Sarah had lain, were wet enough that they "dripped" and "soaked through" the bottom of the brown paper grocery sacks that contained them. "It soaked through the back of the carpet, kind of wicked through the back of the carpet," the scientist said.

When Ryan heard that testimony and saw the water-stained bags, he thought vindication was on its way. *So much for everything being "dry."*

Now the jury had two sets of contradictions to sort out: Wet or dry? Was Sarah face-up or face-down? And of what significance were those circumstances?

As testimony continued, Braley told the jury that he returned to the Widmer home to do further investigation two days after Sarah drowned. And that's when he initially dusted the tub and saw the apparent finger marks appear.

Next, the prosecution used witnesses who knew Sarah to wave some of those Tiny Red Flags: hints of possible marital problems or motives for Ryan to commit murder. They also tried to dispel notions that Sarah's sleepiness or other symptoms were of any significance.

Dr. John Becker, the dentist for whom Sarah worked as a hygienist in Fort Thomas, Kentucky, testified that she would nap in her car during her lunch hour twice a week. But those naps were planned, he said. Becker never saw Sarah fall asleep at inappropriate or unexpected times. She never fell asleep while working on a patient. She did, however, report that she felt sick at work just hours before she drowned. But Becker said he didn't detect anything particularly alarming or unusual about Sarah's achy stomach, head and neck.

Becker said he had little interaction with Ryan and didn't know a lot about their relationship, although Sarah had told him that she didn't like Ryan's smoking cigarettes and drinking beer.

Still, no one testified that Ryan had a drinking problem. And testimony later revealed that Sarah had purchased the beer-dispensing kegerator—an odd gift for her to give to Ryan if she was concerned about his drinking.

Becker testified next about something that some people considered another Tiny Red Flag: Sarah had requested information about her employer's retirement and life insurance benefits just a couple weeks before her death, in late July 2008.

Sarah had stated that Ryan was "really on her ass about this"—referring to the entire benefits package, Becker said.

Unbeknownst to Becker—and to the jury—Ryan and Sarah had consulted with a financial adviser around the time of their wedding; life insurance and retirement accounts were discussed.

Because no information about that meeting was presented, it was disquieting when Becker revealed that Sarah, while asking about life insurance, had stated that "if something happened to her, she didn't want to have her mother pay for her funeral."

Becker said he would have expected a newlywed to say she wouldn't want her *husband* to foot the funeral bill.

"It just struck me as odd that someone who is recently married would think that her *mother* would have to pay for her funeral if something happened to her," Becker said.

Was Sarah's unusual statement a subtle signal that she feared Ryan would kill her? Or was Sarah merely echoing words of a financial adviser stressing the importance of life insurance?

But, Becker confirmed, no life insurance policy was in place at the time of Sarah's death.

Grieving mom takes the stand

As Day Three drew to a close, Exhibit 1, the Christmastime photo of Sweet Sarah, appeared on the courtroom screen again.

Sarah's mom, Ruth Ann Steward, took her turn in the witness chair to identify the picture of her beloved daughter.

Assistant Prosecutor Travis Vieux repeatedly asked whether Sarah had suffered from seizures, irregular or fast heartbeat, chronic migraines, dizziness, numbness, or loss of consciousness.

Each time, Ruth Ann answered, "No."

Asked whether Sarah ever fell asleep during a conversation, Ruth Ann responded, "No, Sarah loved talking."

Ryan thought: *Well, she did fall asleep in mid-conversation in front of me, not that long ago. You didn't see her as much as I did. Now, I look back and realize she must have had something wrong with her. That's why she died.*

Ruth Ann discussed shopping with her daughter and said that, as soon as Sarah would get back into the car, "Ryan would be calling," questioning whether Sarah really needed the items she had purchased. Ruth Ann suspected Ryan was habitually monitoring Sarah's purchases somehow.

Ryan could hardly remember the incident that Ruth Ann had described because he thought it was so trivial.

Then it came to his mind: *Gosh, that only happened one time. And she's trying to make it sound like I checked on Sarah's spending all the time. Are you kidding me?!*

Sarah asked me to keep track of her bank account, and I just happened to check it and saw she had just bought something. I called to tease Sarah about it, kind of like, "Are you SURE you really needed to spend a hundred bucks at Target?"

My gosh, I was JOKING! I didn't CARE if she spent a hundred bucks. I mean, it's not like it's ten thousand bucks. She made more money than I did, anyhow.

It's not like this was a sign we had trouble in our marriage. And it sure as heck wouldn't be a reason to kill someone. Give me a break.

Winding down her testimony, Ruth Ann said Sarah didn't discuss life insurance with her. Because Sarah had no life insurance, her funeral had to be paid by other means.

Vieux asked, "Who paid for Sarah's funeral?"

Ruth Ann responded, "I did." Just as Sarah had feared she would.

Those final words from Ruth Ann struck a chilling note at the end of Day Three. Rittgers had no questions for her.

DAY FOUR

THURSDAY, MARCH 26, 2009

Photos told a tale

When the Warren County coroner, Dr. Russell Uptegrove, took the witness stand, spectators sat on the edge of their seats, waiting to hear precisely what injuries transformed Sarah's drowning from a tragic accident into a murder.

Uptegrove worked for a decade as a full-time forensic pathologist—a medical doctor who investigates deaths—and became the Warren County coroner in April 2007. After getting that part-time job, he continued to work at a regional death investigation center in nearby Dayton, Ohio. That was where Uptegrove performed the autopsy on Sarah Widmer on August 12, 2008, the morning after she died.

The night before, Uptegrove had heard from his investigator, Doyle Burke, about the basics of the case: 24-year-old female, reportedly drowned in the bathtub, most likely would be pronounced dead on arrival at the hospital. That, Uptegrove said, was "an alarming story, so it's not something that routinely happens."

Yet there was no obvious sign of trauma to Sarah's body, Burke had told Uptegrove.

As Uptegrove began talking about the condition in which he first saw Sarah in a morgue, jurors were shown a photo: Sarah's lifeless body on a shiny metal table, clothed in a light blue hospital gown.

Paper bags covered her hands to preserve DNA that might have gotten under her fingernails as she tried to defend herself.

An intravenous tube protruded from the left side of her neck; a blue strap encircled her neck, securing a breathing tube inside her mouth.

Her head was elevated on a small block, beside a square, black sign with her case number, 2933, in white, plus the year, 2008.

What a sad, dehumanizing contrast to the Sweet Sarah picture.

The photographs became more graphic as Uptegrove testified.

Images from Sarah's autopsy were projected onto the courtroom's big screen for the jurors and spectators to see—if they could stomach them. Many people winced. Ryan held up a hand to shield his eyes.

When Uptegrove described areas of hemorrhaging in the front of Sarah's neck and upper chest, it mostly looked like a sea of red, at least to untrained eyes.

Uptegrove's autopsy report says the neck hemorrhage spanned about four inches; a two-inch contusion, or bruise, was found "in the deep muscle overlying the superior aspect of the chest, at the top of the sternum."

In his opinion, those areas had either been compressed or had been struck.

He testified that the injuries were not consistent with CPR, not even "aggressive" CPR, which was done on Sarah for about forty-five minutes. Chest compressions are performed on the breastbone, below the area where the suspicious injuries were located, he said.

Uptegrove said he wasn't an emergency-medicine expert, but he denied that medics could have caused injuries as they performed a "Sellick maneuver." That involves applying pressure on the neck cartilage, which helps medics to see where to "intubate"—or insert a breathing tube through the patient's mouth into the windpipe. The Sellick maneuver is supposed to be done gently, he said, concurring with earlier testimony from medics.

Uptegrove also commented on a picture showing cuts inside Sarah's upper lip. It looked like Sarah's beautiful, straight, white teeth had pressed into that tender tissue, tearing it. "I've never seen injuries to the lip like this from an attempt at intubation," Uptegrove said. But he said it would be *possible* for life-saving efforts to cause such an injury, and another prosecution witness said he had seen that happen.

Sarah also suffered three minor injuries of unknown age, caused by either pressure or "blunt force:"

1. a faint bruise on her right forehead near the hairline

2. a trio of small bruises on the right side of her scalp

3. a superficial bruise at the nape of her neck

None of those bruises would have been created by a blow powerful enough to knock Sarah out, Uptegrove said.

Many things, he said, were *possible.*

One thing was certain: the cause of Sarah's death. Fluid in her lungs and sinus cavities was undeniable proof that she drowned.

But the manner of her death—homicide, suicide, accident, natural, or undetermined—required further exploration, especially because of the additional injuries noted during the autopsy, Uptegrove said.

Sarah was young, seemed healthy, wasn't drunk or on drugs. "How do people like that supposedly drown in a bathtub?" Uptegrove asked.

"This whole scenario didn't make any sense from the very beginning," Uptegrove said.

A lot of people agreed with the coroner about that.

"I think" it was homicide

After the autopsy, Uptegrove listened to the 911 call, met with Sarah's family and spoke to police and medics. He also reviewed Sarah's medical records from the medics and from the hospital. Uptegrove found no evidence of any medical problem that would have caused Sarah to drown.

In addition, he had reviewed photos from Dr. Werner Spitz's autopsy on Sarah. In those photos, taken three days after Uptegrove autopsied Sarah, an additional small bruise appeared on the right side of Sarah's neck. Sometimes, fresh injuries don't show up right away on a deceased person; more injuries may materialize because of decomposition.

Prosecutor John Arnold asked: Was that oval-shaped bruise "about the size of a human thumb?"

Yes, roughly about that size, Uptegrove said.

That projected another vision in jurors' minds: *A thumb was pressing into Sarah's neck while she was forced underwater.*

That vision came into sharper focus after Arnold asked Uptegrove about a maneuver called "the carotid sleeper hold."

Ryan had never heard that terminology before. *What in the world are they talking about?*

Uptegrove went on to explain that the carotid sleeper hold is a technique used to compress one or both carotid arteries in the neck, cutting off blood flow to the brain. That can render a person unconscious in thirty seconds—or much faster, within three or four seconds, Uptegrove said, if the attacker has martial-arts training.

Ryan couldn't believe the prosecution was trying to insinuate that he was some type of martial-arts expert, thinking: *That's not something they teach you in the sports I played, like baseball.*

Arnold wound up: Did Uptegrove have an opinion about the manner of Sarah's death?

"I think the manner of death was homicide," Uptegrove stated flatly.

Nothing stronger than "I think?" It was as if Uptegrove had only scored a double when the crowd was clamoring for a home run.

Defense attorney Charlie Rittgers rose and took his turn at Uptegrove.

Rittgers confronted Uptegrove about reaching conclusions quickly, before he reviewed records from the Hamilton Township medics, the hospital or Sarah's personal physicians.

Rittgers also pointed out a large discolored area in the crook of Sarah's right elbow, where medics tried to insert an intravenous line, but failed.

How could a tiny prick from a needle create such a large, bruise-like appearance?

Uptegrove conceded that "hemodilution," water infiltrating a drowning victim's bloodstream, could have exaggerated the appearance of some injuries found on Sarah.

And Uptegrove agreed it was possible that a break in a blood vessel, caused by some type of pressure during resuscitation efforts, could look worse because of the hemodilution and CPR-induced blood flow.

Rittgers thought it was persuasive: Sarah could have suffered innocuous injuries that looked more severe than they really were. And he thought Spitz's upcoming testimony would support that.

He tried to contrast Spitz's long list of credentials with Uptegrove's lack of board certification; Uptegrove didn't undergo an extensive test to prove his competency but he had asserted his years of experience made him good at his job.

Uptegrove replied that the American Board of Pathology "doesn't issue a certificate strictly for people like myself, who do just forensic pathology." In addition, his job didn't require him to obtain certification. So, he didn't see the point of studying for a year "for some test that I don't need about material that I don't use."

Rittgers got Uptegrove to agree that a large number of people have died after suffering witnessed seizures—but their brains appeared normal. And Uptegrove conceded, "it really takes a neuropathologist to find something." No neuropathologist examined Sarah's brain. That left open the possibility that Sarah had suffered a seizure, but it went unwitnessed and left no trace.

Rittgers asked whether the small bruises on Sarah's head could have been caused by her removal from the tub. "Unlikely," Uptegrove said.

Next, Rittgers grilled Uptegrove about the injuries to Sarah's neck—and the lack thereof. There were no injuries to her throat cartilages, nor to her hyoid bone, a fragile, u-shaped bone. If that bone is fractured, it's considered a telltale sign of strangulation. But Uptegrove said strangulation can happen without fracturing that bone.

Finally, Rittgers confronted the coroner: "Are you telling the ladies and gentlemen of the jury that these bruises on her neck were the result of strangulation?"

Uptegrove replied: "I cannot rule that out."

That was also Uptegrove's response when Rittgers asked whether he was claiming that Ryan "grabbed Sarah from the back" and caused the neck injuries.

So, what was the prosecution's theory to explain the pattern of injuries on Sarah—and how she drowned? Based on the testimony from Uptegrove and other prosecution witnesses, it remained unclear.

Inspired by that uncertainty, Rittgers decided to make a bold move that would knock prosecutors off-kilter the next day.

DAY FIVE

FRIDAY, MARCH 27, 2009

"It *has* to be a homicide"

With each passing day of the trial, the crowd of spectators burgeoned. By Day Five, about ninety people had packed into the courtroom.

Anticipation ran high as the prosecution prepared to call its twentieth—and final—witness.

Batting cleanup: Dr. Charles Jeffrey Lee, a forensic pathologist in central Ohio.

Prosecutors asked Lee to review Uptegrove's findings versus Spitz's findings, making Lee a sort of "tie-breaker."

After the criticism of Uptegrove's lack of board certification, prosecutors also may have hoped that Lee, a board-certified osteopathic doctor, would bolster Uptegrove's findings.

Lee testified that he performed about 250 autopsies a year as chief forensic pathologist and deputy coroner in Licking County, Ohio. He did not conduct an autopsy on Sarah but reviewed records about her.

He concurred with the main points that Uptegrove made and expounded more forcefully than Uptegrove had.

Upon viewing a picture of the thumb-shaped bruise on the lower right side of Sarah's neck, Lee stated: "I think someone grabbed her neck with their right hand." That added another detail to the mental movie depicting how Sarah could have been forced to drown.

And while Uptegrove had testified that none of Sarah's head bruises would have come from a blow severe enough to render her unconscious, Lee stated that Sarah *could* have been knocked out. Unconsciousness is a possibility from any blow to the head, Lee said.

After hours of sometimes-conflicting medical testimony, the cause and relative importance of Sarah's injuries seemed still unclear.

Yet it was crystal clear what prosecutors were trying to show: *"HOMICIDE!"* Just like the red letters projected on the screen during their opening statement.

Deciding manner of death requires considering all the circumstances, Lee said.

"The more information you can get, the better you can evaluate it all," he said. "If there's some hidden piece of information out there, it may sway my idea of what actually happened."

The defense would later use those statements against Lee.

For now, Lee remained confident as he ticked off his thoughts about the five possible manners of death for Sarah:

"It is certainly not natural, because drowning is not a natural cause of death."

"It is not accidental because we have many unusual, peculiar injuries ... plus, we have what appears to be inflicted injuries—maybe to the back of the neck but definitely to the front and right side of the neck."

"I've only seen one suicidal drowning, and that's also very rare."

"So, it *has* to be a homicide."

That declaration had much more impact than Uptegrove's qualified "I think."

But Lee discussed only four possible manners of death. He omitted the fifth: "undetermined."

Still, Lee's testimony did what it was supposed to do. It hardened suspicions about murder.

Rittgers had his game face on as he stepped up to cross-examine Lee. He was far more confrontational with Lee than he was with any other prosecution witness, eliciting multiple objections from prosecutors and even a couple scoldings from Judge Neal Bronson.

Under the prosecution's questioning, Lee spent ninety minutes enumerating reasons he believed Sarah's injuries arose from foul play.

In the ensuing forty minutes, Rittgers unleashed one bold question after another. For a while, Lee stood firm.

Then, with a bit of swagger, Rittgers asked, "What's the purpose of your testimony?"

"Objection!" bellowed prosecutor John Arnold.

"Sustained," said the judge, stopping the witness from answering.

Rittgers recalled Lee's assertion that gathering information is paramount when assessing a death. Rittgers shifted gears and asked whether Lee knew various facts about the case.

Lee knew some of the answers. But some questions—like this one—caught him off-guard: Did he know that the carpet samples, taken from under Sarah's body, were wet?

"What samples were those?" Lee responded.

Finally, Rittgers decided to throw his best curve ball. But his windup was interrupted—twice.

"Doctor, we've been sitting here for a week, listening to the State's witnesses, including you, and we have still not yet heard—"

Arnold objected because lawyers aren't supposed to "testify." They're supposed to just ask questions.

"Ask a question, please," Judge Bronson told Rittgers.

The tension in the courtroom escalated several notches. Everyone wondered what Rittgers was going to ask. Then he let it fly: "Please tell us the State's theory as to how Sarah died?"

Objection. Sustained. Judge Bronson said: "He's here to answer questions, not theories. The State's presenting the case, not the doctor. Ask questions about his testimony."

Rittgers asked for a private conference with Arnold and Judge Bronson at the bench, whispered so the jury and spectators couldn't hear. Such "sidebars" happened about fifteen times during the trial, including three during Lee's testimony.

After the first sidebar, Rittgers returned to his lectern and said, "Doctor, I'll rephrase the question." He leaned forward on an elbow, stared down the witness and asked: "Do you have an opinion as to how Sarah drowned?"

The courtroom was silent, hanging on Lee's answer.

"I think she was pushed or held with her head under water, either over a sink or a tub or in the toilet," Lee said.

Whoa. Sink? Toilet? Wasn't the bathtub the star of the trial?

The prosecution's Bill of Particulars, a legal document that specifies an accusation, stated that Ryan was accused of drowning Sarah in the bathtub. There was no mention of a toilet or a sink. How would the prosecution reconcile that?

Lee continued, "I don't think she was fully immersed, and it may have been running water rather than a pool (of water) or a sink full of water." And he said she was pushed "either forward or backward."

Rittgers probed the possibilities further. He got Judge Bronson to allow Lee to step down from the witness stand, to demonstrate on Rittgers' son how Sarah could have been forced into the water. The younger Rittgers, playing "Sarah," did forward bends and backbends near the jury box.

It was extraordinary to see such a demonstration during the prosecution's presentation of evidence—especially because Judge Bronson had blocked the prosecution from presenting a "re-enactment" video, with actors depicting "Ryan" and "Sarah" in possible drowning scenarios.

The sudden suggestion of multiple drowning locations shocked just about everyone, including Ryan: *That's just mind-blowing. It's not even physically possible, some of the things he said. I mean, c'mon, backwards, in the toilet?! Think about that. Maybe now people will see the prosecution's case for what it is: ridiculous!*

Rittgers seemed to have zapped the prosecution's momentum. He had been brazen enough to break an unwritten rule among trial attorneys: Never ask a witness a question unless you know the answer. When he asked Lee to describe how Sarah drowned, Rittgers had no idea how Lee would respond.

Rittgers felt good; his gamble had paid off. Lee's home-run testimony was snatched from the air before it could get out of the ballpark.

Rittgers persisted, exposing holes in the alternative theories.

How could Sarah be drowned in the toilet, yet suffer no skinned-up knees? How could she be drowned in a sink yet leave no water splashed onto the mirror? If she wasn't taking a bath, why were her wedding and engagement rings placed on the vanity countertop, as some people do before bathing?

Lee took a few stabs at answering. But he appeared to be scrambling.

Finally, Lee stated, "There could be one person surprising another person and a struggle." Then Lee reiterated his bathtub-toilet-sink-other hypothesis and concluded: "I don't know that anyone can tell you what happened in a struggle prior to that, other than Sarah and her husband."

After Lee stepped down from the witness stand, the prosecution rested its case.

When court went into recess, there was a lot of excited murmuring about Lee's testimony.

A couple hours earlier, I had sensed that the case might be headed for a conviction. But after Rittgers' cross-examination of Lee, I thought: *They have a guy on trial for murder, yet they have no earthly idea what really happened.*

The headline on my *Enquirer* story the next day read, "Homicide certain, investigator says." We gave the prosecution its due. And I had a hard time sleeping that night.

DAY SIX

MONDAY, MARCH 30, 2009

Dr. Spitz answers the call

After the first week of testimony, Rittgers believed that he had decimated Lee and that the prosecution's case had almost collapsed. At the least, he had exposed two gaping holes: No solid motive and no specific scenario to explain Sarah's drowning.

Anything the defense presented would score bonus points, Rittgers thought.

Rittgers called Dr. Werner Spitz as his first witness.

Although Spitz, a German-American, had immigrated to the United States more than four decades earlier, he still spoke with an accent, making his words difficult to discern at times.

The white-haired, bespectacled expert matter-of-factly described his fifty years of experience conducting autopsies in Europe and in the United States. He had authored ninety-five scientific articles, and in 1972, published the first edition of his famous forensic science textbook, plus several updates since then.

Spitz had testified thousands of times, appearing in courts in every U.S. state.

Spitz also said he had been involved with or supervised about 60,000 autopsies.

And, without necessarily realizing it, Spitz jostled the thorn in the prosecution's side when he mentioned he had been board-certified in forensic pathology since 1965, contrasting with Uptegrove's lack of board certification.

Then Rittgers cut to the chase and asked about Sarah's death. Spitz responded with a lengthy lecture on drowning. When blood vessels in the lungs absorb water, that increases blood volume and blood pressure. Water swells the red blood cells until they "explode," Spitz said, releasing "loose hemoglobin" throughout the body.

Because of those processes, if a person is injured just before, during or after drowning, "there will be a lot more bleeding" than normal, Spitz said, and injuries will appear exaggerated.

That's why medics' "tiny" needles, about the size of a human hair, left large areas of bruising along the crooks of both of Sarah's elbows, he said.

As Spitz testified, I noticed many jurors feverishly jotting in their notebooks—a memory aid allowed for this trial but forbidden in some courtrooms. Even with good notes, it would probably be difficult for laypeople on the jury to sort out the tedious, hours-long medical testimony. And medical jargon was even harder to digest when Spitz served it up with his German accent.

But there were jurors who had medical backgrounds. Maybe they would help clear up any confusion that might surface in deliberations.

To Spitz's credit, he injected a bit of wry humor at times. The human body has trillions of air sacs, Spitz said, a number "bigger than the national debt."

In examining the three small bruises on the right side of Sarah's head, Spitz thought "they looked like they were all developed from a single impact against a curved surface ... like the bottom part or the side of a bathtub." Spitz also said he doubted the blow that created the bruises would have been severe enough to knock Sarah out.

It soon became clear: There were few differences between Spitz's findings and Uptegrove's. After Spitz had testified for about an hour, Rittgers posed the key question: Why did Sarah drown?

"Cause of death is drowning. Manner of death, I think, in my opinion, is undetermined," Spitz said.

Just as Uptegrove had qualified his response with "I think," so did Spitz.

I wondered how the jury would weigh those two opinions, considering they were both less-than-insistent.

Spitz detailed why he labeled the manner of Sarah's death "undetermined":

- No signs of a violent struggle in her surroundings or on her body.

- No wounds on her accused killer (Ryan).

- She had injuries "produced by resuscitation—intense, aggressive resuscitative procedure."

- The injuries on Sarah all appeared exaggerated because the drowning process causes changes in the blood.

Shifting to cross-examination, prosecutor Travis Vieux almost immediately asked whether Spitz was being paid for his testimony. Spitz corrected him and said, "Well, I'm paid for my *time,* yes."

Spitz said his standard fee was four hundred dollars for each hour of consulting work; he charged prosecutors a $1,200 fee to cover three hours he spent with them when they visited his office in January 2009.

"I don't discriminate ... anybody who uses the time pays four hundred dollars an hour," Spitz said.

He charged five thousand dollars per day for work that took him away from his office in Saint Clair Shores, Michigan—and that's what he was charging the defense for appearing in Ryan's trial.

Spitz wasn't the only expert who charged a fee—even though it came across that way. The defense didn't ask—and the prosecution didn't volunteer—that they paid their experts, too. Each of the prosecution's experts received a total fee in the $4,000-$5,000 range, according to figures disclosed much later, after I made public-records requests.

As Vieux continued questioning Spitz, he confronted the doctor with various passages from Spitz's own book. Notably, the book said hemorrhages in the front neck muscles "do not occur in drowning and should always raise the suspicion of foul play." However, Spitz maintained that the hemorrhages in Sarah's neck and upper chest had leaked from the intravenous line that medics stuck in her neck. "The blood will progress to areas of lesser pressure" between layers of tissue, he said. "That's what you're looking at."

Uptegrove had opined that the IV did not cause all of the neck-chest bleeding—a major point of contention between him and Spitz.

Spitz also said it was possible that Sarah may have suffered a first-time seizure in the tub. He noted that only about one-quarter of people with seizure disorders will exhibit signs that a pathologist could detect. Or a sudden heart disruption may have overtaken her, he said.

Any of those possibilities could have rendered Sarah unconscious, culminating in her death by drowning, Spitz said.

Vieux scored some points when he got the doctor to admit that he had not spoken directly to police, to medics nor to Sarah's family in evaluating her death. Vieux confronted Spitz about the importance of considering all circumstances—the same criticism that Rittgers had leveled against Lee, the prosecution's final witness.

Vieux confronted Spitz with two letters he wrote to the prosecution team, indicating he had no opinion as to the manner of Sarah's death.

Spitz responded: "Actually, the way I would like to say it is that the manner of death is not really 'undetermined,' because that would mean *by me.* But it is undeterminable ... by *anyone* under these set of circumstances."

Spitz and Vieux skirmished over the newer edition of his book deleting references to how drowning exaggerates the appearance of injuries. Spitz said that removing or condensing passages does not suggest that the earlier information was invalid. Rather, Spitz said, if the text delved into detail about every topic, "you would not be able to carry this book." It already weighed more than nine pounds.

Shortly after that exchange, the doctor's cellphone rang. Spitz apologized for the interruption. Vieux said he was done questioning anyway. Judge Neal Bronson excused Spitz from the witness stand.

On that awkward note, the three-hour testimony of the world-renowned death investigator concluded.

How sleepy, how sick was Sarah?

Just when the jurors surely needed a respite from turgid medical testimony, they got it. Rittgers began calling people who knew Ryan and Sarah, to testify about the couple's relationship and about Ryan's character.

Most of them testified only briefly, partly because legal rules limited their testimony to information they knew first-hand, showing the defendant was unlikely to have committed the alleged crime.

Several were friends of Sarah—and, if they had reason to believe he had killed her, they would have been motivated to portray him in the worst light possible.

That didn't happen.

Sarah's friends had nothing but good things to say about Ryan. A couple of them also supported defense points about Sarah's sleepiness and headaches.

Katie Cook, Sarah's best friend since they were 4 years old, testified that she and Sarah talked about how they had both fallen asleep in the tub, lending credibility to Ryan's 911 statement that he believed his wife had fallen asleep while bathing.

In a police file about the Widmer case, a note says Sarah's brother, Mike Steward, told a detective that his sister had a history of falling asleep in the tub before Ryan and Sarah were married.

(Jurors weren't told about that note, dated August 14, 2008, three days after Sarah died. And Mike didn't testify.)

Besides figuring out what significance, if any, to attach to Sarah's purported sleepiness, the jurors also would have to weigh statements of people who talked about conversations with Sarah, including several who said she complained of feeling blah the day she died.

Sarah's friend from dental hygiene school, Amy Karabaic, was the last person to ever talk to Sarah, other than Ryan.

Sarah had called Amy and left a message around 5 p.m. that day. About two hours later, Amy returned Sarah's call. Amy could hear Ryan in the background. Neither Ryan nor Sarah sounded angry.

But Sarah did say something that may seem significant, in hindsight. "She had stated that she had a headache and the back of her neck was hurting ... She didn't sound like she felt very good," Amy said.

That description differed from a phone conversation Sarah had with her mom during that same 5 p.m.-7 p.m. timeframe. Ruth Ann Steward testified that her daughter made no mention of a headache nor any other health complaints.

Had Sarah kept her illness to herself to avoid worrying her mom?

Perhaps.

And there was additional testimony about Sarah's strange symptoms on prior occasions. One witness even testified that almost every time he saw Sarah socially, she would doze off.

Sarah's friend, Dana Kist, the matchmaker who formerly worked with Sarah, testified: "She complained of migraines. She would even say sometimes that she had blurry spots, visual disturbances, where she would go in the middle room of the office and turn the lights out and sit and try to get her migraines to go away."

Spitz had stated that migraines could precede epileptic seizures.

But witnesses made no additional emphasis on that point.

So far, little about the case seemed to make sense.

Mostly "yes" or "no" answers

The defense team called six more witnesses to fill the rest of Day Six: three of Ryan's co-workers, a neighbor, his mom, and a friend of Ryan—the defense lawyer who had urged Ryan to hire an attorney.

Five of those six witnesses were held on a tight rein. Prosecutors objected frequently, and Judge Bronson sustained most of them. The witnesses were shut down whenever they started to describe how Sarah's death affected Ryan—or when they tried to volunteer opinions about how "cute" Ryan and Sarah were as a couple.

Several of the witnesses looked puzzled. They didn't understand why they could not "Tell the truth, the whole truth, and nothing but the truth," as they knew it.

They didn't know about the narrow, sharply defined boundaries for character witnesses. They could say little beyond "yes" or "no" to many of the questions.

Their consensus in response to the defense team's questions:

Yes, Ryan and Sarah seemed happy. Yes, Sarah seemed awfully sleepy. Yes, Sarah would have told her closest friends if she and Ryan were having any significant disagreements.

No, Ryan didn't have a drinking problem or an anger problem; he was "calm," "laid-back." No, Sarah never complained that he was "controlling." No, there weren't signs of financial problems, marital problems or extramarital affairs.

Then prosecutors confronted them, asking: Had they ever seen Sarah experience a seizure? No, they all said.

Almost invariably, prosecutors ended questioning of these witnesses by asking: Were you present in the Widmer home on the night of August 11, 2008? Each said no, they weren't there the night Sarah died. The point was clear: No one except Ryan and Sarah knew what happened that night. And Sarah was gone.

Ryan's mom, Jill Widmer, was given more latitude. She started by speaking fondly of Sarah. Even though Sarah was just 22 years old when they first met, Sarah seemed "wise beyond her years," Jill said. "I instantly fell in love with Sarah. She was like a daughter to me. I loved her like a daughter."

Sarah would never hold back the way she felt about anything, Jill said. Several other witnesses, including three of Sarah's friends, made similar statements, implying that there was no way Sarah would allow someone to hurt her—or to drown her—without a fight.

Jill also recounted the night Sarah died: Ryan called her around 11 p.m., sobbing so hard that Jill could barely understand him. Ryan said he thought Sarah had fallen asleep in the bathtub and she might be dead. Ryan told his mom to come to the hospital.

Jill described how moments after she and Ryan learned that Sarah had died, the coroner's investigator showed up to ask Ryan questions. Judge Bronson didn't allow Jill to talk about that interview.

When prosecutor John Arnold got his turn to question Jill, he began by saying: "I apologize for the loss of your daughter-in-law."

Jill stared at him blankly. Lord only knows what she was thinking.

Then Arnold raised some eyebrows: Did Jill know if there was "any other woman present" at Ryan and Sarah's house the night Sarah drowned? No, Jill didn't know.

So, Arnold said, "as far as you know, there's no reason to explain the DNA (from) the unidentified female under Sarah's fingernails, is there?"

No, Jill said, there wasn't.

Earlier testimony had revealed no trace of Ryan's DNA in scrapings taken from Sarah's fingernails. But tests instead found DNA from an unknown female. Despite tests on four women who were around Sarah, no match for the DNA was identified.

Even though neither prosecution nor defense emphasized the mystery DNA, this tidbit titillated some Widmer Watchers. They wondered if Ryan and Sarah had been involved in a *ménage à trois* with a mystery woman.

No evidence ever came to light to support that theory. But that didn't stop gossip about the DNA, another item on the growing list of "things that just didn't add up."

DAY SEVEN

TUESDAY, MARCH 31, 2009

Interpreting the evidence

Earlier in the trial, police testified they had found two envelopes in the Widmers' bedroom marked, "In Case of a Marriage Emergency"—one labeled

"Sarah" and the other, "Ryan."

For prosecutors, the envelopes could be viewed as evidence that the couple's relationship wasn't as ideal as friends and relatives insisted.

But after the defense provided context, it was questionable why the envelopes were considered evidence at all.

Defense witness Monica Peppard testified that she and her husband were the church-assigned premarital counseling sponsors for Ryan and Sarah. The Peppards gave such envelopes, which included marriage-support brochures, to *all* the couples they counseled.

When police found the envelopes, both were sealed and unopened in the Widmers' nightstand drawers—right where the Peppards had advised the young couple to put them for future reference.

The mysterious envelopes turned out to be meaningless distractions in an already convoluted case.

But before Monica left the witness stand, Arnold used her to reiterate one of his main points: "As outsiders, we don't always know what goes on inside a marriage, do we?"

"Correct," she said.

Next, Rittgers called witnesses who would try to expose the ambiguity of the prosecution's evidence. Rittgers was trying to show that nearly every piece of allegedly incriminating evidence could also be viewed innocuously.

Dr. David Smile, a Cincinnati area board-certified emergency medical doctor, testified that *all* of the injuries on Sarah's body could be attributed to medical intervention. Smile said: "I was actually surprised that there was not more evidence of injury on the body."

That's because resuscitation "is not a delicate process," particularly outside of the hospital ER's controlled conditions. When working on an unresponsive person, medics must apply "a lot of force" during certain procedures, including chest compressions, manipulating the head and using devices to help the person breathe, Smile said.

In one procedure, a medic must put downward pressure on a mask while pulling up on the patient's jaw at the same time, he said.

Although prosecution witnesses had testified that "minimal" or "gentle" pressure was needed to perform the Sellick maneuver, pushing on Sarah's neck cartilage, Smile testified, "I would say it requires quite a bit of force." Studies have shown about ten pounds of force typically is exerted during that technique.

Mistakes are made in "nearly every resuscitation," Smile said. Hands can miss their mark during chest compressions or while applying pressure during intubation attempts, Smile said.

Rittgers ticked off Sarah's "suspicious" injuries one by one—and Smile answered what could have caused them.

In addition, Smile delved into more detail about the "sudden death syndrome" that Dr. Werner Spitz had mentioned.

These unexpected deaths strike all age groups, Smile said, adding, "As emergency physicians, we encounter this quite often, unfortunately."

About 300,000 such deaths occur per year in the United States, he said, about 1 percent to 2 percent of those involve "young people," under age 35. One-third of those victims have a "normal autopsy," revealing no apparent cause for their deaths.

Each month, two or three people under the age of 35 die mysteriously in each U.S. state, he testified.

A few people in the courtroom murmured about that startling statistic; it did seem to increase the believability that a health problem could have befallen Sarah.

When Arnold questioned Smile, he asked if he had seen some of Sarah's medical records. Smile apparently meant to say Rittgers hadn't provided those records. But Smile referred to Rittgers as "my attorney."

Arnold jumped on the slip. "So, he (Rittgers) represents you as well?" Arnold asked, dripping with sarcasm.

Smile retorted: "The attorney that I'm working with."

Smile had already testified that prosecutors as well as defense lawyers had sought his help in other cases. But his misstatement let Arnold imply that Smile was prejudiced for the defense.

Smile's testimony concluded with Rittgers and Arnold taking turns as they asked him to agree with their contentions:

Yes, if Sarah was pulled from a tubful of water, then her body should have been wet.

Yes, if the water was drained from the tub before Sarah was lifted out—as Ryan asserted during his 911 call—her body would be expected to be drier.

Yes, the more time that elapsed between Sarah's removal from the tub and her being found on the floor, the drier she would be expected to be.

Then Arnold scored a point merely by phrasing a final question this way: "And if her body was never submerged in the tub, only her head?"

Yes, Smile said, that would mean the rest of Sarah's body would have been dry.

And on that note, jurors and Widmer Watchers were left to ponder a scenario in which only Sarah's head was submerged, just as Dr. Charles Jeffrey Lee, the forensic pathologist, had suggested on Day Five.

Lee's testimony was still fresh in the prosecutors' minds. Because, unbeknownst to just about everyone in the courtroom, prosecutors had fixed the problem that Lee's testimony created for their Bill of Particulars, the document that specifies how a crime allegedly occurred.

That document, filed months earlier, on October 8, 2008, alleged that Ryan "caused the death of Sarah Ann Widmer by drowning her in a bathtub." Yet Lee had testified that Sarah could have been drowned in the bathtub, toilet, sink or other container.

Eight minutes before Smile started testifying, a brand-new Bill of Particulars was time-stamped "9:39 AM" with the date "09 MAR 31" in the Clerk of Courts office down the hall from Judge Neal Bronson's court.

I discovered it at lunchtime, when I made my usual stop at the clerk's office to check for new filings. One of my favorite clerks greeted me with a smile. "Got somethin' for you, Janice," she said. "Here you go."

I thanked her and grabbed the two-page document bearing the familiar caption, "State of Ohio vs. Ryan K. Widmer."

As I read it, the realization hit: A phrase had been added to the Bill of Particulars, so it now alleged that Ryan drowned Sarah "in a bathtub, *or some other water-containing fixture.*"

What was going on here?

Three days earlier, in my *Enquirer* story about Lee's testimony, I had pointed out that the Bill of Particulars limited the murder scene solely to the bathtub, which didn't fit Lee's tub-toilet-sink-other testimony.

Suddenly, the Bill of Particulars neatly meshed with Lee's testimony, instead of conflicting with it.

Was it a technicality? Or was the very foundation of the Widmer case shaky?

Either way, prosecutors could now expand their closing arguments to encompass possible murder scenes beyond the bathtub—and the jury would be none the wiser.

Expert tested himself

A late addition, Dr. Michael Gregory Balko, would be the final witness for the defense—unless Ryan testified.

Rittgers emphasized Balko's triple certification—again, in contrast to Uptegrove, the county coroner, having none—by asking Balko: "Did I hear you correctly, you have *three* board certifications?"

Balko said the American Board of Pathology not only certified him as a forensic pathologist (death-investigation doctor), but also certified him in two more specialties: anatomical pathology (organs and tissues) and neuropathology (brain and nervous system).

Balko performed all brain and heart autopsies for the Kentucky Medical Examiner, and also served as a deputy coroner in Cincinnati.

Balko had reviewed records of both autopsies on Sarah, and his opinion about the most suspicious injury on Sarah differed from Uptegrove's opinion, just as Spitz's had. While Uptegrove thought there were two separate areas of bleeding in Sarah's neck and upper chest, Balko said, "The blood is continuous" between those two areas, coming from the intravenous catheter that medics placed in her neck.

Balko also saw no pattern of injuries on Sarah that would correlate with a struggle.

Balko agreed with Spitz: The manner of Sarah's death was "undetermined or undeterminable."

"We just don't have a clear-cut picture," Balko said.

When Rittgers was finished, prosecutor Travis Vieux questioned Balko in one of the most memorable exchanges of the trial. Vieux asked whether a body, if removed from a tubful of water, would be expected to be wet a few minutes later.

"I don't know the answer to that question," Balko said. Then he described his attempt to find an answer, setting the courtroom abuzz:

That morning, after he climbed out of the shower, Balko stood there to see how much time it took for his skin to dry.

"I realize it's not a scientific experiment," Balko said, "but I was curious."

He was dry in seven minutes. That was only about thirty seconds longer than Ryan's call to 911, a point Rittgers underscored when he got the chance; it was reasonable for Sarah's body to be dry within that allotted time frame, he said.

Balko's revelation about his body-drying test appeared to have stunned Vieux.

Vieux asked Judge Bronson to strike Balko's answer from the record, on grounds that Balko admitted that his little test was unscientific.

But Judge Bronson refused and responded curtly: "If you're asking him a question beyond the medical realm, Mr. Vieux, you'll have to live with the answer."

Trying to regain ground after that, Vieux confronted Balko with two photographs that Rittgers had shown to Balko earlier. Vieux tried to get Balko to admit that he had misidentified the "body parts" depicted there. Balko replied that one photo depicted bodily tissue, not a body part; the other photo lacked "landmarks" to identify what it depicted.

Before Balko left the stand, Rittgers asked Judge Bronson, "Do I get to ask him a question?" The judge said no. Arnold, from his spot at the prosecution table, shot back: "Nice try, Charlie."

With that, the defense's case ended. Court adjourned. No testimony from Ryan; lots of people were disappointed about that. Some concluded he was a guilty man cloaking himself in silence.

Jurors were sent home early, at 2:24 p.m. They would need their rest. The next day, they would hear closing arguments. Then they would begin the laborious process of sorting through the evidence.

After hearing six days of testimony, Kim Widmer, Ryan's stepmom, wrote in her journal: "I honestly don't think they have proved anything ... Please, Lord, continue to be with us and give us strength. And most of all, please may the jurors see that the evidence is just not there to convict an innocent man."

Others who had listened to the same testimony were just as convinced that the evidence showed Ryan was guilty.

And other Widmer Watchers were puzzled and didn't know what to think.

None of the observers envied the jury's task.

DAY EIGHT

WEDNESDAY, APRIL 1, 2009

Spinning the evidence—literally

After days of tiresome testimony, the electrically charged atmosphere returned to Judge Bronson's courtroom as jurors filed into the room and settled into their seats, awaiting the attorneys' final pitches.

Spectators and news reporters would hang on every word, while scrutinizing jurors' faces for reactions—any hint as to whether they were inclined to convict Ryan or to acquit him.

Rittgers' summation would be sandwiched between arguments from both prosecutors. To compensate for the heavy "burden of proof" that the law places upon the prosecution, prosecutors get the first word and the last word.

So, with The Bathtub, the prosecution's biggest, best prop sitting nearby, Vieux launched into his closing argument.

Vieux listed the evidence: the "wet hair/dry body" descriptions of Sarah; Ryan's alleged lies and odd reactions on the 911 call; Ryan's contradictory "face-up," "face-down" descriptions of Sarah; the two bloodstains on the carpet; TV sets tuned to the wrong stations; the "number and extent" of Sarah's injuries.

Then, Vieux said, the scene was staged to cover up what had really happened in that little bathroom. During the struggle, toiletry bottles were knocked off the ledge of the tub, then replaced, based on circular markings and a "forearm print" overlaying those, Vieux said. Magazines and clothing found on the floor beside the tub were dry, Vieux said, indicating that "those items were placed there after Sarah Widmer was removed from the bathtub."

The Lysol Wipe was used to clean the tub, but left behind the haunting fingertip streaks, which were created when "someone fell into the tub hands-first" or was pushed, Vieux said.

Sarah's unwrinkled fingers and toes indicated that she was out of the tub by the time Ryan called 911. Or maybe Sarah had never been in the tub and Ryan lied about her still being in the tub when he called 911.

Vieux hit especially hard on Ryan's 911 call. His wording, "I think she's dead," and his failure to specifically say, "I need help," aroused suspicion, Vieux said, declaring: "He's already accepted her death."

The "natural response" would have been to immediately remove Sarah from the tub, Vieux said. Why would Ryan wait for a dispatcher to tell him to get her out?

That was probably the single most frequent suspicion people cited about Ryan's 911 call. Many men insisted that a husband, upon finding his wife unconscious in a bathtub, would instinctively pick her up.

Vieux challenged the notion that twenty-nine seconds, recorded on the 911 call, was long enough for Ryan to lift Sarah out of the tub and move her into the position where she was found.

Therefore, Vieux asserted: "She was already on the floor" when Ryan dialed 911. That would explain Sarah's "wet hair/dry body/no pruning" that emergency responders described.

Then Vieux said something stunning.

He reminded the jurors about those two bloodstains on the carpet, created by the fluid that flowed from Sarah's mouth and nose—and that a stain, identified as feces, was found near her head.

The jury could therefore infer that Sarah's buttocks were previously in the spot where her head ended up, depositing the fecal stain—and that her feet were once pointed toward the bedroom, not toward the bathroom. Her body had been spun 180 degrees, Vieux suggested.

It was a puzzling assertion. Why would Ryan have spun Sarah's body? How would that conceal a murder? Vieux offered no guess about that.

As Ryan listened, he thought: *That's just stupid. It's ludicrous. Just like everything else these people are saying. That's what this whole case has been, just tossing things out there that are meaningless, to see what will "stick."*

Vieux's interpretation of the evidence surely contributed new scenes into various murder "movies" playing in the jurors' heads.

Vieux drew an objection from Rittgers when he claimed that rigor mortis, stiffening of a dead body, had begun to manifest on Sarah's body. Vieux asserted that was proof that Sarah had been dead well before Ryan called 911, had been out of the tub longer than Ryan claimed, or that her body "was never fully in that bathtub."

Rittgers declared the evidence did *not* indicate Sarah's body was exhibiting rigor mortis; no one had asserted that during testimony.

But Judge Neal Bronson ruled that Vieux could continue making the rigor mortis claims because, "The jury will determine what the evidence is."

Vieux reminded the jury about the medics' testimony: Sarah's chin kept retracting to its original position when they tilted it upward during intubation attempts. From that, the jurors could surmise that Sarah's body was in the throes of rigor mortis, Vieux said, noting such stiffening can occur thirty minutes to an hour after death.

To conclude, Vieux minimized the testimony of the defense's experts. They had only agreed that it was *possible* that Sarah had suffered from a seizure or heart problem, not *probable*—and they all admitted that her medical history betrayed no sign of such disorders.

While Sarah's mom listened, Vieux paused and adjusted his oval, rimless eyeglasses and declared:

"The only reasonable conclusion is that Sarah Widmer was forcibly held with her head under water until she was dead." Therefore, Ryan murdered Sarah: "I ask you to return a just verdict in this case. Find the defendant guilty of aggravated murder."

His closing argument made no mention of toilets, sinks or "some other water-containing fixture" now incorporated in the Amended Bill of Particulars.

Vieux's focus remained on The Bathtub.

With that, court paused so the tub could be carried out of the room. Its time in the spotlight was over. At least for now.

Five or six theories, no motive

Rittgers began his closing with a simple, powerful statement: "The State wants you to believe that no water on the floor and a dry body equals murder." Yet, he said, if Sarah's body had been wet and water was everywhere, those conditions also would have been interpreted as evidence of murder. "They can't have it both ways."

Rittgers then began disputing the prosecution's arguments. If everything was so dry, explain how the carpet samples were so wet that the water leaked through the evidence bags? And then there were the *Star* and *People* magazines, which had been lying on the floor next to the bathtub. Prosecution witnesses described those as "dry," yet Rittgers pointed out that police collected the magazines two and a half hours after Ryan called 911—and the pages were crinkled, an indication that droplets of water had dried on them.

He defended the way Ryan behaved after finding Sarah. He "did what any one of us would do ... he pulls the drain plug as he is pulling her up, the torso out of the water." That was what Ryan had told Rittgers from the beginning—but the jury didn't know that.

Arnold objected to Rittgers' description because no one had testified about it. But Judge Bronson ruled to let it stand because it was "argument," not evidence.

Then Rittgers tried to turn the tables, using the prosecution's own argument about "what's reasonable."

When Ryan called 911, he had no way to know what the dispatcher would tell him to do with Sarah's body.

If Ryan had lied about Sarah's location, he would have risked quite a predicament:

"What if she wasn't in the tub, like they want you to believe …What, if based on their scenario, the 911 operator said, 'Wait right there. Don't touch the body. Don't do anything. We'll have help there?'" Rittgers asked.

Ryan would have been saddled with a dead body on the floor, with police en route, expecting a body still in the bathtub. Ryan would have had to scramble to put her back into the tub, while still talking with the 911 dispatcher.

Several people in the courtroom nodded their heads in agreement. "Good point," someone whispered.

Rittgers also said that, if you assume Sarah's whole body was never in the tub, "if he dunked her head in the tub and he was a killer, why wouldn't he lift her up, put her body in the tub, fill it with water, call 911? … It all fits then. Think about it."

That would have been the way to "stage" a bathtub drowning, Rittgers said.

And, he asked, would it really have made sense for Ryan to wipe down the tub? Vieux had noted that no blood was found on the Lysol Wipe, but said "perhaps the purpose was not to remove blood but just to remove evidence of a struggle."

Rittgers pointed out that pictures of the tub, taken before fingerprint powder was applied, showed no visible marks—yet prosecutors were alleging Ryan wiped away marks that he couldn't have known about?

And the marks had no significance, Rittgers said, because no one was able to say when the marks were made, nor by whom.

So how did we end up with Ryan accused? Rittgers' voice intensified as he argued that authorities' suspicions were ill-founded.

"The only thing Ryan knows is she fell asleep in the tub … But they jump on that and say he's a liar. That's what this is all about. That's what started it," Rittgers said, setting his jaw.

The defense agreed "one hundred percent" that the evidence showed it would have been virtually impossible for Sarah to merely fall asleep and drown, he said. The defense never argued that she fell asleep; that was just Ryan's supposition when he first found Sarah.

Then suspicions arose because first-responders saw no pruning on Sarah's fingers and toes, Rittgers said. He was exasperated: "Pruning, pruning, pruning—I don't know how many times we've heard about pruning."

Pruning takes time to show up. Maybe about a half-hour, the testimony showed. During his 911 call, Ryan told the dispatcher, "She was in here for at least fifteen minutes to a half-hour, somewhere in there."

No one knows whether Sarah drew her bath and climbed into it right away, Rittgers said. Yet prosecutors wanted the jury "to assume that, as soon as she went upstairs, she jumped in the bath, she was there for a half hour, forty-five minutes, whatever, and she should have had pruning," Rittgers said.

Rittgers explained why the upstairs TV was turned on and tuned into the Bengals game: "What's so bizarre about Ryan walking into his bedroom, getting undressed and turning on the TV before walking into the bathroom?" Yet police were suspicious because Ryan said he had been watching the game downstairs, not upstairs. Ryan was merely trying to answer the dispatcher's question ("How long was Sarah in the water?") by stating he was downstairs. That was his way of saying he didn't know—because he was not with her when she climbed into the tub.

About nine hours after Ryan's 911 call, Uptegrove autopsied Sarah. With Lieutenant Jeff Braley "in his ear," Uptegrove quickly labeled Sarah's death a homicide based on the bleeding and bruising he found, Rittgers said. Yet three doctors, all board-certified, said resuscitation efforts could have caused those injuries, he pointed out.

A day after the autopsy, Ryan was charged with murder.

Seven months later, Ryan finally got to hear the evidence against him. Yet it took until Day Five of the trial to hear any theory about how he allegedly killed Sarah, Rittgers said.

And that was only after Rittgers asked the prosecution's witness, forensic pathologist Dr. Charles Jeffrey Lee, to describe how Sarah may have been forced to drown. Lee then described various theories.

Based on one prosecution theory, Ryan approached Sarah from the front and grabbed her throat to force her underwater, causing the bruising on the front of her neck. Then, in a bit of play-acting, Rittgers asked whether Sarah would have responded by tilting her head back and saying, "Ok honey, strangle me?"

"Hell no."

Then his voice rose and accelerated.

"She's going to be grabbing that arm. She's going to be ripping at it. She's going to be ripping at him. She's going to be losing her French-manicured nails. None of that! There's no evidence of that at all!"

"It makes no sense," he said, pointing at prosecutors, "*their* theory. None!"

Even if there had been only a thirty-second struggle, it would have been desperate and intense. "Can you imagine how many marks would be on Ryan?" Rittgers asked. He invited the jury to set their watches to thirty seconds and envision what damage could be inflicted to both Ryan and Sarah if they struggled for that length of time.

Yet Ryan was unscathed. And Sarah suffered no classic "defensive wounds," injuries to her knees, feet, toes or elbows. "Based on any one of the five or six theories that they've got, you would see injuries to any one of those places," Rittgers said.

Prosecutors had "a big problem in this case, and they've known it from the beginning," he said: the lack of signs of a struggle, and the lack of motive.

So, what happened to Sarah, if Ryan didn't kill her?

Well, "sudden death syndrome" does claim two to three young lives per month in each U.S. state, Rittgers reminded the jury.

"Am I saying it happened (to Sarah)? We don't know," he said. "I know one thing: Ryan Widmer had nothing to do with his wife's death."

He told the jurors that he hoped they would agree Ryan was "not guilty of any wrongdoing," and would acquit him.

Maybe the science didn't matter

Prosecutor John Arnold strode to the lectern. It was time for him to bat cleanup.

He began by acknowledging some legal analysts' opinions that the Widmer case was "all about the science." But, ultimately, Arnold said, maybe none of the forensics would matter. Maybe it would boil down to common sense.

Dr. Werner Spitz, "the highly hyped defense witness," didn't provide a definitive answer about what happened to Sarah. "The best he will do is come in here for five thousand dollars a day and say he doesn't know what happened," Arnold said. "For that amount of money, ladies and gentlemen, if this was not a homicide, he should come in here and say that to you."

Arnold downplayed the medical testimony—even though it dominated the trial.

"If her body wasn't wet, if her body wasn't submerged in that tub when she was killed, then all that speculation, all the possibilities … don't matter," he said.

Arnold told jurors to think about the circumstances: Ryan and Sarah were alone at home that night. "No burglary, no forced entry. So, it must have been some fatal event that came and visited upon Sarah that night—some unimaginable, fatal event."

Arnold advised jurors to reject the sudden-death theory as improbable: A medical problem would have struck Sarah at just the right moment, while she was in the bathtub, and it also would be undetectable after death.

"Whatever this malady is, it's kind of like the story of Goldilocks—it has to be 'just right,' doesn't it? Not too soft, or Sarah would survive. Not too hard or she would have died instantly without filling her lungs with water," he said. "Goldilocks, of course, is an imaginary story. And so is the defense theory in this case."

Arnold, however, validated Rittgers' assessment: prosecutors considered a dry body and a dry drowning scene to be prima facie evidence of murder.

Arnold told the jury: "If you believe that Sarah's body was not wet, then that means she was intentionally held under the water that night—then that is a homicide."

Arnold was lacking some visual aids. The Bathtub was absent. Prosecutors had decided against trotting it out again.

And an equipment failure prevented Arnold from projecting the Sweet Sarah photo onto the courtroom screen again.

Arnold apologized for the glitch. Then he said: "We know that, on the night of August eleventh, the wonderful life that was Sarah's is gone. We're going to ask you to accept what is reasonable and reject what is unreasonable."

Finally, he came right out and made the explicit request that he had skipped at the trial's outset, his voice rising: "We ask you to return a verdict of guilty, that Ryan Widmer is guilty of the aggravated murder of his wife, Sarah."

Then he grabbed the Sweet Sarah picture and it held up one last time.

Jury goes to work

After closing arguments, Judge Neal Bronson asked jurors whether they wanted to take a break. No break needed, the jurors agreed.

The judge spent the next half-hour instructing them how to evaluate the evidence: testimony of thirty-five witnesses, plus dozens of exhibits—photographs, documents, pieces of carpeting, and, of course, The Bathtub.

The courtroom was filled to capacity, mostly with Ryan's supporters, as Judge Bronson explained legal concepts such as "reasonable doubt…a doubt based on reason and common sense … not mere possible doubt because everything relating to human affairs or depending on moral evidence is open to some possible or imaginary doubt."

To convict, all twelve jurors would have to agree that the evidence "firmly convinced" them that Ryan was guilty "beyond a reasonable doubt," of either aggravated murder or murder.

Both charges alleged that Ryan purposely caused Sarah's death. But the aggravated murder charge accused him of acting "with prior calculation and design." That means there was some degree of planning and "a calculated decision to cause the death." A "spur-of-the-moment" decision to kill would be insufficient to support the aggravated murder charge, Judge Bronson explained.

With that, the jury began its work.

Ryan thought that if the jury was logical, he would be acquitted. "I thought we disproved their case," he said later. Still, there was no way he could feel at ease. He had been told something that I knew as a news reporter: Juries are unpredictable.

My editors and friends kept asking me: "What do you think the verdict will be? And how long do you think it will take?"

I gave them my stock answer: "I don't know. I don't have a crystal ball."

Just as prosecutors had argued that no one knows what goes on behind the closed doors of a marriage, neither does anyone know what goes on behind the closed doors of a jury room.

Maybe the jury would arrive at a true consensus with little or no pressure from their fellow panelists. But jurors with strong personalities also have been known to overwhelm the rest of the group—especially in a case such as this, with so much disputed evidence, no solid theory and no motive.

True, the prosecution did not have to prove motive to get a conviction. Still, Judge Bronson's instructions to the jury did say: "The presence or absence of motive is one of the circumstances bearing upon 'purpose,'" an essential element of the crime of murder, or aggravated murder.

From what I could see, public opinion was sharply divided. While some insisted an innocent man was being railroaded on flimsy evidence, others lobbed nasty barbs degrading anyone who doubted his guilt.

In the end, the only opinions that mattered would be the opinions of twelve jurors, ordinary folks now tasked with an extraordinary puzzle.

How would they reconcile the conflicting testimony? How would they weigh the circumstantial evidence? How would they sort out the complicated scientific evidence? Or, would they agree with Arnold and decide that the science didn't matter?

The wait begins

The jury was dismissed to begin deliberations just after noon on Day Eight.

Soon after deliberations began, the jurors asked to examine The Bathtub. They viewed it in private, in a back hallway between the jury room and the courtroom. Judge Bronson's bailiff stood guard until the jurors informed him they were done. Then they were escorted back to the jury room.

All the while, Sarah's mom and brother remained out of sight, as did prosecutors. They seemed quietly confident about their case.

If friends of Sarah—other than Dana and Chris Kist, the couple who played matchmaker—were among the spectators, they didn't make their presence known.

We news reporters had a hard time finding anyone who would go on record with an opinion that Ryan should be convicted. Most people who hung around waiting were Ryan's friends and relatives.

Among Ryan's most fervent supporters were his uncle and aunt, Kevin and Jackie Cronin. They were the ones who consoled Ryan and his mom, Jill— Jackie's sister—at Jill's house into the wee hours the night that Sarah died.

Now, while waiting for a verdict, they mulled over everything that led up to this point.

On the night of Sarah's death, Kevin and Jackie heard Ryan tell how he had found Sarah with her face staring up at the ceiling from under the water. They heard him say that the first-arriving officer helped move Sarah's body. They believed what he had told them. He was in too much shock to make up a story; he kept repeating: "I can't believe this happened."

When Ryan was charged with murder two days later, the Cronins were as stunned as the rest of the family was.

A couple months later, in a dose of irony, Kevin was chosen as a juror in a murder case in an adjacent county.

While Ryan was still awaiting trial, Kevin and eleven other Butler County jurors unanimously convicted the defendant, James O'Hara. He was sentenced to life in prison with no chance of parole.

In the O'Hara case, the victim had been stabbed repeatedly—and cops found a murder weapon. A trail of blood and footprints led to the suspect. And there was a motive: robbery.

The evidence was clear-cut, Kevin said. He expected the same quality of evidence in Ryan's case.

Kevin took notes at the start of Ryan's trial; he almost felt like he was a juror again.

But he kept hearing "opinions, as opposed to the factual data that I heard in the other trial."

In disgust, Kevin wadded up his notes and threw them in the trash.

Ryan's case was light on facts, heavy on speculation and completely missing a motive, Kevin said.

Above all, this was Ryan—one of the least-aggressive, most agreeable and honest young men that Kevin and Jackie had ever known. And his love for Sarah was undeniable.

Surely Ryan would be acquitted, they thought, if there is such a thing as justice.

Day Eight, however, ended without a decision. Around 11:45 p.m., the weary jurors informed Judge Neal Bronson that they wanted to quit for the night.

He sent the jurors home, with orders to return at 9 a.m. the next day, saying, "Have a very good evening, even though it will be a very short evening."

DAY NINE

THURSDAY, APRIL 2, 2009

Watching from near and far

Besides dozens of people waiting at the courthouse for a verdict, untold thousands were following the trial from a distance—via word-of-mouth, the live blog and other media reports.

One of them was Shirley Bonekemper. She was the head of the Convention & Visitors Bureau where Ryan worked, and she had gone through the nerve-wracking process of testifying on his behalf in court. Yet she was unable to say many of the things she had wanted to say.

During her testimony, prosecutors objected five times, about once a minute. Judge Bronson sustained four, leaving Shirley able to say little more than: Ryan was a good employee, Ryan and Sarah seemed happy, and she never saw Ryan angry.

Shirley was not permitted to reveal her staunch opinion that the Real Ryan— the one she knew—could not, would not have killed his wife. She held out the possibility that maybe there was a hidden side of Ryan.

But after the evidence was presented, Shirley was not swayed. She thought nothing solid was proved.

"There was no shred of physical evidence connecting Ryan to what happened to Sarah," Shirley said. "And she was a hefty and strong young woman ... you're going to get a heck of a fight out of her."

Even though Sarah stood only five-feet-one, she was 142 pounds at the time of her death, ten pounds above the generally accepted healthy weight for her height. Ryan did outweigh her by about fifty pounds and was thirteen inches taller than Sarah. Still, Shirley said, Sarah would have not succumbed easily.

To Shirley, the dry bathroom and other evidence seemed to support the contention that an illness preceded Sarah's drowning.

"In that tiny bathroom, for there to be no bruises, I just thought that was very strange," Shirley said.

Shirley also knew it was possible for someone to have a seizure and drown in a bathtub—because that's precisely what happened to one of her own relatives.

That case also happened in Warren County, decades earlier, claiming the life of her cousin's wife. That drowning victim had been a diagnosed epileptic, and Shirley wondered whether Sarah's sleeping episodes could have been small seizures or precursors to seizures.

Besides knowing Ryan personally, Shirley had another connection to the case: She had been a schoolmate of Warren County Prosecutor Rachel Hutzel and her siblings. "I saw a side of her in this trial that I was not impressed with," Shirley said. "I saw that she was hell-bent on a conviction."

Hutzel's friends, however, would say that she was simply passionate about getting justice for Sarah—and that the Widmer case caused her a lot of sleepless nights.

How much doubt?

As the jury resumed deliberations on the morning of Day Eight, Ryan and his supporters were feeling fairly confident that an acquittal might be on the horizon, considering prosecutors had proven no motive and hadn't singled out a specific homicide scenario.

Kim Widmer, Ryan's stepmother, told him, "Ryan, there's no way they're going to convict you."

Kim kept picturing Judge Neal Bronson's visual demonstration of "reasonable doubt" when the jury was being selected. He held his hands up, mimicking a pair of imaginary scales. One side of the scale represented the probability that the defendant did commit the crime; the other side, the chances that he did not. The scales would have to tip in an extremely lopsided fashion to support a conviction "beyond a reasonable doubt."

If the jurors believed Ryan "probably" did it, that would not support a conviction, Ryan's lawyer Charlie Rittgers had said during his closing argument, reminding jurors about Judge Bronson's illustration.

As the deliberations wore on, Kim grew more hopeful. Maybe there were a couple holdouts who wanted to convict and the rest of the jurors were trying to talk sense into them, to persuade them to acquit.

On the previous day, the jurors had deliberated about eleven hours before calling it quits. The longest deliberation anyone could remember in Warren County was about nine hours.

Rittgers told Ryan that a longer deliberation was usually good for the defense.

Regardless, Ryan said, "All I was thinking was I wanted this to be over. I was scared to death and the butterflies in my stomach never went away ... Imagine butterflies in your stomach that don't stop for days at a time."

He thought the truth was on his side. But if all twelve jurors were unable to unanimously convict or acquit, they would be declared deadlocked.

As Day Nine wore on, speculation grew about a hung jury.

Everything changed

As twilight approached, Ryan's supporters, who were passing time in the courthouse parking lot, saw dark clouds begin to roll in. They saw lightning flashing. They heard thunderclaps in the distance. One hell of a thunderstorm was on its way.

An intense foreboding washed over Kim Widmer.

"The best way I can describe it is this: I felt like this was an omen, that something evil was coming," Kim said. "The day had started out gorgeous. But when the sun was low in the sky, it got real windy and dark. It was getting ugly out. And then you could see everyone scrambling, and somebody said the verdict was in."

Everyone ran into the courthouse and breathlessly made their way into the courtroom.

Other reporters and I were still in our seats when we learned the jury had reached a decision.

At 8:26 p.m., I sent a message to my editors: "Verdict. Dunno what it is yet."

My hands shook as I sat in the back row of the courtroom, scribbling in my notebook, with my computer propped open on my lap, ready to fire off an email that would inform my editors: guilty or not guilty. They were waiting to spread the news on Twitter (which was fairly new then) and on Cincinnati.com.

I scratched out some math and figured the jury had deliberated about twenty-three hours.

At 8:28 p.m., I wrote that four deputies were standing guard. I also jotted down some observations: "intense, tense, quiet, nearly packed, 80 ppl."

When the jury returned, they weren't looking at Ryan at all—in my experience, lack of eye contact was usually a sign that the jury had convicted the defendant. Usually. But not always.

As court was called to order, everything happened at warp speed.

"The defendant will please rise," Judge Neal Bronson said.

Ryan and his lawyers stood up. The judge read the verdict form on Count One, aggravated murder:

"We, the jury in this case, duly empaneled and sworn or affirmed, find the defendant, Ryan K. Widmer is..."

Ryan's chin dropped to his chest.

"...not guilty of aggravated murder."

At 8:32 p.m., I sent a message telling my editors about that.

Ryan squeezed his eyes shut and started to cry.

Sighs of relief and a burst of applause filled the courtroom.

Then Judge Bronson held up one hand in a "stop" gesture and admonished the gallery: "Ladies and gentlemen, you're going to have to hold your—contain yourselves, please." Rittgers pushed his right hand backward to shush the crowd that was sitting behind him.

Ryan lifted his head, licked his lips and glanced at the jury. Maybe the jurors' lack of eye contact hadn't meant anything. Maybe they had acquitted him and didn't want to telegraph their decision.

The Count One verdict form bore the previous day's date, April 1, 2009. Judge Bronson said the date was an apparent error, but then he said perhaps the jury had reached the Count One verdict on that date. Some jurors nodded their heads, indicating yes, that was correct.

An ironic date, I mused. April Fool's Day. But there was no prank here.

Upon hearing the "not guilty" verdict, Kim Widmer looked upward and said, "Thank you, God." It seemed her prayers had been answered. But Kim and everyone else knew that Judge Bronson was still holding the second verdict form, for Count Two, murder.

Was the case headed for a full acquittal?

Thunderclaps echoed outside, as Judge Bronson began reading and supporters of Ryan prayed and clutched hands.

"We, the jury in this case, duly empaneled and sworn or affirmed, find the defendant, Ryan K. Widmer is…"

My hands hovered above the keyboard, trembling, ready to send another message to my editors.

"…guilty of the lesser included offense of murder," Judge Bronson read.

People burst into wailing sobs and Ryan doubled over. Rittgers stood stone-faced, head down, but placed a comforting hand on his client's back.

I typed "g-u-i-l-t-y-o-f-m-u-r-d-e-r," and fired off that message to my editor at 8:33 p.m.

I was stunned. After the "not guilty" on Count One, I expected to hear another "not guilty" on Count Two. I think most reporters were as surprised as I was.

One reporter seemed particularly taken aback. Later, when I watched a video of the verdict, I heard an unidentified reporter, apparently from a TV or radio station, made a phone call to tell her boss about the verdict. She then hung up and exclaimed, "Oh my God" repeatedly, apparently unaware that a microphone was picking up her outbursts.

At 8:34 p.m., I sent a message to my editor, reporting the reactions: "Supporters are weeping, groaning, moaning. My God!"

A woman near me whispered, "This is devastating."

It was as if someone had flicked a switch, turning relief into grief. For anyone who was there, the emotional flip-flop was unforgettable.

During Count One, Prosecutor Rachel Hutzel was nowhere to be seen. But upon Judge Bronson's pronouncement of "guilty" on Count Two, Hutzel stepped into plain view in the courtroom.

Years later, Ryan's memories of some details had faded. But the moment he heard "guilty... of murder" remained painfully vivid: "It felt like I had been hit in the stomach with a sledgehammer." Way worse than the butterflies he had felt for days.

I wondered what facts had convinced the jury that no "prior calculation and design" was involved in Sarah's death, resulting in the acquittal for aggravated murder. And what, specifically, led them to conclude that Ryan had purposely killed Sarah and was therefore guilty of murder? Later, some jurors would reveal their rationale in interviews.

As the wheels of the justice system continued to turn mechanically, the cauldron of emotions boiled over for Ryan and many of his supporters.

Ryan covered his eyes with closed hands, sobbing. Trembling, he kissed the wedding band he still wore on his left hand—inscribed with, "I love you most," from Sarah.

Judge Bronson thanked the jurors and said he would immediately proceed with sentencing Ryan. "Counsel, if you'll step forward with your client," he said to Rittgers. Ryan and his lawyers walked toward the lectern.

Someone shouted, "Put an innocent man away!"

Ryan's uncle, Kevin Cronin, couldn't hold back. He shouted, "Small-town justice!" and flung open the courtroom door, slamming it into a wall as he exited in a huff.

Kevin heard the judge's voice behind him: "Take that man into custody, please."

And the unidentified reporter gasped loudly.

Ryan's twin brother, Ayran, sat in the front row, next to their mom, Jill, and covered his face with his hands. Jill had kept her head down, with the side of her fist pressed into her forehead while Judge Bronson read both verdicts. She stared straight ahead as Judge Bronson declared that the only sentence for the crime of murder was fifteen years to life. The unidentified reporter muttered, "Oh my God, I don't believe that."

Judge Bronson asked Ryan whether he wanted to say anything.

Ryan's head was bowed as he kept his lips pressed to his wedding ring. He shook his head sideways in disbelief. Then he looked up at the judge and declared, "I love my wife. I did not hurt her."

I noticed Ryan spoke of Sarah in present tense, not past tense. I wondered if he hadn't come to grips with her death yet.

Over the years, covering hundreds of tragedies, I had noticed that grieving relatives often spoke of deceased loved ones in the present tense. It was as if using past tense would make their death too official, too real. And, as Ryan spoke, Rittgers' earlier words echoed in my mind: "He hasn't had a chance to grieve for his wife because of the charges."

But people who lacked that context saw his wording as an attempt to skirt around the murder accusation. Those critics saw "I did not hurt her" as a weak denial. A truly innocent man would declare, "I did not kill her," they thought.

Perhaps Ryan hated the thought of Sarah being killed so much that he couldn't even utter it. That's what some of his friends said later.

As Ryan spoke, the courtroom crowd was in rapt attention. This was the first time he spoke publicly.

"I was never given a chance. The day after she passes away, they charge me with murder," Ryan said, the palm of his left hand facing up, pleading for understanding.

Then he said, "I didn't," and interrupted himself with a deep breath and said, "If I had an answer, I would give the answer to what happened to her. But I can't."

Then he breathlessly emphasized his next words: "I... was... not... in... the... bathroom... with her."

Judge Bronson asked Ryan if he wanted to say anything else. Ryan shook his head sideways, looked straight at the judge and repeated: "I love my wife and I did not hurt her."

As the judge explained that Ryan had the right to appeal and he would be transported to jail, then prison, the unidentified reporter told herself: "I'm way too emotionally involved in this case."

Deputies converged on Ryan and pulled his hands behind his back. One put handcuffs on his wrists and squeezed them snug, making that unique ratcheting noise that tells a convicted man, "Your freedom is a thing of the past."

Just a few feet away, Ryan's mirror image, his twin brother, Ayran, remained a free man—a poignant irony.

Jill wanted to give Ryan a goodbye hug. Deputies refused. She rushed behind Ryan and the deputies into the hallway.

As Jill entered the vestibule, she flung her umbrella against a wall. Ayran tried to coax Jill to leave quietly so she wouldn't end up in custody alongside Ryan's uncle Kevin.

Kevin had the car keys, so his wife, Jackie, didn't know how she would get home.

"It was like the whole world was falling apart," Jackie said.

The deputy who caught up with Kevin in the courthouse hallway apparently could see the anger in his eyes because all that deputy said to Kevin was, "You go with me."

Kevin was detained in a holding cell. The deputies told him that Judge Bronson took mercy on him, and the judge was allowing Kevin to go free because it had been such an emotional trial.

But before Kevin was released, the deputies brought Ryan into an adjoining cell. Kevin couldn't see his nephew. But Ryan was crying so loudly that Kevin could hear his sobs through the concrete wall that separated the two of them.

Kevin was in anguish. He wanted to comfort Ryan. But he was powerless to do so.

Weeping, Ryan blurted: "I have been good all my life. I would never hurt anyone, especially not kill someone. How could this happen to me?"

Those words will torment his uncle Kevin. Forever.

Sarah and Ryan Widmer on their wedding day, April 19, 2008.

The home of Sarah and Ryan, Hamilton Township, Warren County, Ohio, as police photographed it on the night she died, August 11, 2008.

"Sweet Sarah" photo frequently shown in court by the prosecution.

"Scary Ryan" image kept in police investigative file, depicting Ryan at his arraignment for murder.

The drowning scene: Bathtub, obscured by door, left; two bloodstains visible beyond doorway of master bedroom.

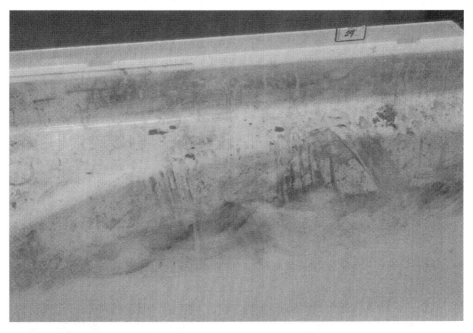

Finger streaks on bathtub. Prosecutors argued these could have been made by Sarah's hands.

Ryan, left, with his mother, Jill Widmer, and twin brother, Ayran.

The Widmer boys: Ryan, Ayran and Kyle, in undated photograph that tugged at their dad's heartstrings after divorce.

Free Ryan Widmer: Ryan's dad, Gary, with his wife, Kim.

"Mystery Witness," Jennifer Crew, as shown in Linn County, Iowa, police photo.

CHAPTER 7
Backlash and Boomerang

Within minutes of the Ryan Widmer guilty verdict, the Warren County court-house went empty and silent, like the eye of a hurricane. Powerful emotions spiraled away from it and a furious thunderstorm raged around it.

Ryan's stunned supporters had scattered from the building. Desperately trying to distance themselves from the verdict, they plunged into the rainy night.

But Ryan's supporters couldn't escape the reality of these three words: "Widmer found guilty." That was the front-page headline rolling off the printing presses in bold, inch-high letters on 175,000 copies of *The Cincinnati Enquirer* that night, ready to land on subscribers' doorsteps the next morning.

Sarah's relatives were ensconced in an undisclosed location, absorbing the jury's decision that the prosecutor, Rachel Hutzel, had relayed via speakerphone. "Nobody knows what they feel; they don't want anybody speaking on their behalf," Hutzel told reporters.

Sarah's family, the Stewards, had left the courthouse after closing arguments. They had no desire to be present for the verdict. It was sure to be emotional, no matter which way it went—and they knew reporters would be asking for comments.

Ryan's family retreated to Jill's house. First, they held hands and prayed. Then they cried. Then they drank themselves into oblivion. They didn't know what else to do.

Ryan's dad, Gary, and stepmom, Kim, drove back to their home in Colerain Township, Ryan's old stomping ground. Kim wept nonstop during the for-ty-five-minute drive, rocking back and forth, repeating: "This is not real. This is not real."

With hands propped on the steering wheel and gaze fixed on the road, Gary was a statue.

He spoke not a single word. Not even after Kim asked, "Gary, are you all right?"

Kim whimpered, punctuating the windshield wipers squeaking, the rain pelting, the tires swooshing.

After Gary and Kim finally got home, Gary's cellphone rang. It was his ex-wife, Jill; their sons needed him.

Kim told Gary: "Yes, go be with your boys."

Gary climbed back into the car and headed toward Warren County again.

Meanwhile, news of Ryan's conviction was blaring across all electronic media and was spreading by word-of-mouth.

Ryan's co-worker Lori Worley was among thousands who heard about the verdict on TV that Thursday night, April 2, 2009. Lori had intended to witness the decision at the courthouse, but a family commitment forced Lori to leave. Drenched in the rainstorm, Lori went home to change into dry clothes, planning to return to the court.

But within minutes, Lori's fiancé, monitoring the TV, yelled: "The verdict's on!"

Lori, her fiancé and her two daughters clustered around the TV screen, clenching hands and praying. The two girls adored Ryan; he made them laugh and feel special when their school bus dropped them off near the office where Ryan and their mom worked.

Upon hearing "not guilty" on Count One, aggravated murder, Lori and the girls started jumping up and down, screaming "yay!"

The three of them made such a ruckus, they didn't hear the "guilty" verdict on Count Two, murder. Lori's fiancé shushed them and delivered the news: "They found him guilty on the other charge."

The celebration stopped. Lori was dumbstruck. She felt like she had plunged into a dense fog. She was too numb to cry at first.

Lori's boss, Shirley Bonekemper, called. Lori went outside to speak privately. She stood under the soffits, shielding herself from the persistent rain.

Lori and Shirley sobbed in disbelief together on the phone.

As the call ended, Lori's emotions gushed out. Her knees buckled. She fell against the side of her house and slid to the ground. The rain pelted Lori as she looked skyward and wailed: "Oh God, why?!"

Now labeled a "killer"

After Ryan was found guilty, a pair of deputies ushered him through the rain and into a waiting vehicle. They drove a few hundred yards to the county jail, the same place where Ryan was locked up when he was first accused of killing Sarah. Now Ryan was being booked in as a convicted killer.

But Ryan wasn't focusing on that unnerving reality. He was unable to focus on *anything*. Trying to concentrate on any one thought or emotion would have been like trying to keep track of ingredients whirring around in a blender. Everything in Ryan's mind had blurred into a big, homogenized mess.

He realized this was the first night of a potential life prison term. Unless a future parole board would take mercy and let him out after fifteen years. Or twenty years. Or... never.

Even so, jailers didn't make Ryan put on the black "suicide vest" that he was forced to wear eight months earlier. Instead, Ryan traded in his business suit for an orange inmate uniform, with "Warren County Jail" printed on back, in big, black letters.

Ryan was glad to be rid of the bulky, uncomfortable suicide vest. But its absence begged the question: Wouldn't a *just-convicted* man be more likely to be suicidal than a mere suspect?

Maybe there was a valid reason for skipping it this time. Or, perhaps Ryan's lawyer, Charlie Rittgers, was right to suspect that the vest was intended to help create the Scary Ryan persona during his client's first public court appearance.

That was the first—and only—time Ryan was forced to wear a suicide vest.

Now that Ryan was adjudicated a killer, his public appearance no longer mattered.

Ryan spent that first night after the verdict virtually sleepless, staring at the ceiling. Only a mattress pad separated his body from the cold, concrete floor of the county jail's holding cell. He had never felt so scared, so alone, so confused. He felt and thought a mixture of just about everything imaginable—except happiness.

After a weekend in the county jail, on Monday, April 6, 2009, Ryan and a few other prisoners were loaded into a van. Together, they would make the seventy-mile trip to Orient, an impoverished central Ohio town that was established as a railroad station.

In Orient, there were fewer than one hundred private residences. There also were a pair of "big houses"—state prisons. One of them, the Correctional Reception Center, or "CRC," served as the "welcome-to-prison" destination for Ryan and 13,755 other men who were sentenced to Ohio prison terms in 2009.

New prisoners typically stayed at CRC for just a couple weeks. Then, based on the seriousness of their crimes and other factors, the new prisoners were assigned to serve their sentences in one of Ohio's twenty-seven other prisons.

Ryan's companions in the sheriff's van were anonymous to him. But he was certain they knew who *he* was. After their ride with Ryan, they could now boast: "When I first got locked up, you won't believe who I was with—that dude who drowned his wife in the bathtub. You know, Ryan Widmer. His case was on the national news and everything."

But notoriety wasn't on Ryan's mind. Fear was.

This was a place where Ryan knew none of the rules and none of the people. He was no longer a free U.S. citizen. He was a ward of the State of Ohio, which was in control of everything he would do from now until his prison term ended.

Ryan was terrified when he went on trial. But this was worse. It was as if the dial on the fright meter was being cranked higher and higher to see how much he could withstand.

Ryan was pretty sure that the other guys in the van were afraid, too. But the men kept their thoughts and feelings to themselves. They were practically paralyzed and hardly uttered a word during the eighty-minute ride to CRC.

Only a fool would admit feelings of fear on the way to the state pen—or while locked up inside a prison. Based on the images shown on TV and in movies, most new prisoners picture prison as an unforgiving place where human bloodhounds detect any whiff of weakness—and hunt it down for dinner. Ryan would later learn that prison life, like life in general, isn't quite the way it's depicted in popular culture.

Finally, the van exited Interstate 71 and slowed down to make its final turns onto residential streets leading to the prison. It gently bounced over one, two, three, four speed bumps, and rolled past rows of ramshackle houses. Around the bend was the area's tallest structure: a water tower, painted white with "Village of ORIENT" in black letters. As the van made one more turn and climbed a slight grade, the sprawling fifty-acre prison complex—the van passengers' new "home"—came into view.

The prison's one-story brick buildings sat behind dual rows of chain-link fences, topped with coils of razor wire—a sight that makes a man say to himself, "This shit just got real."

The van pulled around to the fence's back gate. An electric motor s-l-o-w-l-y slid the gate to the left, making way for the van to roll through.

What sort of hell awaited inside?

Ryan could only guess.

Guards ushered Ryan and the other new prisoners out of the van, ordering them to form a single-file line as they headed for "intake." That's where prisoners were required to remove all their clothing for the dreaded "strip search," to check for drugs and other prohibited items. Guards aimed miniature flashlights into the prisoners' mouths, underarms and ears. Then they commanded the nude prisoners: "Bend over and cough."

Each new arrival also got a new mugshot and, in a way, a new name: a unique inmate number.

Just as the coroner's office had labeled Ryan's wife, Sarah, Case No. 2933, the state prison system labeled Ryan Inmate No. A599952.

Those numbers symbolized a certain bleak finality for both of them.

Sarah had been deprived of her life, and the legal system stripped away her humanity. It reduced her to a soulless mass of tissues to be poked and prodded and analyzed. She lived only in the hearts and minds of people who loved her. Ryan counted himself among the members of that club, whether he was welcome or not.

Ryan's identity, his freedom and his self-determination vanished. The Ohio Department of Rehabilitation and Correction had taken complete control of the tattered remnants of his life, quite possibly for the rest of his days.

Supporting a convicted killer

The morning after the verdict, Friday, April 3, 2009, reactions were coming in hot and heavy—except from Sarah's family. The Stewards kept away from the fray. They apparently had become convinced of Ryan's guilt, and were trying to heal their broken hearts in solitude.

Ryan's family and closest friends felt almost paralyzed. What do you do after someone you love is sentenced to fifteen-to-life? Could an appeal overturn the verdict? How does any of that work, anyhow? And what was happening to Ryan? How would a naïve guy like him deal with prison?

Several of Ryan's relatives wrote letters to him the day after the verdict, including his cousin, college football coach Sean Cronin. "I don't know where to start and I have no idea what to say," Sean began. A lot of letters to Ryan started that way.

"No matter what happens, all I know is that God took Sarah, not you. Which means He still has work for you to do," Sean wrote. Sean had no clue as to God's purpose for Ryan's incarceration, but he was sure there must have been one.

In another letter, Sean followed up on that thought: "Maybe this happened to you because there is nothing evil in you ... Everyone who has met you loves you and maybe that is why. Maybe God knows that you can bear this burden because you will have support."

Sean tried to keep Ryan entertained, too. Ryan's lack of appetite had left him looking painfully skinny. But Sean joked with Ryan: "I hear you are not allowed to smoke but they put money in your account so you can get candy bars and stuff. Not being able to smoke plus candy bars is going to result in getting you fat. You will look like me in a week."

As for the public, the verdict wasn't sitting well. Radio talk shows and the internet were blowing up with comments from people denouncing the verdict as unjust.

The county prosecutor, Rachel Hutzel, had a public-relations crisis—and before the day was over, Hutzel would make statements that ignited more controversy.

Within hours of the verdict, more than five thousand people had voted in the *Enquirer's* unscientific online poll: "Do you agree with the guilty verdict for Ryan Widmer?" Fifty-eight percent of the people said, "No."

That type of response was unparalleled, as far as I knew. It would be more likely for people to complain about an acquittal—the bad guy "got off scot-free"—rather than express concern about a possible wrongful conviction.

After the Widmer verdict, local Facebook pages exploded with comment. Inspired by that outrage, a local internet guru started the FreeRyanWidmer.com website.

No one in Ryan's family knew the founder, Mike Mayleben, but they welcomed his help—cautiously. They worried whether he had an agenda. But Mike told Ryan's family his sole motivation was to help right a perceived wrong: Ryan shouldn't have been convicted.

Mike had latched onto a phenomenon.

FreeRyanWidmer.com, online the day after the verdict, drew fourteen thousand pageviews in its first two days; within a month, more than one hundred thousand—impressive numbers for a small, independent local website.

Even people who were strangers to Ryan expressed how deeply the verdict affected them. One commenter wrote: "After keeping up with the entire trial from Day One, I was sure there was no way this jury of twelve could come back with 'guilty.' …Then there came the verdict of 'guilty' and instead of feeling the knot in my stomach relax, it actually felt like it double-knotted. Tears stung my eyes … I have a sadness over me, for the loss of Sarah and for the loss of Ryan. I truly hope these knots loosen soon. My thoughts, prayers and heart go out to Ryan and the Widmer family."

One supporter said his family prayed for Ryan every night at dinner. Playing off of the nickname for Cincinnati football fans, "BengalNation," he wrote: "You have a RyanNation supporting you and fighting the fight with you …We are here to support you, to support your family and to do everything we can to make the truth known. We also want to make sure this will NEVER happen to anyone again! We all 'heart' Ryan Widmer!"

T-shirts, pins, wristbands and bumper stickers were soon being printed with

"Free Ryan Widmer." Proceeds went to Ryan's legal defense fund. Candlelight vigils, golf outings and other fundraisers drew hundreds of supporters—usually the type of events reserved for murder *victims*, not for convicted killers. The outpouring for Ryan was unprecedented. No one could remember seeing greater outrage over another Cincinnati-area murder conviction.

Later, FreeRyanWidmer.com, Facebook and the *Dateline* TV show all would produce unexpected—and unintended—consequences for Ryan.

Doubts about reasonable doubt

Ryan's friends and acquaintances believed he wouldn't hurt a fly—and they had a hard time figuring out how the jury saw proof of Ryan's guilt "beyond a reasonable doubt."

That's an amorphous concept that most people, including jurors, struggle to grasp.

The Widmer jury was ordered to rely on the definition that Judge Neal Bronson gave in these four sentences:

Reasonable doubt is present when, after you have carefully considered and compared all the evidence, you cannot say you are firmly convinced of the truth of the charge.

Reasonable doubt is a doubt based on reason and common sense.

Reasonable doubt is not mere possible doubt because everything relating to human affairs or depending on moral evidence is open to some possible or imaginary doubt.

Proof beyond a reasonable doubt is proof of such character that an ordinary person would be willing to rely and act upon it in the most important of his or her own affairs.

Based on his understanding of the Widmer case, a high school buddy of Ryan, Brett K., thought there were boatloads of doubt.

The verdict perplexed Brett and upset him so badly, it caused him nightmares. He pictured himself and his family facing a similar situation. His wife was a stranger to Ryan but she wept for him.

One factor weighed particularly heavily on Brett's mind: the prosecution's emphasis on the dryness of Sarah's body and her surroundings. Why was that so damning, considering that Ryan had stated he pulled the drain plug as soon as he found Sarah in the tubful of water?

"If he already drained the tub, she was already starting to drip-dry" by the time Ryan called 911, Brett said. "Everybody thinks he pulled her out of the tub and she was going to be soaking wet."

The lack of wetness was a big factor that persuaded the jury to convict Ryan, according to a juror, Raymond D., who granted interviews to several news outlets including *The Cincinnati Enquirer.*

No one relished finding Ryan guilty, he said, but each one was confident that was the correct verdict.

Ryan's courtroom demeanor was the first thing that Raymond cited in his interview with WLWT-TV, Channel 5: "He was totally expressionless."

The jurors didn't know that Ryan's lawyer had advised him to avoid reacting. The jury also didn't know that Ryan typically showed less emotion than the average person. Because Ryan's character witnesses were blocked from revealing specifics—and because Ryan didn't testify—jurors were left with only a black-and-white sketch of Scary Ryan.

Jurors found no "prior calculation and design," which explained their acquittal on the aggravated murder charge. They decided to convict Ryan of the lesser charge, murder, after deciding that Ryan and Sarah must have quarreled about something, maybe over money, because of his alleged policing of Sarah's spending. Then, in the heat of the moment, Ryan drowned his wife, Raymond said, and apparently panicked and attempted a clumsy coverup.

But the scenario Raymond described didn't seem to match the legal definition of *murder:* purposely causing another person's death. Taking a life in a sudden fit of rage fits the definition of voluntary manslaughter, *not* murder, under Ohio law.

And Judge Bronson told the jurors that the law required prosecutors to prove that Ryan acted with "a specific intention to cause the death of Sarah Widmer."

But absent any other charges to weigh, the jury was faced with this dilemma: Either convict Ryan of the lesser charge, murder, or turn loose a guy who was "hiding something," Raymond said.

Despite that apparent contradiction with the law, Raymond asserted that the jurors meticulously dissected the evidence. They even used a timer to analyze whether statements on the 911 call corresponded with known events and conditions, Raymond said.

Using the timer and their logic, the jury concluded that Ryan's 911 call was replete with fabrications.

Another key to the verdict: The jury concluded Ryan had feigned removal of Sarah from the tub. They thought she was already on the floor before he called 911 based on two things: 1. Only twenty-nine seconds elapsed on the 911 call while Ryan was supposedly removing her body from the tub. 2. Her body was dry when first-responders arrived minutes later—too quickly, they thought, for the moisture on her skin to evaporate.

And, Raymond declared to a suburban Cincinnati newspaper, *The Western Star:* "I don't care how flustered you are, or excited or anything. If your loved one is underwater, you're going to get her out."

But Raymond didn't seem to consider that a dry body might be expected if Ryan was truthful when he told the 911 dispatcher, "the water's draining ... the water's completely drained."

Rittgers had argued that it made sense for his client to sit Sarah upright while the water drained, but the jury apparently disregarded that argument, perhaps because Judge Neal Bronson had warned: *arguments are not evidence.*

Yet the jury did buy a claim from the prosecution's closing argument. Raymond said they believed that Sarah's body showed signs of rigor mortis when her chin retracted during medics' attempts to reposition her head.

Additional conclusions the jury reached, according to Raymond:

- Ryan drank more than the four beers he had acknowledged to police, possibly fueling an angry outburst that culminated in Sarah's death.

- Sarah's French-manicured nails were made of acrylic and therefore were incapable of inflicting scratches, which could explain why there were no marks on Ryan.

- Ryan seemed to be "controlling" when he checked on Sarah's store purchases. Maybe he did that because he was frustrated that Sarah earned more than he did, and he wasn't getting pay increases. Maybe that fueled the argument that led to Sarah's death.

But facts contradicted the rationale and assumptions that Raymond described, avid Widmer Watchers said:

- No one testified that Sarah's body was stiffening from rigor mortis. Dr. Werner Spitz did say rigor mortis would be "a possibility" when an intubation is difficult. But Spitz made that statement in response to a general, hypothetical question. Spitz did *not* say that happened in Sarah's case. The prosecutor, Travis Vieux, was the only one who claimed there were signs of rigor mortis.

- No one testified that Ryan seemed drunk the night Sarah drowned. No one testified Ryan got angry when he was drinking. In fact, there was unrefuted testimony that Ryan was extra-quiet and more laid-back when he drank.

- No one testified that Sarah's pink-and-white French nails were acrylic. In fact, Sarah's French manicure was painted on her *natural* fingernails—a detail that was revealed after Trial One.

- No one testified that Ryan was frustrated with his salary and his career advancement. Although Sarah's mom mentioned Ryan failed to get an expected raise, Ryan had been promoted to sales manager nine months before Sarah drowned. And his boss testified that he was progressing through the ranks.

While it's fair game for jurors to make an *inference*, or reasonable conclusion, based upon a fact, jurors are not supposed to pile inferences on top of each other. Specifically, the Widmer jury instructions stated: "You may not draw an inference based entirely on another inference."

Yet, according to juror Raymond D.'s statements, inferences were being stacked like blocks in a Jenga tower, mingled with confabulations. Before long, disclosures from one of Raymond D.'s fellow jurors would cause the whole construct to topple.

Justifying the verdict

Prosecutor Rachel Hutzel sent out a post-verdict news release covering the usual bases. She commended her staff's hard work and praised jurors for their "deliberate and careful analysis of the facts."

The news release heralded Ryan's murder conviction and made no mention of his acquittal on the aggravated murder charge—a sign that Hutzel's office was putting the best possible spin on the trial's outcome.

Hutzel discussed the verdict on 700 WLW radio with talk show host Bill "Willie" Cunningham.

Hutzel declared that justice was done, citing the "very conflicting information on the 911 call," the face-up/face-down contradictions by Ryan and the dryness of the drowning scene.

When Cunningham, an attorney, asked whether that was "real evidence of guilt," Hutzel replied, "I think that's an indication of guilt."

She conceded: "I do not know exactly how the murder took place."

Hutzel said she thought it was a mistake that Ryan didn't testify. "I think that the jury needed to hear from Ryan," she said. That comment bothered many in the legal community because a defendant's right not to testify is supposed to be sacrosanct.

When Cunningham asked whether Hutzel wanted to see Ryan spend the rest of his life behind bars, Hutzel paused. Then she replied, "I don't know. I think that he has taken an innocent life. That's a tough thing. He needs to pay his debt to society and to this family."

Later, Hutzel publicly released information that Judge Neal Bronson had blocked from Ryan's trial: A possible motive.

Hutzel told me and other reporters that Ryan had repeatedly visited an adult "swingers" website; Sarah might have discovered the online activity, triggering a fight that turned deadly.

Defense lawyer Charlie Rittgers, still licking his wounds, was livid that Hutzel would try to justify an unpopular verdict by publicly releasing information that the judge had excluded from the trial for good reasons.

Rittgers said his client only looked at "racy pictures," and Ryan never tried to meet any of the women on the "Adult Friend Finders" website. Rittgers said a computer expert's report would verify those assertions.

To settle the he-said, she-said, I asked Hutzel for a copy of the report; she refused, repeatedly.

When Hutzel revealed the porn-surfing motive the day after Ryan's conviction, she commented that such activity did not portend well for a new marriage.

People who concurred with the guilty verdict also seemed to agree with Hutzel on this point. Aha, they thought: Now this guy is exposed as the creep we believed him to be. What kind of guy would frequent a "swingers" website when he was just married to a lovely young bride? And surely Sarah's family found the whole situation repugnant.

But Hutzel's critics denounced her as a prude and an overzealous prosecutor. They said lots of young men look at sexy pictures—and sometimes couples even enjoy looking at titillating images together. Even if there was a disagreement over porn-viewing, would it have been serious enough to turn a laid-back, ordinary guy into an enraged killer?

Hutzel took another post-trial step that further agitated her critics. She publicly released a video "re-enactment" of scenarios that could have ended Sarah's life—the proposed exhibit that Judge Bronson had rejected. It would have been the first time that such a video was used in a Warren County murder case.

Rittgers later wondered whether he made a mistake by fighting to exclude the video from Ryan's trial. Maybe the video could have shown the implausibility of various theories, Rittgers said, because the marks that the video "victim" would have suffered did not match those found on Sarah.

When Hutzel was bashed for releasing the re-enactment video and the internet-porn-surfing "motive," Hutzel retorted that she was responding to news reporters' requests.

Dozens of Ryan's supporters vented their displeasure with Hutzel—and with the verdict. They sent messages to the Ohio governor at the time, Ted Strickland, and to Hutzel's office email account.

Michelle D. wrote: *How dare you continue to slander an innocent man after you or your henchmen couldn't even decide on which theory you wanted to use on how poor Sarah died. I was in the courtroom and you did not have enough FACTS/EVIDENCE to convict. You had no motive ... so you had to "make one up." I am very disappointed in the Warren County justice system.*

Cheryl C. gave this well-written critique:

- *The arrest, trial and conviction of Ryan Widmer has shattered my faith in the justice system and I find it terrifying that someone can be put through what Ryan has with no hard evidence.*

- *The prosecution presented what they "think" happened—not hard, factual evidence of what did happen. Such evidence did not exist, for either side, in this case. No one knows why Sarah is not here. The entire case is based off of theory and conjecture.*

- *To gain public favor in the wake of an outpouring of support for this supposed "killer," prosecutors release a video of theoretical scenarios and "guesses" on an argument that may or may not have taken place ... the prosecutors just seem to be making a desperate, ridiculous spectacle of themselves as they try to preserve their image in the public eye.*

- *Outspoken jurors are admitting to creating their own theory of what they think happened in the bathroom that night, and then convicted Ryan based on this theory.*

- *What happened to "beyond a reasonable doubt?" If there isn't reasonable doubt in this case, I don't know what case has it, then.*

- *People who know the law, believe in the law, studied for years to uphold the law and don't know Ryan at all are expressing shock and disbelief at this verdict.*

Cheryl C.'s conclusion:

- *Warren County has single-handedly shown citizens across the nation, who have been following this case, that the justice system in this country is very broken and is not designed to protect them. This is not how I understood the justice system to work in this country and I do not feel proud to be an American today.*

When people came out in support of the verdict, they mostly made short comments such as this one on Cincinnati.com, crediting the coroner for the conviction: "Guilty! Thank you, Russ Uptegrove."

Another: "Let the man rot in prison. HE IS A KILLER...If you do not like our judicial system, then get the heck out of our country."

Crisis of conscience

Ryan's lawyer, Charlie Rittgers, felt compelled to do *something*. He had grown quite fond of Ryan and was absolutely convinced of his innocence. He was distraught that he had somehow failed. Rittgers filed a motion asking the judge to set aside the verdict—something Rittgers had never done before in more than three decades as a lawyer.

Rittgers said the guilty verdict stupefied him because "I thought everything went our way." Rittgers had lost other big cases, but never one he believed in this much.

Rittgers held little hope that his "motion for acquittal and new trial" would find favor with Judge Neal Bronson, but he had to try.

A week after Ryan was convicted, Rittgers filed his eight-page motion, arguing that evidence against Ryan was insufficient.

Prosecutors presented no specific theory about how Sarah died "because no theory would withstand the facts established in this case," Rittgers wrote, noting prosecutors amended their Bill of Particulars "to fit with their changing theories."

To convict Ryan, the jury ignored the facts and "shifted the burden to the defense to show why Sarah drowned, or lowered the state's burden," he said. "The prosecutors never linked their experts' testimony to any theory as to how Ryan allegedly killed his wife. Nothing presented by the prosecutors added up to murder."

When juror Raymond D. told *The Western Star,* "We found so many holes in the defense's stuff," that sure sounded like the jury expected the defense to prove Ryan's innocence, rather than forcing the prosecution to prove his guilt.

And because Raymond said the jury believed Sarah's body was in rigor mortis, that showed the jurors had accepted the prosecution's "rigor mortis" argument as fact—even though "not one witness, expert, EMS worker, layperson or any medical record indicated that rigor mortis was an issue," Rittgers wrote.

Hutzel's office dismissed Rittgers' concerns as nonsense.

But Hutzel and her team had no inkling about the crisis of conscience that was tormenting a Widmer juror—Jon C., the one Rittgers had almost kicked off the jury.

Jon recalled the jurors being admonished to follow rules—including this one: *"Make no independent investigation or attempt any independent investigation."*

With that in mind, Jon C. was troubled by things that happened during deliberations. His concerns kept him awake at night. He chronicled them in diary entries that eventually were filed as public records in the Widmer case.

On Friday, April 3, 2009, the day after the verdict, Jon wrote: "Having questions about several jurors doing (their) own tests on how quick a body can dry and telling the results to the entire jury."

While the uproar over Ryan's conviction and Hutzel's post-verdict revelations escalated during that weekend, so did Jon's inner turmoil, as his diary revealed:

Monday, April 6: Jon consulted a lawyer for advice. That lawyer urged Jon to contact Judge Bronson's office. The judge's secretary, acting as a go-between, replied the judge could do nothing about it now; she suggested Jon could share his concerns with a lawyer in the Widmer case.

Jon wrote: "Now what the hell do I do? Although I still think he is guilty, do I suffer in silence and forget about this? Or does my strong need to be fair, honest and my deep need to keep my integrity compel me to act upon this?"

Tuesday, April 7: "Still not sure what to do … After a short internet search today, I found a lot of information about this … Seems no matter which way I go, I end up the bad guy. Guess I will give it another day."

Wednesday, April 8: "Going to talk to some close friends about this after work today to get their input on what I should do."

Thursday, April 9: "Talked to a close friend about this last night. He had the same moral dilemma about this as I do … Keep quiet and have the thought in the back of your mind forever that you may (have) compromised your honor or speak up and suffer the storm that will follow. Either way, I need to do something very soon."

Later, Thursday, April 9: "My decision is made. I faxed a cover letter and account of what happened to the defense attorney, stating if this was of any significance, he could contact me, and if it wasn't, I would consider the matter closed."

That was a week after the guilty verdict. It also was the same day that Rittgers filed the motion for acquittal or a new trial.

Rittgers' wife, Ellen, also an attorney in the family law firm, walked into his office and handed over a fax. Its cover sheet read something like, "For Charlie Rittgers' eyes only. I need to talk to you about the jury."

Rittgers was astounded to see that the fax was from Jon—the juror who had given Rittgers a bad gut feeling.

And Rittgers' jaw dropped when he read why Jon had contacted him: Several jurors had experimented on themselves to find out how long it takes a freshly bathed body to air-dry. Then they told other jurors about the results, possibly swaying votes to convict Ryan.

Jon's revelation reinforced Rittgers' contention: the jury had lost its way.

"Whether you think Ryan is guilty or not guilty, how the jurors could believe the government proved their case beyond a reasonable doubt is beyond my comprehension," Rittgers said years later. "I had police officers—I know a ton of them—who came up to me and said, 'We don't know if he was guilty or innocent, but how the jury found evidence of guilt beyond a reasonable doubt is baffling.'"

The jurors who did the experiments were, in essence, acting as witnesses against Ryan inside the cloistered jury room, not in open court; there was no opportunity for Rittgers to attack their findings. And it would have been impossible for the experiments to have been valid or reliable. No one at the scene had measured airflow, room temperature and humidity the night Sarah died—all factors that affect evaporation.

Rittgers' son, law student Charlie M. Rittgers, was struggling emotionally after the verdict as much as his dad was. But when he learned about the jurors' experiments, a glimmer of hope shined through. He viewed Jon C.'s revelation as "a gift." One that dramatically increased Ryan's chances for a new trial or acquittal.

The elder Rittgers lurched into high gear. He interviewed Jon by phone, then directed a law firm employee to type an affidavit, a sworn written statement, based on the conversation.

Later that day, Jon stopped by Rittgers' office on his way home from work and signed the statement.

That eased Jon's torment. That night he slept peacefully for the first time since the verdict.

Friday, April 10: Rittgers rapidly crafted a four-page addition to the motion for acquittal or a new trial, along with Jon's two-page affidavit. "Ohio law is clear that any independent inquiry or experiment by a juror about the evidence violates the juror's duty to limit his considerations to the evidence, arguments and law presented in open court," Rittgers wrote.

News reporters pounced on the story. The weird Widmer case had suddenly become even weirder. Soon after Rittgers filed his document, we quoted it in our online stories, and the story hit radio and TV.

Jon recorded his dismay in his diary: "Crap. My statement is out along with my name. I knew this was going to happen sometime, but I sure as hell didn't expect it this soon."

News crews showed up at his house and tried calling him.

"Most don't seem to understand why I will not do an interview," he wrote. "This is by far the hardest decision I have ever had to make. Talking to the media only turns the focus to me and not the situation in question. What happened is what needs to be addressed, not the person that brought it out."

He felt suffocated. He needed an escape. So, he hopped on his motorcycle and took a ride to clear his head.

Jon's wife and friends commended him for maintaining his integrity. But others wondered why he didn't report his concerns before the verdict.

Saturday, April 11: Jon's critics couldn't understand what it was like to be in the jury room while the other jurors were revealing their wet-dry experiments, Jon wrote: "When this happened, I did feel uneasy about it. But it didn't seem to bother the other eleven people in the room, or at least they didn't say it did."

"I know now that I should (have) said something at the time but that is with 20-20 hindsight. If any of those on the outside think this was easy, I will gladly trade places with them right now."

Even after Jon blew the whistle, his conscience wasn't entirely clear. He worried about "The Big 'What-if?'" *What if Ryan would be set free and would commit another murder?* "Then I will have to live with that," Jon wrote. "Anyone (who) thinks that this is something you can decide and do in a day is at best, uninformed, and, at worst, a fool."

Indeed, timing was everything

Here's what Jon revealed:

- At least three of the twelve jurors had tried to find out how long it takes a just-bathed body to air-dry.

- A fourth juror discussed purposely checking on bathroom conditions several hours after bathing a child—and observing that everything was still wet.

- All four of those jurors shared their results with the rest of the jury, influencing several jurors and ultimately helping them to find Ryan guilty.

Despite the rules, jurors apparently couldn't resist seeking their own answers because no one had presented evidence about how long it *should* have taken for Sarah's body to air-dry—a natural point of curiosity about the case, considering the emphasis on first-responders' quick arrival and their observations that the conditions shouldn't have been that dry already.

Even before news about the jurors' experiments broke, several Cincinnati.com readers reported timing their own air-drying. Some news reporters confided that they, too, had done such experiments. I chuckled when I pictured half the Greater Cincinnati populace wet and naked, staring at clocks.

Everyone who did the tests seemed to get different results—proving that many variables could have affected Sarah's drying time.

But, then again, drying-time was less-relevant if Sarah was sitting in a completely drained bathtub, as Ryan stated during his 911 call.

Regardless, Jon C. held firm to his belief: The jury was *right* to convict Ryan, but just went about it in the wrong way.

Still, the younger Rittgers said, "I think it was his conscience telling him that he had doubts."

How many verdicts could be tainted by such jury misconduct cannot be known. Because few jurors would likely be as forthcoming as Jon was.

Experiments or not?

The jurors' drying-time experiments fanned the brushfire of discontent with the Widmer verdict.

Posts such as these flooded FreeRyanWidmer.com and local news websites:

"After thinking, OK, perhaps the jurors know more than I, they were there in the courtroom... I was wrong! The jury did not do their civic duties! In fact, I feel they did quite the opposite!"

"Our justice system may be horribly flawed but with citizens such as ourselves that refuse to give up in the face of injustice, we can make a difference.... Remember, if this can happen to him, it can happen to any of us. Something needs to change!"

Mark Godsey, law professor and director of the Ohio Innocence Project at the University of Cincinnati, said that at least a dozen people had urged him to take on Ryan's case. But his group works to exonerate wrongfully convicted prisoners only after appeals are exhausted.

Based on what he knew—that no one knew what scenario killed Sarah—Godsey told me he worried about a possible miscarriage of justice: "Not knowing what happened is a far cry from proof beyond a reasonable doubt."

Ryan's family retained Godsey, outside of the Innocence Project, to work on Ryan's appeal. Godsey and his wife, Michele Berry, were Ryan's first visitors at the Correctional Reception Center.

Ryan felt renewed hope when Godsey and Berry discussed the jurors' drying-time experiments. Godsey said he thought it amounted to juror misconduct and should force a retrial—but not without a fight.

The weary defense team was reinvigorated; prosecutors weren't budging. The intense legal battle over the juror experiments and other issues filled five hundred pages.

In an attempt to stifle Jon C.'s revelations, prosecutors cited Ohio's *aliunde* rule. Under that rule of evidence, Judge Neal Bronson shouldn't even consider Jon's statement, prosecutors said.

Translated from Latin, "aliunde" means "from another person or place"— meaning evidence of juror misconduct must come from *outside* the jury room.

Rooted in old English law, the rule was established "to protect the finality of verdicts and to ensure that jurors are insulated from harassment by defeated parties," prosecutors wrote. "Courts must preserve the integrity and privacy of deliberations to ensure that future jurors will engage in deliberations with the utmost candor and without fear of later public scrutiny and embarrassment."

Furthermore, prosecutors contended that "the alleged actions of some of the jurors can hardly be considered 'experiments.'… They were simply life experiences."

For more than a week, Jon C. worried that his fellow jurors might leave him standing alone; some jurors hired lawyers. But a private investigator working for Rittgers secured affidavits from two other jurors, who largely corroborated Jon's statements.

Juror Angie R. stated that, before the second day of deliberations, "I got out of the shower and allowed myself to air-dry for five minutes and discovered that I was still wet." Another female juror took similar actions. Angie said she didn't think she had done anything wrong, nor did she think her statements would sway other jurors' votes.

But Juror Stephanie S. said that the air-drying times *did* influence her to judge Ryan guilty. Stephanie said discussions were "contentious," and that "jurors who thought Ryan was guilty were trying to convince jurors who were undecided."

One of the women reported a fifteen-minute drying time, Stephanie said. If that was true, then Ryan's reported activities on the 911 recording must have been fabricated, Stephanie said, "because Ryan would have had to have taken Sarah out of the tub much earlier for her to be dry by the time the first responders arrived."

After news broke about the alleged jury misconduct, public opinion shifted even more in Ryan's favor. Eighty percent of people in an *Enquirer* poll said he should get a new trial based on the jurors' alleged experiments—22 percentage points higher than the percentage that initially opposed the guilty verdict.

In late May, a month and a half after Jon C. first came forward, Judge Bronson issued a complex ruling. It spanned sixteen pages and cited twenty court cases.

He sided with the prosecution on three main points:

- A juror's public quotes weren't evidence of anything.

- The prosecutor's statement about rigor mortis was an over-reach but it did not affect Ryan's rights, because jurors were instructed that closing arguments were not evidence.

- By law, trial evidence must be viewed "in a light most favorable to the prosecution." The evidence passed muster, the judge said. He didn't elaborate.

But would Ohio's aliunde rule block the jurors' affidavits from being used?

Judge Bronson wrote: "If the statements about air-drying and timing accurately reflect the actions of jurors, then they were 'manufactured' life experiences" and "independent inquiries outside the evidence." He also was convinced that the experiments *did* affect the way the jury considered the bona fide evidence.

Therefore, the judge agreed to consider jurors' affidavits that Rittgers had filed; prosecutors would have three weeks to file counter-affidavits.

The judge's decision was positive for the defense, although it wasn't a slam-dunk. Still, it wasn't good news for the prosecution.

Bright spots amid darkness

While lawyers were busy dictating legal documents, Ryan was getting writer's cramp as he replied to supporters' letters.

After his first couple weeks at the Correctional Reception Center, he was transferred to Warren Correctional Institution, so named because of its location in rural Warren County, about six miles west of the courthouse where he was convicted.

Mail is delayed for new prisoners for a week or more—and it had been piling up for Ryan. He couldn't believe his eyes when he saw a stack of cards and letters several inches thick. He wondered: "Who is all of this from?" He thumbed through it and saw a bunch of names he didn't recognize, mingled with daily letters from two cousins, Missy Parker and Sean Cronin, the college football coach.

Missy's letters always included entertaining photographs and news items; Sean's often were accompanied by a page that simply said: "NEVER GIVE UP," printed in giant letters that filled a full sheet of typing paper. It sounded like something that Coach Cronin might say to his football players—but now it meant much more.

Ryan was receiving about a dozen letters a day. One frequent writer was Debbie Cupp, a fellow Bengals season ticket holder who sat in front of Ryan and his brothers at Paul Brown Stadium for years. Ryan affectionately nicknamed her "Bengal Mom."

Debbie wrote to Ryan on April 14, 2009, twelve days after his conviction: "My Dear Ryan, I can only imagine what pain, anger, hurt and confusion you are feeling right now ... You are in my mind and in my heart (that is truly turned upside-down) every day, and it is hard to think of anything else."

Debbie attended Ryan and Sarah's wedding; she was aware that their first wedding anniversary would have been April 19, five days after the date of her letter. "I know there is a difficult date this week," Debbie wrote, "and I will pray for good memories to fill your mind that day."

Ryan replied: "Getting the mail is one of the few bright spots during my days."

"It is truly amazing to see what so many people are doing for me ... the letters I get are so kind and uplifting ... It is simply amazing how so many people can see the TRUTH and injustice, yet because of the judgment (or lack thereof) of a few, I am stuck in this world I don't belong in."

Debbie is a woman of deep Christian faith, so Ryan knew she would be glad to hear that he was attending church services in prison. One of his biggest surprises about prison: Quite a few prisoners had expressed kindness and support, especially as the battle over a possible retrial continued. Ryan wrote to Debbie: "On Sunday, one guy passed me a note which reads, 'I pray your conviction is overturned! God loves you and He is the Truth!'"

Ryan asked, "Please continue to pray ... it's in God's hands and He will protect me and help the TRUTH to prevail!"

He closed: "I cannot wait to see all of you again. I just pray continuously and trust He will make that time much sooner rather than later. Thank you! For Everything! Love, Ryan."

Ryan tried to write back to everyone. Sarah had been big on thank-you notes; in a way, many of his replies were a tribute to Sarah. He often wrote about his love for her.

Supporters ranged from young husbands who sympathized with Ryan, to older women who identified with his mother, and many others in between. In a few cases, the letters sowed the seeds of everlasting friendship.

Marilyn Schnebelt, then in her mid-60s, got involved with Ryan's cause, along with her daughter, who was a couple years older than Ryan. Both women lived in the Cincinnati area and both had become fascinated with the Widmer case. Neither had ever felt so emotional about a criminal case.

Both vividly remembered the night Ryan was convicted.

Marilyn was fixing dinner. From a small TV on her kitchen countertop, she heard an announcer say that the Widmer jury had reached a decision.

She put down the spoon she was using to stir the food she was cooking, removed the skillet from the stovetop and stood in front of the TV in rapt attention.

"My reaction was, 'Oh my God.' I sat down in a chair and I started to cry," Marilyn said. "They ran that video of him crying, and he said, 'I love my wife...' He couldn't believe this was happening. By the way he talked, she was still alive to him. He put his face down into his hands. And I sat down and I cried with him."

Across town, Marilyn's daughter was exercising on her elliptical stepping machine. The verdict made her stop in her tracks. Too upset to continue her workout, she called her mom and said, "I can't believe they did this to him!"

They both kept repeating, "Oh, this is awful."

"I couldn't get Ryan out of my mind the whole night," Marilyn said. "I just kept seeing the vision of the news... they're leading him out of there in handcuffs, and I was just haunted by that picture."

Ryan's "open, trusting, boyish face" reminded Marilyn of her own son. "I guess that's why I emotionally connected with him," she said.

And Marilyn had personal knowledge of three local cases in which young people, Sarah's age or younger, had died suddenly:

- One young man, who had a history of headaches, suffered an apparent first-time seizure in a swimming pool and drowned.

- A young lady slipped in the bathtub, knocked herself out and drowned.

- A 21-year-old man took a nap and never woke up.

Those deaths happened within about a decade of Sarah Widmer's drowning, Marilyn said. "So, when the prosecution was saying, 'Healthy young people just don't die suddenly,' I was thinking, 'Oh yes, they do!'" Marilyn said. "If there were three cases that I know of, how many more are out there?"

The day after Ryan was convicted, she and her daughter both joined the FreeRyanWidmer.com community.

Soon, both women started writing letters to Ryan as he sat in prison. They also started attending FreeRyanWidmer.com events.

They missed the first candlelight vigil in April 2009 but went to fundraisers for Ryan's legal defense fund, starting with the "Circle of Love" held in June 2009 at a business on Cincinnati's east side, across town from where Ryan grew up.

As Marilyn watched folks eating and playing cornhole, she thought the gathering resembled a nice family picnic—except for the large crowd of 150 and the Free Ryan Widmer T-shirts being sold.

"I said to myself, 'This is a good family. This is the sort of thing that could happen to any family—*our* family,'" Marilyn said.

Before long, Marilyn and her daughter felt they had become part of Ryan's virtual "family." Later, the two women would meet Ryan in person; they would remain among his most loyal advocates.

"A living hell"

As the summer of 2009 wore on, Ryan's case continued making headlines; on June 10, prosecutors asserted that the jurors' actions were not improper, "but even if they were, such was harmless error."

In response to three juror affidavits from the defense, prosecutors plunked down affidavits from *seven* jurors, including Angie R., who had first written a statement for the defense.

In her prosecution affidavit, Angie said she was "preoccupied" by the deliberations and had absent-mindedly failed to dry off after showering—and noticed she had remained wet after about five minutes. "I did not make a conscious decision to do this," she said.

Angie complained that media attention, the public's negative reaction to the verdict, and being contacted by the defense team "made my life a living hell."

Ryan vented his thoughts on four pages of graph paper that another prisoner gave to him: "My life has been a living hell, not theirs. They shouldn't have convicted an innocent man and should have followed the instructions and the law!"

He disputed the notion that the drying-time experiments were discussed only a few minutes during deliberations and were insignificant. Four jurors made wet-dry observations, Ryan wrote, so "no doubt discussions were way longer."

Although prosecutors had repeatedly emphasized Sarah's suspiciously dry skin during trial, they attempted to minimize the significance of that point after the juror-experimentation allegations surfaced. Ryan thought that was B.S. Ryan's written notes quoted Judge Neal Bronson's May ruling: Prosecutors had written thirteen paragraphs summarizing facts of the case and "six of those paragraphs reference (Sarah's) dry body," the judge had written.

By late June, two months after Ryan was convicted, two of the twelve jurors swore in affidavits that the other jurors' experiments *did* influence their decision to vote Ryan guilty.

Stephanie S. was one; Jon C., the juror who first blew the whistle, was the other. His original affidavit made no mention of his own vote being influenced by the deliberations—an omission that prosecutors attacked.

His follow-up affidavit said, "I have heard how some of the jurors are now trying to say that what they did were not 'experiments.' You can use whatever word you want ... but what was done and told to the other jurors were tests and experiments, plain and simple ... these experiments that I have discussed affected my decision and impacted my decision to vote guilty."

The filings and counter-filings continued like an interminable game of volleyball.

Finally, in early July, three months into the fight over the jurors' actions, Rittgers declared: "The time has come to grant Ryan Widmer a new trial."

Four days after that, Judge Bronson filed a document labeled, "DECISION AND ORDER." We reporters rushed to the courthouse to get the document, thinking that Judge Bronson had finally ruled whether Ryan would get a new trial.

The document was only two pages long but it wasn't easy to interpret.

One TV reporter told her boss on the phone, "Um, I just read it and I don't know what it means. Hold on, let me see if anyone else can figure it out."

I took a look at Judge Bronson's wording and said, "I *think* it means he's headed toward granting a new trial but stopped short of doing that right now." I double-checked by faxing the document to a judge in another county. He agreed.

This was the key sentence Judge Bronson wrote: "The affidavits submitted fail to dissuade the court that there were external matters introduced into the jury room."

In other words, Judge Bronson didn't buy the prosecution's contention that the jurors' experiments were harmless observations of "life experiences." He believed they were "external influences" outside the trial evidence—which would mean Ryan *could* be entitled to a new trial.

But under the law, either side could request a hearing to explore the issues further.

So, the decision wasn't *really* a decision... yet.

On the outside, looking in

Ryan's family and close friends stayed busy trying to figure out how to best help Ryan.

They did interviews with news reporters and spoke up for Ryan on radio talk shows.

On April 10, 2009, eight days after Ryan was convicted, Ryan's mom, Jill, and his twin brother, Ayran, were guests on Willie Cunningham's talk show on radio station 700 WLW. Prosecutor Rachel Hutzel had been on the air with Cunningham the day after the verdict.

Jill did most of the talking. She described Ryan's side of the story, how he pulled Sarah's head out of the water and started draining the tub. She made two assertions that matched the Rittgers law firm notes:

- "I don't think Charlie (Rittgers) ever told the detectives that Ryan wouldn't talk to them."

- The first-responding officer had told Ryan something like, "Let's get her all the way out on the carpet," then he helped Ryan move Sarah.

Jill was sympathetic toward Sarah's family: "They're going through a horrible grieving because they lost a beautiful daughter."

Jill, Ayran and Ryan's other relatives also worked on vigils and fundraisers. They met with attorneys and private investigators for Ryan's appeal and possible retrial.

They brainstormed about things that bothered them during the trial: they thought questioning during jury selection could have been more rigorous and thought they saw some jurors dozing off during testimony.

They met with prisoner advocates so they could figure out how to navigate all the rules for contacting Ryan—and how to advise him to cope with life behind bars.

They warned him: Don't talk to guards too much; you could appear to be a snitch even if you're not. Don't share any information that other prisoners could use against you to get their own prison terms reduced. Don't borrow anything or loan anything.

They encouraged him: Get involved with education programs. Get a prison job. Get into a routine. Know we are doing everything possible to get you home.

Ryan's dad, Gary, wrote: "We are fighting for you and will not ever give up ... Ryan, you know I am not a very good person with words. This whole thing has left me speechless. Just continue to have hope that we can overturn this."

Ryan's friends and relatives had to wade through the red tape that envelops the prison system. They had to learn what they were allowed to send to Ryan and how to send it. No greeting cards decorated with glitter; none that played music. Yes, pictures, but limited to three, no larger than four inches by six inches. Yes, Ryan could receive pre-stamped envelopes and blank paper for correspondence, within limits; he might have to barter extra paper and envelopes to get a pen or pencil from another inmate.

No incoming calls could be made to Ryan but he could call people who agreed to pay a collect-call fee.

To visit Ryan, loved ones had to apply—and undergo a criminal background check. Once approved, they had to learn specific procedures for visitors.

His mother was the first relative to visit him. "It was great being able to finally touch someone I loved again," Ryan recalled. "It was very surreal and sad to see her go."

After Jill left, an emptiness washed over Ryan. He was again alone. Just Inmate No. A599952—no one's son, brother, cousin, friend. Just A599952.

On May 21, 2009, Ryan's dad, Gary described his first prison visit with Ryan in a posting on FreeRyanWidmer.com:

I have never been so touched in my entire life by such a courageous, strong, caring young man...I have never seen the display of love like I saw this evening. After spending two hours with Ryan, I went to my car and just cried my eyes out.

He is my hero! *Imagine that, a father calling his son hero.... with the love of God and you, he is able to endure this tragedy.*

Please do not give up! ... Thank you from the bottom of my heart and God bless you all.

Love, Gary

Meanwhile, Ryan's family also was trying to figure out what to do about practical matters on the outside—settling bills, figuring out what to do about his student loan, car and home insurance, bank and credit accounts; distributing and storing his personal possessions. The list went on and on—no doubt similar to the list that Sarah's family had to tackle after her death.

Because Ryan had been jobless while awaiting trial, he couldn't keep paying the mortgage on the house he and Sarah owned. It was going into foreclosure. "Who cares? Good riddance," Jill wrote in a letter to Ryan.

She had become a woman on a mission. She went back to work at Luxottica to earn money to keep things afloat. Aside from that, she spent every spare minute working on Ryan's case—working on fundraisers, researching legal matters and studying disorders that might have befallen Sarah.

Jill was distraught over Sarah's death, over Sarah's family turning their backs on Ryan—and above all, over Ryan's prosecution and conviction.

To numb the ever-present pain, Jill drank alcohol. Lots of it.

Starting the night of the guilty verdict, Jill started binge-drinking. That night, she passed out on the couch after downing copious amounts of Stolichnaya, a Russian vodka. The next morning, as soon as she opened her eyes, she tried to reach for a glass of wine. Jill's other sons, Ayran and Kyle, cut her off and told her, "No, you can't be drinking like this." Especially since the whole family was headed to the Rittgers law firm that day to figure out what, if anything, could be done to help Ryan.

However, Jill's sons couldn't always be around to police her drinking. So, it continued. And it worsened.

Jill tried to put a positive spin on her communication with Ryan. But every so often, she would drop hints about the toll that Ryan's situation was taking on her—mingled with expressions of a mother's unconditional love: "I would take all of your pain and trade my life to get you back home," she wrote a few days after Ryan's conviction. "Know that I think about you with every waking moment—which is most of the time, as it's hard to sleep."

Jill felt like she was overdosing on heartache—and it kept coming. On May 5, 2009, she found Ryan's beloved dog, Annie, dead in his room. The dog was lying on his clothes, as though she were waiting for her master to come home. Ryan had been imprisoned for a little more than a month at that point.

Jill shared a message about the dog's death with FreeRyanWidmer.com supporters:

She was a beautiful "pound pup" that we had the privilege to adopt 9 years ago. She was in such ill health when we adopted her that they didn't think she would live.

When I talked to Ryan today and told him he said, "Mom, just remember Annie's condition when we adopted her and how great a life we gave to her."

Thank you to all who continue to support my family in all of this sadness.

Chris and Dana Kist, the close friends who had introduced Ryan and Sarah to each other, were inconsolable after the guilty verdict.

Chris' first letter to Ryan began, "I seriously can't believe I am doing this right now. It is hard for me to sleep at night knowing you are in jail ... I have literally been sick since it went down last week."

Chris said he was sorry he missed a phone call from Ryan. He didn't answer because he assumed it was a news reporter calling again; Chris was too distraught to talk to reporters.

"I will make sure I answer next time," Chris wrote. "Your message was all broken up and I couldn't hear most of it, but I could tell you were pretty upset like the rest of us. I still can't believe that crazy verdict. Were those jurors in the same courtroom we were?! What could they have possibly been thinking?"

At Ryan's request, Chris and Dana granted an interview to *Dateline NBC*. "I think the show will help you get your story out there and it will be very positive for you," Chris wrote.

Chris was only partly right about that.

On April 18, 2009, sixteen days after Ryan was convicted, Chris received his first letter back from Ryan and responded: "We got your letter today and I have never been so excited to get a piece of mail in my life."

"It is good to know that you are doing well considering the situation that you are in ... This just really sucks because we miss you greatly and we took for granted being able to just call you or show up at your house ... I hope to see you soon in person because I am sick of seeing you on TV."

Dana and Chris read Ryan's first letter at least three times the very day it arrived, Dana wrote back: "We just need something to make us feel close to you. We love you so much and are praying for you daily. You really are on our minds all day."

Everyone who knew Ryan fretted about his life behind bars.

Was he okay? Were prison guards merciless? Was Ryan able to make himself eat? Was the food horrible? Would he just keep getting thinner and thinner?

Were thugs beating him up? Making him their "prison bitch?"

And how was he holding up mentally? How was he *not* losing his mind?

Although many of those concerns remained, Ryan's supporters felt some relief whenever they heard from him.

People would share updates about Ryan on FreeRyanWidmer.com, along with their comments on the latest news. The jurors' experiments looked like the answer to their prayers, to set Ryan free—or to at least give him a second chance with a new jury.

Ryan clung to that hope like a man overboard clings to a life raft.

Turning point

On the morning of July 22, 2009, Inmate No. A599952 (Ryan) was ordered to report to an administrative office inside Warren Correctional Institution. He had no idea why.

When Ryan arrived, a prison administrator was on the phone with someone. As the conversation continued, the administrator scrawled on a yellow Post-It note and slid the paper toward Ryan.

It read: "You get a new trial."

The administrator, who had apparently been talking with one of Ryan's lawyers, hung up the phone and said, "Congratulations."

Finally, Ryan thought, *something is going the right way: Maybe this wrong done to me will be made right. Maybe this is the beginning of the end of this nightmare.*

Ryan received the news shortly after Judge Bronson's much-anticipated ruling was filed at 8:12 a.m.

This time, the "DECISION AND ORDER" filled twelve pages, in contrast to the two-page "DECISION AND ORDER" that merely hinted which way the judge was leaning.

This time, the judge's wording was unequivocal and straightforward:

"A new trial must be granted."

Judge Bronson explained that he ruled that way because the guilty verdict may have at least partly resulted from "external influences"—the jurors' drying-time experiments—in violation of Ryan's constitutional and due-process rights.

Judge Bronson didn't buy arguments that the experiments were done as "an afterthought."

Rather, he concluded that the experimenting jurors had offered their observations for a specific purpose: to attack the credibility of "the only evidence on drying time," the testimony of the defense witness who described a seven-minute air-drying time after his shower. That timing more closely matched the timing of events on the 911 recording, yet jurors had chosen to instead believe their peers' longer air-drying times.

Juror Stephanie S. consistently claimed that the drying-time discussion influenced her to vote guilty, Judge Bronson noted, which convinced him that "improper external evidence" played a role in her decision to convict Ryan.

Within three hours of the judge's ruling, Prosecutor Rachel Hutzel responded with a motion asking Judge Bronson to rethink it. An appeals court had ruled in another murder case that "one juror's affidavit alleging misconduct of another juror may not be considered without evidence aliunde (from another source) being introduced first."

But the judge didn't budge. Later that afternoon, he filed a one-sentence denial of Hutzel's request. He also ordered state prison officials to transport Ryan back to the Warren County Jail, where he would be held "until further order of the court."

He set Ryan's bond at $1 million.

To get him released, Ryan's family would need to post $100,000 with a bondsman. That seemed insurmountable on top of Trial One defense costs—about $250,000, according to Ryan's mom, Jill.

Sarah's relatives maintained their public silence about the extraordinary turn of events. Prosecution and defense alike said they couldn't recall another case in which the trial judge tossed out a jury's guilty verdict before the case reached an appeals court.

Ryan's supporters were elated.

His lawyer, Charlie Rittgers, said the day Judge Bronson granted Ryan's new trial was one of the happiest of his life, exceeded only by the day he married his wife and the dates their two children were born.

For three months, Rittgers had been in the doldrums. "It seemed like forever, and I wasn't the one in prison," he said later. "Getting that conviction thrown out meant the blood was no longer on my hands. I was just so thankful that he was not going to be in prison anymore."

Friends and family poured out their happiness in cards and letters to Ryan.

"Wow! What an emotional rollercoaster the past few days have been," Ryan's brother, Kyle, wrote in small, cramped handwriting that resembled Ryan's. "I am so happy things are starting to move in the right direction. It still sucks that you still have to sit in jail for nothing."

Kyle's co-workers had been reluctant to discuss the case. He thought they were supportive but too "timid" to broach the subject. "I was right!" Kyle wrote. "After the big decision by (Judge) Bronson, there have been a lot of people approaching me to congratulate you. They were very happy about the decision … and they also believe this case was messed up."

The excitement, however, was tempered by yet another delay.

Hutzel wasn't giving up; the retrial order was put on hold while the prosecution appealed.

And Ryan remained jailed while supporters tried to scrape together bond money and his lawyers tried to get the amount reduced.

Ryan's family had recruited one team of lawyers to handle appellate court action and another team to handle the bail issue and retrial.

The one-year anniversary of Sarah's death, August 11, 2009, came and went without a decision from the appeals court—and with only a minimal statement from Sarah's family. Sarah's relatives were privately celebrating her life.

Mike Mayleben of FreeRyanWidmer.com created a new website, RememberSarahWidmer.com, where people who loved and missed Sarah could express their feelings.

Meanwhile, prosecutors were making doomsday predictions about the ramifications of Judge Bronson's retrial decision.

His ruling had "flung open the doors of the jury room" and invited chaos and uncertainty to intrude, they said. It "compromised the finality of every jury verdict in Warren County, past, present and future, and has left jurors defenseless from the harassment of defeated parties."

Ryan's lawyers retorted: "Judge Bronson did not toss the Warren County jury system into a state of lawless anarchy." They alleged that prosecutors were "invoking inflammatory rhetoric as a substitute for law." The ruling didn't set any sort of a precedent; it was applicable solely to Ryan's case.

The good news for Ryan was tempered somewhat by the escalating concerns about Ryan's mom, Jill.

In August 2009, Ryan's uncle, Kevin Cronin, wrote a letter to Ryan, telling him that his mom was out of money and "her mental state is fragile, at best, right now." Ryan should lean more on his dad, Gary, Kevin advised.

"This is a tough letter for me to write to you but it needs to be said by someone and you can be mad at me, but these are the cold, hard facts," Kevin wrote.

Actually, Kevin was holding back details. He knew that his correspondence, sent to Ryan in the county jail, was not private; he didn't want word to spread that Jill was spiraling downward.

But eventually, there would be no way to keep Jill's deterioration a secret.

Released, but not freed

Six weeks after Judge Bronson ruled to throw out Ryan's conviction, the Ohio 12th District Court of Appeals in Middletown made its decision: The appeals court refused to consider the prosecution's contention that Judge Bronson's decision was a mistake.

Prosecutor Rachel Hutzel was unhappy; just when it seemed as though the Widmer case was heading out of sight, it boomeranged into her front yard again.

After the appeals court's decision on September 3, 2009, things happened fast.

The next day, Judge Bronson reduced Ryan's bond from $1 million to $400,000. Ryan's family didn't have the required 10 percent to post, so they offered several properties as collateral.

They just desperately wanted Ryan to be *home*.

Within two hours of the bond-reduction order, Ryan's mom and dad, both wearing white plastic bracelets reading, "Free Ryan Widmer – An Innocent Man," were hugging their son in the jailhouse lobby.

And Gary was holding the door open for his son to walk outside into the bright afternoon sunshine. Seeing Gary making that thoughtful gesture tugged hard on my heart because of a running joke between Gary and me.

Gary had habitually opened the courtroom door for me and others each day of Ryan's trial back in March and April; he and I spoke very little because of the situation. But we would smile at each other as Gary insisted upon holding the door. In jest, I would say we ought to tip Gary for being the courthouse "doorman."

Despite Gary's shy grin, I detected a deep sorrow in his eyes—the same type of sadness I saw in everyone at the heart of this case.

But on this day, Gary, Ryan and Jill were joyful—unbridled but for the fact that Ryan was not yet an entirely free man.

Ryan still faced a murder charge; he was still under a curfew and other restrictions, including, for the first time, an order forbidding contact with Sarah's family; they again declined to comment.

Ryan had a hard time describing how happy he was to get *out*.

As anyone who has been through "the system" knows, time drags in the county jail because there are so few activities to divert inmates' attention. Ryan was going stir crazy in the county jail during the six weeks following the new-trial order.

He was so close to freedom—at least partial freedom. Yet he could do nothing except wait—and worry. What if the appeals court disagreed with Judge Bronson? What if there was no money for his bond, leaving him stuck in this godforsaken place, bored out of his mind?

Ryan kept wait-wait-waiting. Then, all of a sudden—BAM!—he was out!

Ryan walked out the jail door, smiling broadly. He barely acknowledged the journalists who peppered him with questions. As I recall, he spoke only a single word—"yes"—when someone asked if he was prepared for Trial Two.

He thought: *This is the last time I'm going to be locked up. Everything is on its way to being all right. Except I still miss Sarah. And I always will.*

It felt so good for him to again be in charge of all the mundane daily decisions that incarceration takes away—what time to wake up, what time to go to sleep, what to eat and when to eat it.

It had been too long since he last enjoyed two hometown favorites: black-raspberry-chocolate-chip ice cream at Graeter's and a steaming plate of Cincinnati-style chili with spaghetti, cheese and onions, known as Skyline Chili's "four-way."

Ryan had few possessions left; he could now fully appreciate what people mean when they say "material things don't matter."

A black plastic bag held his belongings—some clothes and lots of mail. Ryan hoisted it into the trunk of his aunt Jackie Cronin's car. Then Ryan settled into the back seat to ride to his mom's house, where supporters greeted them, arriving throughout the day and night.

A grilled steak dinner would fill Ryan's appetite. Love would fill his heart. And his head would rest on a fluffy pillow in a comfortable bed—for the first time in the thirteen months since Sarah's death.

After Sarah died, Ryan had refused to sleep in a bed; he preferred the couch because being in bed made him miss Sarah too much. For the seven months leading up to Trial One, he slept on his mom's couch. Following the guilty verdict, he slept on bunks, mats and cots in the county jail and in the state prisons.

But now he decided to climb into a bed.

His longing for Sarah had not abated. But Ryan had finally accepted the reality: Sarah was gone.

And he knew that before he could begin rebuilding his life, he would have to wage a war for his freedom—for the second time.

Instinctively, he knew: Now was the time to rest. He needed to be ready for the fiercest fight yet.

CHAPTER 8
Stalemate

Ryan Widmer felt out of place when he was the center of attention. His twin brother, Ayran, usually served as spokesman for the two of them when they were growing up.

So Ryan was content to take a back seat to the take-charge personality of Sarah Steward, the woman he married.

After Sarah drowned, Ryan was thrust into the public spotlight—first as the widower-turned-accused-assailant, then as a convicted killer who tearfully protested his innocence.

When Ryan finished the first phase of Ohio prison orientation, he was transferred to the prison where he would likely serve the rest of his sentence, Warren Correctional, in the same county where he had stood trial.

Shortly after his arrival, inmates shouted his name; his fellow prisoners seemed to be *greeting* him. Ryan thought that was strange. But he was pleasantly surprised that the other prisoners weren't taunting, attacking or threatening him.

He was apprehensive when a big, intimidating guy approached him. To Ryan's amazement, the inmate was offering help: "Let me know if anyone tries to mess with you."

Other prisoners seemed to be living vicariously through Ryan, hoping the justice system would work in his favor.

Even if only 4 percent of inmates were wrongfully convicted—according to some scholars' estimates—that would account for *two thousand innocent people* behind bars in Ohio. Ryan has continually claimed to be one of them.

On Friday, September 4, 2009, Ryan was released on a $400,000 bond to await his retrial. But once set free, he rarely went out in public. He didn't want strangers to recognize him as the guy whose murder case was all over the news.

He longed for his private, low-profile life.

But that died with Sarah.

Sarah's family, the Stewards, continued grieving privately. They shunned Ryan and his family and turned down media requests for interviews.

Ryan's family struggled emotionally and financially. Any semblance of normalcy seemed out of reach; they rode on a carousel of chaos.

Meeting with lawyers. Meeting with supporters. Dealing with news reporters. Trying to boost Ryan's spirits and his appetite. Grappling with alcohol-induced outbursts from his mom. Fretting over the impending retrial. Brainstorming ways to cover the soaring costs of defending Ryan.

Every bit of money helped; no fundraiser was too unconventional. Ryan's supporters even resorted to a campaign called "Trash for Cash." They collected aluminum cans and other metal to sell to a scrapyard.

Most of the funds for Ryan's defense came from his mom and dad, ordinary middle-class folks. Both had sacrificed their retirement accounts and remortgaged their homes. Ryan's mom, Jill, said she was willing to sacrifice everything she owned. If she ended up living in a cardboard box, that would be OK, as long as her son was acquitted.

Hundreds of people contributed ten or twenty bucks apiece. Donations via FreeRyanWidmer.com spiked after *Dateline NBC* aired its episode about the case.

"The Mystery in the Master Bedroom" ran on September 18, 2009, two weeks after Ryan was freed to await Trial Two. The story was so compelling that *Dateline,* on the air since 1992, chose the segment as its season premiere.

Ryan and his family clustered around the TV at Jill's house to watch. Although surrounded by people who believed in him, Ryan felt oddly self-conscious.

It was weird turning on the TV and seeing himself, knowing that untold thousands of strangers were watching at the same time. He had become a cause célèbre for all the wrong reasons.

In my own living room, a couple miles away from Ryan and Sarah's old house, I watched *Dateline*, too.

During that hour, my thoughts drifted to Sarah's relatives. I imagined they probably *weren't* watching. I doubted they would force themselves to confront pictures of Sarah's smiling face on national TV—painful reminders that she would never again be there to smile at them in person.

I thought *Dateline* portrayed the story fairly—and more accurately than some other media outlets had.

But Ryan and his family took issue with aspects of the *Dateline* program. They thought the show lent too much credence to the "wet hair/dry body" suspicions, without giving equal weight to Ryan's claim that he sat her up and drained the tub. To Ryan and his relatives, that was a no-brainer explanation for Sarah's dry skin.

In defense of *Dateline,* it may have been difficult to reflect Ryan's explanation considering that he didn't testify—and he had declined to grant an interview, on advice of his lawyers.

Yet, even without airing Ryan's account, *Dateline*'s coverage raised enough doubts that many viewers sided with him. With a few computer-mouse clicks, dozens of viewers landed on FreeRyanWidmer.com—where pageviews soon would surge above 750,000.

Later, a trio of *Dateline's* long-distance viewers would be pulled into the Widmer drama, playing roles that even Nostradamus never could have predicted.

The Real Ryan

When Ryan was released on bond, some of his Cincinnati-area supporters decided to make good on promises they had made while he was locked up.

One of them was Mollie Mihalik.

Mollie was among the advocates who felt as though she knew Ryan, despite never having met him. She knew many friends and co-workers of Ryan's mom, Jill. "Everyone that I knew didn't think he did it, and everybody was so appalled that he was found guilty," Mollie said.

As Jill's alcoholism continued to debilitate her, Mollie was able to fill the void as somewhat of a mother figure to Ryan. Mollie contributed lots of time, money and effort to the Free Ryan Widmer movement.

After learning that Ryan's conviction was being set aside, Mollie wrote to Ryan on a cheery, bright green notecard: "What a wonderful day today! You are getting a new trial. Can't describe the emotions. I promised you a drink and dinner when you get out… Can't wait to meet you in person and give you a big hug."

Within weeks of his release, Ryan accepted Mollie's invitation to have dinner at her house in West Chester, a few miles from his mom's house in Mason.

As Ryan enjoyed prime rib, Yorkshire pudding and conversation with Mollie and her family, Mollie thought he fit right in. She liked how unassuming and down-to-earth he was. "With him, what you see is what you get," she said.

Mollie now saw for herself: The Real Ryan was the polar opposite of Scary Ryan.

With his boyish charm, Ryan even won over Mollie's relatives who had looked askance at the unusual circumstances of Sarah's death. He was good-natured about taking a ribbing. He blushed easily.

Was this guy a hardened killer? They didn't think so. But Sarah's family originally had that same sense about Ryan, too.

While the Stewards were now keeping their distance from Ryan, people like Mollie were drawn to him. They believed in his innocence. And they felt compelled to help him.

After that initial meeting, Ryan did odd jobs for Mollie. Over lunches together, he often spoke of his love for Sarah. Each time, Mollie was moved to tears.

Ryan wished Mollie could have met Sarah. "She would have liked you a lot," Ryan told the fiery redhead. "Sarah was a lot like you because she wouldn't take crap from anyone, either."

Mollie, a mother of three grown children, felt so close to Ryan, she started calling him "my fourth kid."

She was certain that the jurors who convicted him had allowed emotion to overtake logic. A registered nurse since 1966, Mollie believed life-saving procedures caused Sarah's injuries. Especially because Ryan was unscathed.

She had followed Trial One from a distance. Now that she knew the Real Ryan, she resolved to personally witness Trial Two.

Marilyn Schnebelt and her daughter also became real-life friends with Ryan after exchanging letters while he was locked up.

When Ryan met Marilyn at a fundraiser, he came up and hugged her. Marilyn was touched.

And right away, Marilyn noticed hiccups in his communication. "Gosh, I can see where he wouldn't do well on a witness stand," she decided. "A prosecutor would just chew him up into little pieces."

His new legal team was forming that same impression as Trial Two loomed.

Inside Ryan's mind

As Ryan's new attorneys started getting acquainted with him, they learned that extracting information from him—about *anything*—was no easy task. He answered every question they asked—but almost invariably gave short, vague responses.

Was Ryan trying to hide something?

Ryan's attorneys soon concluded that he was forthright; he just didn't express a lot of thoughts or feelings unless he was prodded.

Because of his demeanor and occasional verbal snafus, putting him on the witness stand would be risky.

But attorney Lindsey Gutierrez prepared just in case. She and Ryan were both in their 20s and they had developed a rapport. If he testified, she would be the one asking the questions.

While Gutierrez was trying to pin down a detail about something related to the case, Ryan said he might be able to find the answer... *in his journal.*

What?! Why hadn't he mentioned that he had kept a diary?

Gutierrez was excited. She anticipated a treasure trove of insights into her client's psyche and details about the events surrounding Sarah's death.

When she and Ryan got together again, Ryan handed over the leather-bound book. Gutierrez retreated to her office to give it her undivided attention.

Her eyes darted across the white, gray-lined pages, searching for deep meanings among the words Ryan had scrawled in blue felt-tip ink. Fifty-nine pages of thoughts that Ryan had never intended to share with anyone.

Gutierrez settled at her desk and began to read.

One of the first entries: January 2, 2009, which would have been Sarah's 25th birthday. Ryan described visiting Sarah's gravesite and singing "Happy Birthday" to her, along with his mom and a niece who adored Sarah. Then Ryan visited his lawyer, Charlie Rittgers. Ryan wrote that he asked Rittgers the same question he always asked: *Why can't they see that things just don't add up to the story that they're making up? Each day is still as painful and as frustrating as the day I lost Sarah... I remain at their mercy.*

They have lied and tried to make me into someone I'm not and something I could never do.

Ryan's pain spilled across the pages and leapt into Gutierrez's heart.

Excerpts from other January 2009 entries:

I'm still sleeping here on the family room couch. I still haven't gained the courage to sleep in a bed...

Every night I lay here on the couch and cry because I miss her so much. And just don't know why she is gone and why they won't back off with the charges and help try to find out what happened to her that night...

We are spending all this money not only to defend my innocence but also to hopefully find out what went wrong...

I just don't understand what I have ever done to deserve this...

When Gutierrez read a passage about Ryan and his family looking for signs that Sarah's spirit was present, she wept.

As sunrays streamed across her desk, Gutierrez read about Ryan's life in the bleak days that followed Sarah's death. He was merely existing, not living.

Longing for Sarah. Losing faith in the justice system. Clinging to faith in God, family and friends. Searching for answers.

Each entry would end with a variant of *Love You More, Miss You Most.* Even the last one, dated just before the start of Trial One.

Gutierrez read the whole thing in one sitting.

It was her private communion with that journal, an experience that would be seared in her memory—vividly, viscerally, no matter how many years elapsed.

Deceptive detective, drowsy dispatcher?

As if the Widmer case already wasn't controversial enough, a pair of scandals simmered behind the scenes.

Ten days after Sarah drowned in August 2008, defense lawyer Charlie Rittgers had learned something potentially damaging about Lieutenant Jeff Braley, the lead investigator on the case.

During routine research, Rittgers heard that the detective's personnel file contained falsehoods about his credentials. Specifically, Rittgers was told that Braley's records fraudulently claimed that he earned a master's degree and had held an inspector's job at the U.S. Postal Service, where he actually worked as a clerk. (Braley later said those statements were indeed false—but he said someone else must have inserted the false information into his file.)

As Rittgers walked into the courthouse on Day One of Trial One, he spotted Braley and asked about the personnel file documents. Braley leaned against a wall and nonchalantly responded: "I don't know how those got in there," according to Rittgers.

Rittgers held onto that tidbit. Unless Braley's testimony turned out to be particularly damaging to Ryan's case, it would be smarter to attack the prosecution's medical experts instead of attacking Braley, Rittgers figured.

The case, Rittgers thought, was largely a battle of experts. He thought it was all about the science—and that the defense had the advantage with better-qualified experts.

But it later became apparent that the Trial One jurors focused on *circumstantial evidence.* That's why Ryan's new lawyers decided to attack the person in charge of assembling that evidence: Braley.

They believed he made flawed assumptions that spread like viruses, infecting the Widmer case from the start. And they thought it would be important for the Trial Two jurors to weigh Braley's qualifications and character.

Prosecutors went to bat for the detective—a de facto member of their team. The lead investigator typically sits with prosecutors at their table, consulting with them and listening to testimony even when other witnesses are barred from doing so.

Prosecutors asserted there was no proof that Braley authored the false statements. They also argued that the documents were irrelevant because they were created long before the Widmer case began.

After a series of closed-door sessions, Judge Neal Bronson sided with the prosecution. He ruled that Ryan's jurors would not be told about the disputed Braley records.

Meanwhile, Warren County officials were quietly investigating the 911 dispatcher's handling of Ryan's call.

Concerns about the dispatcher surfaced during a training session in April 2009, the same month that Trial One ended, but results of an internal investigation didn't go public until a report was released that October, as Ryan awaited Trial Two.

The report criticized the Widmer dispatcher for "long moments of silence and lengthy pauses where even the caller had to confirm that (the dispatcher) was still on the line." The dispatcher also failed to provide guidance after Ryan said he knew little about CPR. And then there was the dispatcher's nonsensical question to Ryan: "Are you *her mother?*"

The Widmer dispatcher admitted he had "dozed" on duty before—and so had his colleagues—but he couldn't remember whether he was asleep before Ryan's call, a report said.

A subsequent investigation concluded the Widmer dispatcher had not been asleep. But until that follow-up report was issued, the allegations were embarrassing for Warren County. A political firestorm ensued; the county's emergency management director resigned.

It was hard to fathom how so many controversies and complications could plague a single court case: Misbehaving jurors, an allegedly drowsy dispatcher and a lead detective with some allegedly bogus credentials.

Yet the Widmer Weirdness was just beginning.

Battle lines drawn

Ryan's new lawyers made it clear: They intended to sear prosecution witnesses to a crisp.

Some people claimed that Ryan's first lawyer, Charlie Rittgers, had been leery of making too much fuss in the backyard where he still had to play ball after the Widmer case was over. But Rittgers' decision to treat Braley and his cohorts with respect was a calculated one, intended to appeal to conservative Warren County values.

Enter Ryan's new legal team: Three outsiders, all based in the "big city," Cincinnati. They didn't care what anyone in Warren County would think of them after the trial ended.

The brashest of the bunch was Ravert J. Clark, known as "Jay." On first glance, Clark appeared innocuous. Average height. Slight build. Pale skin. Auburn hair. Long, oval face. Small, somber eyes, usually with dark, puffy circles underneath from lack of sleep.

But in court, Clark was a tour de force. He trampled over witnesses like a combine harvester laying waste to cornstalks. That was just his style. And he made no apologies for it, not even at the risk of irritating jurors. "I'm not there to play nice in the sandbox," he told me.

The perfect counterpoint to Clark's scorched-earth approach came from co-counsel Lindsey Gutierrez: Petite, soft-spoken, fresh-faced with doe-like eyes and long, chestnut-brown hair.

Gutierrez was also exceptionally bright and articulate. She was disarmingly charming—which made her a formidable interrogator despite her young age. She was a velvet hammer.

Gutierrez would sweetly ask difficult questions with a smile—and before the witnesses knew it, she had waltzed them into a corner.

The third member of the new Widmer team, Hal Arenstein, cut an imposing, intellectual figure. He was one of the tallest guys in the courtroom, with salt-and-pepper hair. Peering over his eyeglasses, Arenstein sized up witnesses the way a chess pro strategizes game pieces.

The defense trio would attempt to discredit virtually every professional who touched the Widmer case. They would ask unflinchingly provocative questions. They would lay bare every goof-up and every statement that differed from the witnesses' Trial One testimony.

The two lawyers who prosecuted Trial One, John Arnold and Travis Vieux, were back in action for Trial Two. And they weren't about to be steamrolled.

As Arnold and Vieux trudged along the familiar pathways heading toward the retrial, they believed the journey would end the same way it had the first time: with a conviction. But the prosecutors also knew they would need to counteract ambiguities in the evidence. They also would need to adjust to the new defense team's no-holds-barred tactics.

The prosecution and defense teams seemed to be fairly evenly matched.

Arnold could be as abrasive as Clark; Vieux seemed as studious as Arenstein. And the third member of the prosecution team, Jason Hilliard, was the male version of Gutierrez: young, smart and confident beyond his years.

During the final weeks preceding Trial Two, exchanges between the two sides became increasingly contentious. Besides fighting to get Braley's employment and education history pulled into the mix, the defense team also pushed to exclude the key piece of visual evidence that had helped convict Ryan: The Bathtub.

Arenstein wrote that the police search warrant was fatally flawed because it never singled out The Bathtub as evidence of an alleged crime: "Nothing in the warrant authorized the tearing out of the bathtub from its foundation." Police "overstepped" their authority, he argued; thus, testimony about the fingertip streaks in the tub constituted "fruit of the poisonous tree and must be suppressed as well."

Prosecutors retorted that The Bathtub was "an instrumentality of the crime," so its seizure was justified. They also argued that a motion to keep the tub out of court was required to be filed within thirty-five days of Ryan's first court appearance. Rittgers had strategically decided against fighting to exclude the tub back then. And Ryan's new legal team was unable to turn back time. Judge Bronson admitted The Bathtub—and the testimony about it—into Trial Two.

Judge Bronson also shot down the defense team's request to exclude the 911 recording. The county's 911 system stops recording during periods of silence, then resumes when voices or noises are detected. Because of this quirk, Ryan's lawyers argued that the recording misrepresented the timing of events the night Sarah died. But prosecutors convinced Judge Bronson that the unrecorded gaps were inconsequential.

In another blow to the defense, Judge Bronson blocked a Cincinnati-based engineer, Michael Birchak, from providing a possible answer to the question that derailed the Trial One verdict: how much time would be needed for a body to air-dry in the Widmer home the night Sarah died.

Birchak analyzed weather data for that date, blueprints of the home and Ryan's statements, and concluded: "There was adequate time for virtually all body surfaces to have dried prior to the arrival of the paramedics."

Prosecutors denounced Birchak's methodology as unreliable, an argument Judge Bronson apparently found persuasive.

That meant the defense had lost four big pretrial decisions: Birchak, the 911 recording, The Bathtub and Braley's credibility.

The defense did win one notable pretrial battle: Judge Bronson agreed to allow an expert to testify whether the pattern of injuries on Sarah—and lack of injuries on Ryan—made sense within the confines of the Widmer bathroom. That witness hadn't been allowed to testify during Trial One.

As time passed, prosecutors got more irritated with the defense team. They accused the defense of filing court documents purposely to manipulate public opinion.

Prosecutors asked the judge to intervene. He did.

Judge Bronson issued a gag order forbidding public comments from "all parties to the case, their counsel, employees, agents, witnesses and employees of the Clerk of Courts." He also blocked release of—and discussion about—Braley's personnel records, any other documents about him or about any other Widmer trial witness.

Gag orders are fairly common in big cases. But this was the most extensive one I had ever seen; my usual courthouse contacts were afraid to even say "hello" to me.

The *Enquirer* and I were convinced that the order was overly restrictive. Township officials refused to provide Braley's personnel records–documents that were unquestionably public—citing the judge's order. The judge later amended his order "to expressly permit" release of documents under Ohio's public records law—but that didn't happen until after the trial began.

As a result, Braley was temporarily shielded from alleged sins of his pre-Widmer past as Trial Two began.

JURY SELECTION and OPENING STATEMENTS
MONDAY, MAY 10, 2010–WEDNESDAY, MAY 12, 2010

Still stung by the Trial One juror misconduct, Judge Bronson and attorneys on both sides took extra pains to screen potential jurors and to emphasize the importance of following court rules.

The jury candidates had to answer ninety-two written questions, about two dozen more than were asked in Trial One.

Judge Bronson also drilled the rules into potential jurors' heads, telling them, verbally, and in writing:

If selected for this case, no communicating about it until the trial ends. Decide the case solely on evidence generated within the courtroom's four walls, coupled with life experiences, reasoning and common sense.

Folks who admitted they had preconceived opinions were questioned individually—a highly atypical procedure.

After two hours of that, lawyers quizzed the remaining potential jurors, trying to sniff out those who were biased or who clearly didn't "get" basic legal tenets such as the presumption of innocence.

Assistant Prosecutor John Arnold focused on how jurors perceived media coverage of the case and how they would evaluate conflicting stories.

Defense lawyer Jay Clark kept asking people about presuming Ryan innocent and what they would think if he didn't testify.

He also asked if the potential jurors understood the lawyers' roles in the case.

One lady told Clark: "You have to prove that your client's innocent." Then, gesturing toward Arnold, she said, "and he has to prove that he's guilty."

Many courtroom observers groaned and shook their heads, disappointed that such a basic principle of American jurisprudence was so woefully misunderstood.

Judge Bronson stated flatly: "The defendant has nothing to prove."

The confused woman was later dismissed.

By the end of Day One, about forty potential jurors remained from the original pool of one hundred.

On Day Two, the twelve-member jury was sworn in—with only eight potential jurors to spare.

On Day Three, the jury reported for duty—and took a field trip to the Widmer home, about ten miles from the courthouse.

This was new; the Trial One jury had not seen the Widmer home.

The Trial Two defense team wanted jurors to see how tiny the bathroom was. Ryan's lawyers thought it would help jurors to see that it would be difficult for combatants to avoid injury in that cramped space.

Clark was convinced that was true after he viewed the Widmer bathroom himself and then set up a mock "bathroom" in his office. He bought a used department store mannequin from a thrift store. The mannequin represented Sarah; he taped autopsy pictures onto the mannequin at the points of injury.

Because Clark's unscientific demonstration wouldn't be allowed in court, the defense would instead present a prestigious expert to testify about the pattern of injuries and the bathroom's small size.

Prosecutors, however, were hoping that seeing the Widmer bathroom would add scenes to the "movie" of a murderous struggle that they were trying to splice together in jurors' minds.

On that drizzly Wednesday morning, Ryan lingered in the garage while jurors and lawyers did walk-throughs of his former home.

To him, the bathroom was not the scene of a crime; it was the scene of a tragedy. Revisiting it would only amplify his agony.

The jurors spent a few minutes inside, then boarded a sheriff's vehicle back to the courthouse for opening statements.

Both sets of lawyers told the jury: Don't speculate.

Assistant Prosecutor Travis Vieux repeated his Trial One refrain: "Accept the reasonable and reject the unreasonable." The phrase was simple. Memorable.

No legal gobbledygook. Just good, old-fashioned common sense. Hard to argue against that.

Vieux summarized the evidence. Ryan's statements. The Bathtub. The two bloodstains. The dry scene. Dry Sarah, with those suspicious neck injuries.

Vieux ended more decisively than his teammate John Arnold had during Trial One. Vieux directly urged jurors to find Ryan guilty.

When defense lawyers got their chance to outline the evidence, they tried to humanize Ryan, to retouch the Scary Ryan portrait that prosecutors painted.

In Trial One, attorney Charlie Rittgers had attempted to do that, too.

But the Trial Two team did it more dramatically.

Attorney Lindsey Gutierrez, who was about Sarah's age, walked around the defense table and stood behind Ryan. She seemed to evoke the ghost of Sarah as she placed her hands on his shoulders and began to speak.

She described how August 11, 2008 was supposed to be just another ordinary day for Sarah, "day one hundred fourteen in a fresh, new marriage with Ryan Widmer, the love of her life."

Sarah's day unfolded in unremarkable fashion—except her head, neck and throat hurt. Sarah still felt crummy that night when, after eating dinner and watching TV, she told Ryan goodnight and "I love you." She retreated upstairs to take one of her soothing baths.

Then Gutierrez said: "That bathroom was very sentimental for her... while this sounds a little different, that bathroom is where Ryan proposed to her."

Journalists shot puzzled looks at each other as we realized: Sarah had died near the very spot where Ryan had knelt on one knee and asked her to be with him forever.

If Gutierrez had revealed one more detail—about C.J. the dog rushing to just-showered Sarah with the engagement ring tied to his collar—that would have helped explain why the proposal happened in the bathroom. But with that question left hanging, Gutierrez sat down.

Defense attorney Jay Clark resumed where Gutierrez left off: "After Sarah took off her rings and laid them on that vanity top, she got in the bathtub. No one knows what happened to cause her to drown. Ryan doesn't know. Police don't know. Prosecutors don't know what happened."

Alleging numerous contradictions and holes in the evidence, Clark said, "It's a case that will leave you with more questions than it will answers."

With so many lingering questions, jurors would have to rely on "imagination, speculation and assumptions" to fill in the gaps, he said, which would not result in a true and just verdict. And, Clark said, that's why "justice for Sarah" demanded that Ryan be acquitted.

THE PROSECUTION'S CASE

WEDNESDAY, MAY 12, 2010–WEDNESDAY, MAY 19, 2010

Turning the tables

In Trial One, prosecutors had apparently assumed that the defense would claim Sarah had fallen asleep and drowned. Thus, they presented a sleep expert to debunk a claim that the defense never actually made.

So, for Trial Two, prosecutors made an adjustment. Their witnesses now included a doctor who covered a trifecta of bases: sleep, epilepsy and neurology. He opined that it was unlikely, though *possible*, that Sarah had suffered a first-time seizure in her bathtub the night she drowned.

As other prosecution witnesses took the stand, Clark relentlessly probed for new information; his former job as a medic helped him to make some strong points.

One document showed medics made only *one* attempt to insert a breathing tube into Sarah, but testimony revealed *five* such attempts—*six* if you count the emergency room doctor's final try, Clark noted.

Clark was trying to persuade jurors that extensive medical procedures could have inflicted trauma on Sarah's body. At the same time, he exposed errors in medical and police records and attacked first-responders' methods.

As the WLWT-Channel 5 live blogger Travis Gettys put it, Clark sometimes seemed like a magician, deftly lifting a handkerchief to unveil surprises for the audience.

Spectators grew wide-eyed as Clark and the other defense team members pulled these rabbits out of a hat:

- A medic was unable to explain why there were two versions of the same patient record on Sarah—and the medic said he never knew different versions existed until a prosecutor told him about the problem just before he testified.

- A medic had been disciplined for "unauthorized release of information" about the case; Judge Bronson prevented witnesses from answering questions about that.

- The ambulance, with Sarah inside, remained parked outside the Widmer home for *twelve minutes* instead of heading straight to the hospital. Clark questioned why.

- First-responders didn't recall seeing a dispatcher's typed note saying, "water drained out of the tub," which would have been sent to a computer screen mounted in their vehicles. The implication: if police and medics had paid attention to that statement, they shouldn't have been surprised that the drowning victim's skin had dried.

- Twenty-one errors riddled Sarah's emergency-room records, including a representation that Sarah was successfully intubated. At autopsy, the tube was found in her esophagus, which leads to the stomach, instead of in her windpipe, testimony revealed.

Clark's colleague, Hal Arenstein, scored a significant point while questioning a police sergeant who worked with Braley.

Under the prosecution's questioning, Sergeant Lisa Elliott testified she saw no pruning—just as she stated during Trial One. She saw no sign that Sarah's skin was wrinkled from being immersed in water. Not even from a "very close" vantage point.

But when Arenstein probed further, Elliott replied she didn't see whether Sarah's fingernails were broken or damaged.

"Well, that's interesting," Arenstein commented.

If she had seen Sarah's finger*tips*, how come Elliott didn't notice the condition of Sarah's finger*nails*, too?

Such questions kept Widmer Watchers' minds circling like lost drivers stuck in a roundabout.

While Clark and his team worked their magic, a few jurors rolled their eyes and shifted uncomfortably. It was hard to tell whether the jurors were troubled by the revelations—or whether they thought the defense was wasting time on minutiae.

The prosecution remained on-task, dropping breadcrumbs that they thought would lead jurors down the path to a conviction.

But Trial Two had barely started when a jury problem surfaced. A juror had reportedly told a third party that he or she was serving on the Widmer case. The judge underscored the importance of jurors maintaining silence, but the loose-lipped juror was neither identified nor punished.

An early witness who came across strong for the prosecution in both Trial One and Trial Two was Coroner's Investigator Doyle Burke.

Burke's testimony seemed damaging to Ryan as prosecutor John Arnold questioned Ryan's words and actions.

But Clark got Burke to admit that he hadn't taped his interview of Ryan. And he strongly implied that Burke may have misinterpreted some of Ryan's words.

When Ryan stated he had "pulled" Sarah from the tub, Clark asked Burke, "You don't know if he meant *pulled her physically out of the tub*, or pulled her face above water and hung her over the edge of the tub, do you?"

Objection. Sustained.

The next several witnesses didn't advance the prosecution's case much. Instead, testimony established that the "golden rule" of crime-scene investigation had been violated repeatedly in the Widmer case. Police are taught to treat a crime scene as though they will only get one crack at it. They're not supposed to touch, alter or move anything unless it's been measured, photographed and catalogued.

Among investigative mistakes the defense exposed: Yellow "crime scene" barrier tape blocked off only three sides of the house. A log of personnel who entered and exited lacked the times they came and went. Police removed the yellow tape, locked the doors and left, only to return two days later with a search warrant. And when they removed the tub, they left the faucet and handles behind.

The defense hoped that, by revealing slip-ups, they could raise doubts about the integrity of the evidence, the competency of the investigators and the validity of their conclusions.

When it came time for the prosecution to call Lieutenant Jeff Braley, prosecutors covered just the basics, avoiding questions that could "open the door" for Clark to delve into Braley's baggage.

Clark grilled Braley for almost an hour and a half, about triple the time the prosecution spent with him. And it didn't go well for Braley.

He declared, "I've had lots of training." But the longer Braley testified, the more Clark revealed deficiencies in training and experience relevant to the Widmer case.

In 2005, Braley had attended *four hours* of training on crime-scene management. Some procedures taught in that class were not followed in the Widmer case.

Notably, during the thirty-one hours that preceded the second search of the home, Braley had no idea who, if anyone, may have entered and disturbed the scene—or whether someone else may have bathed or showered there.

Braley also didn't follow a checklist and failed to note temperature or humidity inside the home—key factors affecting water-evaporation timing, one of the biggest points of contention in the case.

Clark also got Braley to admit:

- People who die unexpectedly, with no obvious cause found, tend to be younger people without prior documented injuries or medical problems—a profile that Sarah Widmer fit.

- A bloody, frothy mix should not be considered suspicious in a drowning, not even in large amounts.

- He never talked to anyone about inconsistencies in Sarah's medical reports.

- He never interviewed Ryan—and investigators were unable to find anything negative about Ryan, let alone a motive for murder.

Clark was trying to show that Braley skipped steps and leapt to conclusions. Clark's efforts seemed fairly successful, legal analysts said. To them, it looked like the prosecution was off to a shaky start. One attorney who attended the trial told me privately: "Some of the witnesses sounded like rats jumping off a sinking ship."

But the prosecution still had more chances to present witnesses who might help the jury see that Scary Ryan was real—and that he had killed Sarah.

Coroner defends ruling

When the Warren County coroner took the stand, he seemed more self-assured than he had been in Trial One. Then, Dr. Russell Uptegrove had said, "I think" Sarah's death was a homicide. Now he declared bluntly: "The manner of death was homicide."

Otherwise, Uptegrove's testimony differed little between the two trials.

Despite Uptegrove's more forceful testimony, the prosecution still seemed to be struggling to pick up momentum.

Clark harped on Uptegrove's lack of board certification. He got Uptegrove to admit he was unfamiliar with procedures done on Sarah. Uptegrove had merely *watched* an intubation—the insertion of a breathing tube—while he was in medical school; he had never performed one. And he had never seen anyone perform "the Sellick maneuver" on a patient's neck.

When Clark displayed pictures of the procedures, Uptegrove refused to concede that the techniques likely were performed in areas that lined up with Sarah's injuries. "I've never seen bruising like that on someone's neck" as a result of medical procedures, Uptegrove declared.

Uptegrove did seem a bit rattled, though, when Clark attempted to show that the coroner ruled too quickly.

Clark asked Uptegrove if he skipped additional tests on Sarah because they were expensive and time-consuming. Uptegrove's response: a journalist at a small community newspaper had "misquoted" him on that topic. Hundreds of genetic tests are available, Uptegrove explained, and he saw no clue crying out for more tests.

Clark produced a copy of Sarah's emergency-room records. They were released a week *after* Uptegrove declared Sarah's death a homicide. When Clark asked the coroner whether he had made up his mind about the manner of death, even without those records, Uptegrove replied, "Yes, I had already."

Uptegrove defended that decision, saying it was based upon autopsy findings, plus Sarah's mother's assertion that her daughter had no significant medical issues.

When Clark asked whether Uptegrove spoke with Ryan about his wife's health, Uptegrove declared Ryan was "unavailable"—and he thought Sarah's mother was better-qualified to speak about Sarah's medical history, anyhow.

But the two women hadn't lived together in several years. So, perhaps Sarah's mom didn't know all the relevant facts about her daughter's health. Maybe she didn't know that Sarah reportedly exhibited a peculiar behavior—including the night she died.

A document describing that behavior was buried in boxfuls of Widmer records kept in a downtown Cincinnati office basement. But the document—and the information in it—would remain unnoticed and unexplored for nearly a decade after Sarah's death.

Playful banter? Or nasty arguing?

Just before Sarah's mom, Ruth Ann, took the witness stand, Ryan's mother, Jill, entered the courtroom, touching off murmurs. Her presence indicated she would not be a witness; all witnesses were barred from listening to other testimony until after they testified.

A tense hush fell over the courtroom as people strained to hear what soft-spoken Ruth Ann would say about Ryan this time versus Trial One.

She took a decidedly tougher tone.

When asked about Ryan and Sarah's interaction before their April 2008 wedding, Ruth Ann replied: "They would argue." No other witness gave a similar description. Not even Sarah's best friend.

But Ruth Ann said the couple argued over trivialities, such as their differences in stature. Ryan stood thirteen inches taller than Sarah.

"They stated their opinion to each other in argument ways," Ruth Ann said.

After hearing that stilted remark, Ryan was in disbelief. He couldn't figure out what Ruth Ann was talking about, except when he had joked about Sarah being a "midget" a couple times. But he couldn't remember a fight over that.

Supporter Mollie Mihalik sat next to Jill. Mollie could almost see steam rolling off Jill's head; through clenched teeth, Jill disputed Ruth Ann's unflattering assertions about Ryan.

Ruth Ann started to cry when she reminisced about Ryan and Sarah's first dance as husband and wife. Judge Bronson offered her a tissue. She already had one. But she agreed to take a sip of water to regain her composure.

Then defense attorney Lindsey Gutierrez approached to cross-examine Ruth Ann—which the all-male Trial One defense skipped to avoid any perception of bullying a grieving mom.

Gutierrez brought a feminine sensitivity that gave her more leeway. But prosecutors objected repeatedly to keep Gutierrez on a tight rein.

The judge prevented her from asking Ruth Ann why she supported Ryan at his first court hearing. That would have been a powerful fact for jurors to consider.

But Ruth Ann did confirm she had visited Ryan in the county jail. And there was a significant revelation about Ryan's conduct on the night Sarah died.

Ruth Ann testified that Ryan called her to say that Sarah was headed for the hospital.

"Are you aware that you were actually *the first person he called?*" Gutierrez asked.

"No," Ruth Ann said.

She also didn't know Ryan tried calling her *five times* before reaching her; phone records proved that was true.

A little jolt hit the courtroom. If this guy had just killed someone, why would he dial the mother of his alleged victim right away? Isn't that how an innocent man would behave? Or could that be a guilty man's attempt to *act* innocently?

After Ruth Ann testified, a pair of doctors wrapped up the prosecution's case. Neither had examined Sarah, but both had reviewed her records and offered opinions about her injuries. Both had also testified in Trial One.

Dr. William Rogers served as a dual-purpose witness—as a board-certified ER doctor and as a police officer. The WLWT-TV blog called Rogers "a doc in cop's clothing."

His apparent role: To shore up the testimony of two key prosecution witnesses whose credentials were under attack, the coroner and the lead detective.

And Rogers did seem to complete that mission successfully; he came across as a highly credible witness.

Rogers agreed with one of the coroner's most damning assertions: Sarah may have received upwards of 4,000 chest compressions—yet all that activity produced no bruises on the area where CPR should be done. It was peculiar that bruises instead appeared in other areas: her lower neck and upper chest.

But the defense would undermine that strong point during cross-examination of Dr. Charles Jeffrey Lee, a deputy coroner in a central Ohio county.

Lee was the Trial One witness who had theorized that Sarah could have been drowned in the bathtub, toilet or sink, prompting the prosecution to change the Bill of Particulars.

This time, in Trial Two, Lee withstood many volleys from attorney Jay Clark but ultimately admitted that, in a photo from Sarah's autopsy, hemorrhaging "does appear to be right on the sternum," or breastbone, the correct target for CPR compressions. And that seemed to conflict with Upetgrove's and Rogers' declarations about *lack* of injuries to that area.

But did the apparent conflict stand out to the jurors? They seemed weary, and some were reclining their heads against the courtroom wall as Lee's testimony approached the four-hour mark.

After Lee finally finished answering questions around 7 that Wednesday night, Judge Bronson told jurors: "Ladies and gentlemen, we'll have four more witnesses tonight."

He was joking. Lee was the prosecution's final witness—just as he had been in Trial One.

Legal experts agreed: This time, the prosecution's case was much weaker than it had been in Trial One. But Ryan wasn't in the clear yet. A lot depended on what the defense witnesses would say—and whether Ryan would be one of them.

THE DEFENSE'S CASE

THURSDAY, MAY 20, 2010–TUESDAY, MAY 25, 2010

In a welcome respite from medical testimony, many of the defense team's initial witnesses were ordinary people who knew Ryan and Sarah—co-workers and friends who reprised their testimony from Trial One.

After three days of such witnesses, the defense dove back into the medical morass.

The world-famous death investigator who had autopsied Sarah for the defense, Dr. Werner Spitz, gave a strong, clear explanation for the hemorrhage on the left side of Sarah's neck.

He called it "a huge bruise that extends down the shoulder and onto the chest," and said it arose from the same mechanisms that caused extensive bruises to appear in the crooks of her elbows.

Medics had pricked Sarah's elbows and neck with needles, trying to administer medication. Those punctures allowed blood to leak into surrounding tissues, then the drowning process made the bruises look more severe. Water diluted her blood, increased her intravenous pressure and burst her red blood cells. Decomposition made the injuries even more visible during Spitz's autopsy, three days after Uptegrove's autopsy.

Spitz was confident that the neck-chest hemorrhage resulted from medical procedures—not homicidal violence, as prosecutors claimed.

If jurors understood Spitz's statement—and found him credible—it seemed they had to acquit Ryan. Her neck-chest hemorrhage was the worst, most suspicious injury—a major reason the coroner ruled her death a homicide. Yet Spitz, the "king" of death investigation, believed the bleeding was caused by medical procedures and drowning-related processes—not by Ryan.

Uptegrove had stated that a body will not bruise after death because the heart isn't pumping blood. In response, Spitz said, "The general concept is correct, but the factual concept makes it actually incorrect." To explain that cryptic comment, he went on to fill three transcript pages.

"Objection, unresponsive," prosecutor Travis Vieux said. Judge Bronson replied: "Let's get to questions and answers, or we'll be here all day."

Defense lawyer Hal Arenstein steered Spitz back on track; Spitz said bruises *can* happen after death if blood seeps out of damaged blood vessels. And CPR chest compressions would surge blood to some extent, causing further seepage.

Based on the absence of scratches, defensive wounds, pulled-out hair, broken fingernails or toenails, or injuries to Sarah's elbows and knees, Spitz again declared that her manner of death was "undeterminable," as he did in Trial One.

When Vieux questioned Spitz, he again emphasized the hefty fees the expert charged and asked: "You are also going to get paid for the time to go back to Michigan, right?"

Spitz retorted: "Well, unless you want to take me in permanently."

The laughter was squelched by Vieux's salty comeback: "I assure you, I don't."

At times, Judge Bronson had to act as referee. "Whoa, whoa, whoa," he interjected, telling Vieux to wait for Spitz to finish answering—and telling Spitz to wait for Vieux's questions.

Vieux challenged Spitz's opinion that Sarah's death was "undeterminable by anybody," but Spitz held firm. He said Sarah's body exhibited enough signs to suggest that "a natural event, leading up to the death by drowning," would be possible.

There was insufficient evidence to blame a seizure or heart problem, yet neither factor could be ruled out.

Dr. David Smile, a board-certified ER doctor who also had testified in Trial One, again strongly asserted that he was surprised Sarah hadn't suffered more injuries during prolonged attempts to revive her.

He also made some intriguing revelations:

- A scholarly study showed that taking a hot bath may increase a person's risk of a seizure.

- The average age for a first-time seizure, with no traceable cause: 23.8 years old—strikingly close to Sarah's age, 24.

- About one person in every one hundred will suffer at least one seizure during his or her lifetime. That countered prosecutors' assertions that Sarah's chances of suffering a seizure were remote.

- A less-serious seizure could turn deadly if it strikes a person in or near a risky environment—such as a moving car, a rooftop, a swimming pool... or a bathtub.

- Many heart and neurological disturbances leave no detectable trace after death.

Smile was far easier to understand than Spitz was.

Vieux had to do *something* to undermine Smile, who had testified unflinchingly for more than five hours. So, Vieux revealed that the defense team had supplied some of the scholarly articles Smile discussed in his testimony. Smile said his commentary would be the same, no matter who gave him the information.

But with that stroke of legal gamesmanship, Vieux managed to smear a little mud on Smile's otherwise crystal-clear testimony.

Two people in a bathroom

The next defense witness was a new one: Dr. Chandler Phillips.

A college professor, Phillips started out as a medical doctor then branched into several engineering fields. Most career biographies are snoozers. But his was intriguing.

211

Phillips had received acclaim for his work on patented technological break-throughs to help paralyzed people regain movement, such as *Superman* actor Christopher Reeve. That work required detailed knowledge of medicine, the human body, injury and how people interact with their environments.

And now Phillips, a Nobel Prize nominee, was asked to analyze how Ryan and Sarah might have interacted in their master bathroom.

Phillips said he reviewed every medical and investigative report, dozens of photos and floor plans. He also went inside the home and took measurements in the bathroom. He drew diagrams of Sarah, who stood five feet one, and Ryan, who was six feet two. Then he analyzed what injuries could have been expected if they struggled in the bathroom.

Considering all of that—and the thirty-seven-inch space between the cabinets and the bathtub—Phillips could not come up with a struggle scenario that would fit the pattern of injuries and non-injuries on the couple.

If Ryan had approached Sarah from behind, outside the tub, that would have folded her body over the top of the tub and put her knees on the ground. Her feet would have been in contact with the cabinets' corner edge. Injuries to her feet, knees and hip bones would have been expected. In addition, at least one arm would have been flailing, at risk of "bruising, tearing, scraping" if it banged against the metal faucet.

If Ryan had approached from the front, trying to choke Sarah with both of his hands, her hands and feet would have been unrestrained; she easily could have won the fight by merely poking him in the eye, Phillips said.

In either of those scenarios, Sarah's instinct to survive would have taken over. She would have grabbed, clawed or kicked Ryan—causing injuries on herself and on him, the expert said.

And what if Ryan had subdued Sarah with the "carotid sleeper hold," which prosecutors suggested? At the beginning of the attack, the victim could still instinctively grab at the attacker's arms or hands before losing consciousness.

Based on all the circumstances, Phillips concluded: "Ryan Widmer did not forcibly drown Sarah Widmer. ... I would have expected to see more injury to Sarah Widmer and I would have expected to see injury to Ryan Widmer if a violent struggle had occurred."

He also would have expected to see "a lot of water," not the dry conditions that the litany of prosecution witnesses described.

After that, the youngest prosecutor, Jason Hilliard, had to figure out how to cast doubt on this sophisticated witness without seeming to be disrespectful of an elder with an impressive background.

Hilliard got in a few digs. He noted that Phillips hadn't been a practicing medical doctor in a long time, and he had last seen a patient with bruises more than two decades ago.

The young prosecutor also tried to portray Phillips' body-measurement diagrams as inaccurate, because the limb lengths of Ryan and Sarah were estimated, not actual.

And just as the prosecution had made Spitz's compensation an issue, the prosecution made sure jurors knew that the defense paid Phillips $300 per hour, or $3,200 per day.

But Hilliard hit a snag when he suggested that the victim might try to "grab something stable, such as the side of the tub." He was hoping Phillips would agree; that would fit nicely with the prosecution's focus on the fingerprint streaks along the back of the bathtub.

But Phillips replied: "I would disagree with that at an instinctual level."

Grabbing at the attacker's hands, rather than at the tub, would probably be the first reaction, Phillips said.

CLOSING ARGUMENTS

WEDNESDAY, MAY 26, 2010

The morning after Phillips testified, the courtroom began filling with spectators—and anticipation. Would Ryan take the stand in his own defense? The only thing the public had heard from him was his tearful protest of innocence at the end of Trial One.

Even Sarah's mom, who avoided Trial Two except to testify, was there. Whispers rippled through the crowd as Ruth Ann Steward and her police-officer boyfriend sat down in the front row, a few seats away from Ryan's parents.

Warren County Prosecutor Rachel Hutzel was watching from the Media Room. Her bid for a judgeship had succeeded without challenge; she would be leaving the prosecutor's post in early 2011. She hoped to exit on a strong note, with Ryan behind bars again.

While the lawyers and the judge met behind closed doors, Ryan sat at the defense table. Lieutenant Jeff Braley sat at the opposite end of the courtroom. Both looked sad, worn out and alone.

Then there was hubbub as prosecutors tested the 911 recording and three of Hutzel's employees carried in The Bathtub.

After court was called to order, the defense rested. No testimony from Ryan. His lawyers thought they had raised reasonable doubt about the prosecution's case. Why risk shining a brighter spotlight on Ryan's stoicism and inarticulate communication?

Ryan's lawyers could only imagine him trying to explain the face-up/face-down contradictions; even a skilled communicator might easily mix up those terms when put into the pressure cooker: the witness chair.

And what could he even say about what had happened to Sarah? He wasn't in the bathroom with her when she drowned, he said, so how could he know what had occurred?

Travis Vieux put up the Sweet Sarah picture. He played the 911 call recording. He repeated his "reject-the-unreasonable" argument and his Spinning Sarah Theory: the two bloodstains and the apparent fecal stain near her head proved that her body had once pointed in the opposite direction.

Based on all the evidence, the defense was "unable to diagnose" Sarah with an ailment, Vieux said, which "only exists if you reject that she was murdered."

In contrast to Vieux's straightforward closing, defense lawyer Hal Arenstein delivered a summation that was almost poetic.

"It was supposed to be the stuff that dreams are made of; it was supposed to be their time to shine." That was Arenstein's refrain as he recounted the Ryan-and-Sarah love story—and how it devolved into a nightmare.

"The last twenty months, Ryan has heard the whispers and the innuendo for a crime that never happened," Arenstein declared.

He criticized Vieux for "telling you what we *didn't* prove instead of what they *did* prove, beyond a reasonable doubt."

He ticked off more than a dozen problems with the investigation and said, "It's not the quantity of evidence, it's the quality of evidence that matters."

Arenstein also emphasized why the bathroom and Sarah were drier than expected: "Once Sarah was removed from the drained tub, there's not water to drip all over the place."

He concluded by saying, "I think that, after ten days of testimony, you know why we said this is a case that will leave you with more questions than answers … it's a prosecution with an ocean of holes."

He ended with an impassioned plea:

"Why should you assume that Ryan did something wrong when all the evidence you have heard here is that he was nothing more than a shy and gentle man? ... You hold this young man's life in your hands. Have your reasonable doubt today. Send Ryan Widmer home to his family so he can finally begin to mourn the loss of his wife … Do justice to the memory of Sarah Widmer—and find Ryan Widmer not guilty."

Given the last word, Prosecutor John Arnold suggested that the defense was trying to put everyone else on trial. "This case, ladies and gentlemen, is the State of Ohio versus Ryan Widmer. It is not the State of Ohio versus the first responders, the police ... the doctors or the nurses in the ER."

The defense's medical-mishap theory was fantastical, Arnold said, leaving murder—by Ryan—as the only remaining explanation for Sarah's death.

"Nobody saw Ryan Widmer kill Sarah on the night of August eleventh, but Sarah is dead of drowning and her body was dry, and the defendant was the only one who was home that night. ...We ask you to accept what is reasonable, to reject that which is unreasonable and to return a verdict that Ryan Widmer is guilty of murder."

DELIBERATIONS

WEDNESDAY, MAY 26, 2010–FRIDAY, MAY 28, 2010

Nerve-wracking boredom sets in for spectators during jury deliberations.

There's nothing to do but wait. Straying from the courthouse could mean missing the crucial moment when the jury foreman presses a buzzer and notifies the bailiff: We have a verdict. Once that happens, people rush into place; minutes later, it's all over.

But sometimes the buzzer gets a workout for other reasons. Jurors are hungry. Or they want a break to smoke. Or they have a question.

And every time the buzzer goes off, people jump.

After two and a half days of intermittent buzzing from the Widmer jurors, news reporters and commentators began to wonder if a unanimous verdict was impossible.

By mid-afternoon Friday, there it went again: "Bzzzzz!"

This time, it felt different. Jurors had reached the twenty-hour mark, not quite as long as the twenty-three hours jurors spent during Trial One.

Within moments, there was a rush of activity. Prosecutor Rachel Hutzel entered the courtroom with a gaggle of her employees. Ryan's family entered, too. Then the letdown: Judge Neal Bronson announced that the jury was having trouble agreeing on a verdict. He urged them to re-evaluate their opinions.

About an hour later, as a storm approached, I overheard attorney Lindsey

Gutierrez tell someone that she heard rain is good luck on a wedding day, "so maybe it's good luck on your verdict day."

I didn't tell her that it rained the night Ryan was convicted in 2009.

Soon, thunderclaps were booming. Ryan's supporters were overcome with déjà vu, fearing the worst: another guilty verdict on another stormy night.

The clock kept ticking. Jurors kept deliberating.

At 4:30 p.m., twenty-one hours...

At 5:23 p.m., "Bzzzzz!" False alarm. Smoke break...

At 6:30 p.m., twenty-three hours...

At 6:37 p.m., court reconvened. Judge Bronson told jurors to enjoy their three-day Memorial Day holiday weekend, then return to deliberate on Tuesday—making sure to avoid discussing the case with anyone.

THE LAST DAY

TUESDAY, JUNE 1, 2010

Jurors returned to the courthouse at 9 a.m., some looking less-than-refreshed despite their break from jury duty.

By 10 a.m., there it was again: "Bzzzzz!" Smoke break. Again. *How many chain smokers were on this jury, anyhow?*

11:30 a.m.: "Bzzzzz!" Lunch break. Deliberations had now exceeded twenty-five hours.

2:25 p.m.: "Bzzzzz!" Never did figure out the reason for that one. Twenty-eight hours down.

4:44 p.m.: "Bzzzzz!" Followed by an insistent second "Bzzzzz!"

The double buzz looked promising, as lawyers scurried back to the judge's chambers. Next came Hutzel. But still no sign of Sarah's family.

Judge Bronson reconvened court and read a note from the jury foreman:

"We have decided that we cannot agree, and that further deliberations would not serve a useful purpose."

After more than thirty hours—the longest deliberation anyone could recall in Warren County history—twelve people were unable to agree whether Ryan had killed his wife.

Spectators stared at each other, dumbstruck. Even normally talkative people seemed to grope for words.

Ryan's mom, Jill, had reportedly suffered a nervous breakdown and was nowhere near the courthouse.

Ryan's dad, Gary, buried his eyes in his shirtsleeve.

And Ryan told news reporters: "I just want this to be over."

No one had any idea how or when that might happen.

CHAPTER 9
Secrets and Revelations

Oh noooooo.

Widmer Watchers let out a collective groan after Trial Two ended without a verdict in mid-2010. They wondered aloud: "What now?"

Ryan's lawyers promptly filed a motion asking Judge Neal Bronson to acquit Ryan without a third trial—a long shot.

While that was in play, the prosecution had three choices, all with potentially negative ramifications:

They could dig in their heels and go for Trial Three. But… if opinion polls were accurate, many people believed Ryan was wrongfully prosecuted on scant evidence—and they would see a third trial as a waste of time, effort and money.

They could cut their losses and dismiss the charges. But… dropping the charges could anger citizens who believed Ryan killed Sarah—and that she and her family deserved justice.

They could try to cut a plea deal. But… after so aggressively pursuing the case against Ryan through two mistrials, a plea bargain might look weak.

In the coming days and weeks, the case traversed a path riddled with landmines—secrets that exploded with every step.

An evil alter ego

Ryan and his family had managed to conceal two big secrets during Trial Two and its aftermath.

Big Secret No. 1: His mom, Jill, was going off the deep end.

She was in and out of treatment centers, hospitals and even psychiatric wards. A doctor told Jill, "You're drinking yourself to death." But she was unable to stop.

Jill had been a go-getter, accustomed to setting goals and achieving them; that was how she ascended from a secretarial job to a vice-president position in the Luxottica eyewear empire in Mason, Ohio.

When her best efforts to help Ryan were thwarted, frustration built—and alcohol turned her frustration into rage.

Jill would send out "nastygrams," scathing emails and text messages in the middle of the night. Anyone could be a target.

Sometimes, she would leave drunken voicemails claiming that Ryan was a "murderer." Those fueled suspicion: Had Ryan told her that he had killed Sarah?

Jill's friends and relatives knew that, deep down, she never doubted her son's innocence. They believed she was suffering from "alcoholic psychosis"—brain chemistry run amok, causing hallucinations, delusions and illogical suspicions.

Ryan felt like he was living with a stranger. The mom he had known and loved his whole life was obscured behind a veil of anger and liquor.

He worried about her constantly. He also worried that, if the prosecution got wind of Jill's alcohol-induced accusations, those would be used against him.

Yet, Ryan didn't let her irrational accusations hurt his feelings. He knew that, as in the classic novella, *Dr. Jekyll and Mr. Hyde,* Jill had an evil alter ego. Ryan blamed Jill's dark "Mr. Hyde."

Ryan was terrified that his mom would die, and he'd be blamed—a fear that intensified after a disturbing incident that followed Trial Two.

He returned home around 9 p.m., in time for his court-ordered curfew. The house was dark. Eerily, music was blaring—and there was no sign of his mom.

His breathing quickened. He turned on the lights, turned down the music—and was horrified at what he saw: His mom's legs sprawled across the floor, protruding from behind a couch.

Ryan's heart dropped. *Was she dead?!*

He rushed to her and called out, "Mom?" No response. Until Ryan hovered directly over her face. Then Jill groggily opened her eyes. He asked what she was doing. "Sleeping," she replied. But Ryan knew she was in a drunken stupor.

Tension between Jill and Ryan came to a head after Jill learned about Big Secret No. 2, a secret about Ryan. It was unrelated to Sarah's death. But it looked bad—the last thing he needed while a judge was considering whether to acquit him.

Jill was so infuriated, she set fire to some of Ryan's clothing in a black cast-iron fire pit—more than once.

"She was completely crazy," Ryan said. "She was just downright mean and lost touch with reality." He got a court order allowing him to live elsewhere.

As Ryan struggled to keep the lid on his own secret, Jill's drinking problem became public in the fall of 2010, when she was arrested for drunken driving near her Mason home.

Police noticed Jill had been driving on a flat tire; smoke was rolling off of it. She failed a field-sobriety test and was caught with an open vodka bottle in her car. She rambled about Warren County being corrupt in her son's case, and told officers that, under similar circumstances, "You wouldn't be in any better shape than I am."

Meanwhile, two more secrets, directly related to Ryan's case, were about to pop.

Fireworks in July

July 2010 began with a firecracker that fizzled—and ended with the biggest Widmer bombshell yet.

Ryan's lawyers filed a document revealing that, in the midst of Trial Two, a witness brought a record to court, showing that Sarah had once been diagnosed with a heart murmur. Yet all previous testimony had indicated that Sarah had *no* history of heart problems.

The heart-murmur record came from the Kentucky dental office where Sarah worked as a dental hygienist and received care as a patient; it was a health-history form she had filled out in 2006, two years before her death.

When Judge Neal Bronson saw the form, he ordered the dental office to release all records about Sarah. The judge had acted so quickly that he didn't wait for his assistant to type the order; it was *handwritten*.

However, Judge Bronson concluded the heart-murmur record contained scant information, wasn't part of Sarah's official patient-care record and could confuse the jury. So, he kept it out of Trial Two. It stayed out of the public eye until Ryan's lawyers cited the heart murmur as a reason Ryan should be acquitted

221

without a third trial. It reinforced the theory that Sarah drowned from a cardiac event.

"HUUUUUUUUGE news in this case," one blogger wrote, referring to my *Enquirer* article about the heart murmur. Some Trial Two jurors said the heart condition could have influenced deliberations.

Prosecutors fired back: When Sarah's mom testified that Sarah was free of heart ailments, that was accurate. Sarah's heart murmur was detected when she was a baby; the condition resolved itself in eight months.

But Sarah never underwent a recommended follow-up with a pediatric cardiologist. So maybe the heart murmur persisted, undetected, Ryan's lawyers argued.

The heart-murmur controversy faded into the background when prosecutors dropped a megaton bombshell: A new witness claimed that Ryan confessed to killing his wife.

Adding to the intrigue, prosecutors withheld the witness's identity under Ohio's just-enacted witness-protection law. The so-called "Mystery Witness" requested anonymity, fearing "bodily harm and intimidation or coercion," prosecutors said.

Most folks suspected that the Mystery Witness was a jailhouse snitch, an ex-cellmate looking to cut a deal. Others who knew about Jill Widmer's drunken rantings wondered: Was she the Mystery Witness?

Ryan told his lawyers he hadn't "confessed" to anyone; he had nothing to confess. And he had no clue who the Mystery Witness might be.

Curiosity about the Mystery Witness skyrocketed. And Ryan's hopes for acquittal plummeted.

Mostly guilty—or not?

In a post-trial interview, a Trial Two juror told radio station WLW that she thought *only two of the twelve jurors would have voted not guilty* if a final vote had been taken. She told the prosecution to "go for it:" plow ahead with Trial Three.

Several not-guilty jurors were irked. According to them, as many as *seven* jurors may have favored finding Ryan not guilty.

Three jurors signed affidavits, supporting the defense motion for Judge Bronson to acquit Ryan without a third trial. Based on the ambiguous evidence, they doubted a future jury could reach a unanimous verdict.

At Ryan's acquittal hearing in August 2010, four "not guilty" jurors sat in the front row in a silent show of support for him.

Two days after that thirty-minute hearing, Judge Bronson ruled: No acquittal. "The evidence, when construed in a light most favorable to the state and without weighing it, was legally sufficient to support a conviction," he wrote.

While Sarah's family still kept a low profile after that decision, Ryan's parents, Jill and Gary, responded with a news conference. Jill said they were determined to defend Ryan as he faced a third trial. She insisted the family had no doubt that Ryan was innocent.

Only a handful of people who heard Jill that day knew about her drunken "Ryan-is-a-killer" rants.

Money and motions

A January 2011 date was set for Trial Three. Ryan's family had no idea how to fund the fight after blowing through a half-million bucks for the first two trials.

While the prosecution had a seemingly limitless armada at the ready, the Widmers could hardly muster a lone gunboat to return fire—until a wealthy benefactor came to the rescue.

A Cincinnati-area businessman believed in Ryan's innocence so much that he offered to cover his attorneys' fees for Trial Three. The businessman, who struck up a friendship with Ryan after they met at a fundraiser, donated $60,000 anonymously.

That was enough to pay for Lindsey Gutierrez and Jay Clark; Hal Arenstein bowed out. In his place: Charlie M. Rittgers, whose dad, Charlie H. Rittgers, was Ryan's first lawyer. The younger Rittgers had become an attorney, too; he joined Ryan's Trial Three team *pro bono,* at no cost.

The prosecution's young Trial Two lawyer, Jason Hilliard, went into private practice, leaving John Arnold and Travis Vieux to finish what they had started.

Asserting that Ryan was indigent, the defense sought public funds for expert-witness fees. Prosecutors fought against that, skeptical that he was out of money because he seemed to have legions of supporters. The Widmers asserted that all "non-family sources" had generated only $81,300 for Ryan's defense.

Most of the defense fight was funded by his parents' retirement funds.

Judge Bronson granted up to $11,000 for two expert witnesses—less than one-quarter the requested amount.

In another blow to the defense, the judge again forbade confrontation of Lieutenant Jeff Braley about his personnel records.

The most critical pretrial ruling: the trial's location. Citing a "media frenzy," prosecutors made a rare request to move Trial Three outside Warren County— something that reportedly hadn't been done in three decades.

Ryan's lawyers fought to stay local. Relocating the trial would rack up additional costs that their client couldn't afford, they said publicly. Privately, they had a strategic reason to stay in Warren County: Public opinion seemed to be on *their* side, based on media polls and talk on the streets.

The defense team thought the odds seemed good that twelve randomly selected people would at least entertain a disquieting possibility: Maybe there was no crime at all in this case.

If that happened, Ryan Widmer just might walk away a free man.

JURY SELECTION and RECESS

TUESDAY, JANUARY 18–TUESDAY, JANUARY 25, 2011

Trial Three almost didn't happen. Prosecutors secretly floated a plea deal.

Maybe they lacked confidence in the Mystery Witness or in their overall case. Or maybe they just wanted to put an end to the Widmer drama without the hassle of another weeks-long trial.

Ryan's lawyers pulled Ryan and his dad, Gary, into a conference room at the courthouse. Everyone sat down. Jay Clark laid out the prosecution's offer: If Ryan would plead guilty to a reduced charge, he would go to prison for five years, max, instead of risking being convicted of murder—again—and serving fifteen-to-life.

Ryan stopped Clark in his tracks: *No. No way am I admitting to something I didn't do. I did NOT hurt Sarah.*

Clark urged Ryan to hear him out. Ryan wouldn't budge. He shook his head emphatically. *Nope. No deal.*

Ryan was never surer about anything in his life: An innocent person shouldn't agree to go to prison for five years. The Trial Two jury had at least moved closer to an acquittal; maybe his odds were improving. He knew he hadn't confessed to anyone—and he believed his lawyers would expose the Mystery Witness as a charlatan. After that, could any fair-minded juror trust the prosecution's case?

The trial went ahead as planned.

Nearly all the jury candidates had some knowledge of the case, yet few admitted having an opinion about it.

That bothered Mark Krumbein, a Cincinnati defense attorney. Fascinated by Widmer plot twists that would put Hollywood scriptwriters to shame, Krumbein attended the end of Trial One and many parts of Trial Two. Krumbein also served as a legal analyst for local media, helping to fill the void that the judge's gag order created.

Everyone he encountered seemed to express a strong opinion about Widmer's guilt or innocence. It didn't compute that members of the jury pool could be so neutral. Krumbein wondered: Were some of them harboring deeply entrenched opinions?

Although many people dread jury duty, some secretly hope to be chosen as a juror on a big case. The process seems fascinating—and comes with bragging rights. The potential for hidden agendas and subconscious biases worried Krumbein and other Widmer Watchers.

And after the history of juror misconduct in Trial One, everyone was hyper-vigilant for any whiff of jury shenanigans.

The first inkling of a problem arose during the second day of jury selection. Judge Bronson had received word that an outsider contacted a jury candidate and discussed "what the outcome of this case should have been." The judge reinforced his order to potential jurors: Do not talk with anyone about the case until you're dismissed.

Many jury-selection questions centered on the Mystery Witness, listed on court documents as "Jane Doe." That revealed the gender of the Mystery Witness. But nothing else had been disclosed—until odd questions from the defense dropped hints: Why might a person contact a criminal suspect who was featured on a TV show? Do you know anyone who lives in *Iowa*? Anyone who worked at *a strip club*? Anyone who had a *problem with drugs or alcohol*?

Bizarre. If the Mystery Witness fit that description, would a jury find her believable? And why would the prosecution rely on such a witness? Maybe she had rock-solid proof, such as a recording of the confession. Something like that would spell C-H-E-C-K and M-A-T-E for Ryan.

As questioning continued, both sides exhausted their peremptory challenges to remove undesirable jurors. Even so, a jury was seated in two days, the same as in Trial Two.

After prosecutors disclosed the Mystery Witness' name to Ryan's lawyers, Judge Bronson sent the newly seated jurors home for several days, giving the defense time to investigate.

At the same time, the case took another improbable twist.

It involved... wait for it... a chicken bone.

On Christmas Eve 2010, Dr. Werner Spitz, the defense's expert who autopsied Sarah, had swallowed a chicken bone. It perforated his bowel. Because Spitz was still recovering from surgeries, he wouldn't be well enough to testify, his office said.

Judge Bronson declared Spitz "unavailable." A stand-in would read Spitz's prior testimony into the Trial Three record.

Prosecutors surely resented that the defense would benefit from Spitz's testimony without having to shell out $15,000 for his services again. The defense also might get a boost if the recited testimony "played" better than Spitz did in person.

On the other hand, stale testimony would pack less punch. And Ryan's lawyers would be unable to ask revised questions.

Ryan worried that, with his luck, this fluke would hurt his case.

JURY VISIT and OPENING STATEMENTS
WEDNESDAY, JANUARY 26, 2011

As in Trial Two, jurors toured the Widmer home; Ryan again chose to remain outside.

Last time, no reporters were permitted inside. This time, because the *Enquirer* won a court battle, I was allowed to go in after the jurors left.

I felt uncomfortable entering the home that was now occupied by another family—people who chose to live there despite knowing its history.

To my surprise, my hands shook as I took notes. As the designated "pool reporter," I was obligated to share my observations with other journalists. I hoped nothing important would escape my notice.

It pained me to see the space where one life was lost and another was wrecked—either by murder or by fate. This was ground zero of the case that had kept me and so many other people transfixed for almost two and a half years.

After entering the front door, I ascended the staircase. Seven stairs. Then a landing. Five more stairs to the top.

I pictured action up and down that staircase the night Sarah died. Ryan running down to unlock the front door. Deputy Steve Bishop vaulting up as Ryan yelled, "Come up here, please hurry up!" Medics rushing in with equipment—and later struggling to descend with Sarah's still-unresponsive body on a backboard.

I noted the three-foot space between the bathtub and the cabinets. Yes, that was a tight space to contain two people in a deadly struggle.

Sadness washed over me as I pictured Sarah lying naked on the carpet. I half-expected to see the two infamous bloodstains on the carpet, even though they, of course, were long gone.

What happened here—a murderous attack? Or a freak accident? I couldn't decide which. Not even after sitting through two previous trials. And now, not even after seeing the scene in person.

I wondered: How in the world would Ryan's third jury find the truth? Would the Mystery Witness give the answer? Or would she only make things muddier?

After the jury returned to the courthouse, prosecutor Travis Vieux again displayed the Sweet Sarah picture for his opening statement. He deviated little from previous scripts—except for his words about the Mystery Witness.

Everyone listened with rapt attention as Vieux described how, after the first trial, a woman in Iowa watched Ryan's case on *Dateline NBC* and contacted Ryan via FreeRyanWidmer.com. She and Ryan exchanged emails, instant messages, text messages and phone calls almost daily. After a little more than a month, Ryan called her and made a drunken confession, Vieux said.

Vieux repeated familiar refrains: "reject the unreasonable…find justice for Sarah…find the defendant guilty."

In her opening statement, defense attorney Lindsey Gutierrez said Ryan and Sarah's "ordinary life turned into an extraordinary tragedy."

Ordinary versus extraordinary. That became the defense team's new theme.

When young people who appear healthy die unexpectedly, extraordinary effort is required to find out what happened, Gutierrez said. Sarah's case deserved extraordinary attention but instead got only "run-of-the-mill work from everyone involved... coupled with mistakes, misunderstandings and shortcuts," she said.

This was a less-abrasive approach, compared with Trial Two. But would it prove more effective?

As for the Mystery Witness, Gutierrez used the prosecution's own argument—rejecting the unreasonable. She asked jurors: Was it reasonable for the Mystery Witness to stay quiet for more than seven months after the alleged confession?

She urged jurors to render "a verdict that would finally allow Ryan Widmer to mourn the death of his young, beautiful wife"—a verdict of not guilty.

THE PROSECUTION'S CASE

WEDNESDAY, JANUARY 26–FRIDAY, FEBRUARY 4, 2011

The prosecution began by bulletproofing weak spots that the defense team had blasted during Trial Two.

Medics admitted to at least a half-dozen mistakes on reports about Sarah, including the number of intubation attempts she underwent.

And they explained why there were two different versions of the ambulance run report: At the hospital, a medic was still filling out the report when an investigator asked for a copy. "Did you try to falsify a separate copy?" prosecutor Travis Vieux asked. "No," replied the medic.

So far, so good. But when defense lawyer Jay Clark started asking the questions, some witnesses became guarded. A few seemed leery of saying anything that might support the defense contention that medical procedures left marks on Sarah.

When Clark asked whether CPR is more difficult on the floor of a home or in a moving ambulance, a medic replied it was "the same."

A few courtroom spectators nudged each other. It seemed logical, as the defense implied, that it would be harder to do CPR in a moving ambulance. Yet this witness wouldn't say so?

When Sergeant Lisa Elliott took the stand, she blocked the defense from casting doubt on her powers of observation again. During Trial Two, the defense wondered why she failed to notice Sarah's undamaged fingernails yet insisted she saw Sarah's unwrinkled fingertips. This time, Elliott pre-empted defense lawyers with an explanation: "As CPR was in progress, I noticed her right hand rolling out."

Another important witness, Deputy Steve Bishop, the first officer to arrive at the Widmer home, told Prosecutor John Arnold that he hadn't moved Sarah.

Even so, defense lawyer Lindsey Gutierrez inquired about that twice more.

> Gutierrez: "Isn't it correct that Sarah Widmer was actually halfway in the doorway and you had to move her because you couldn't work on her?"

> Bishop: "Absolutely not."

> Gutierrez: "You don't remember that?"

> Bishop: "It didn't happen."

Unless Ryan testified, the jury wouldn't know that, all along, Ryan had been alleging that the officer had helped him move Sarah.

Despite Bishop's denials, Gutierrez hoped that her questions might help some jurors to picture Sarah's body being moved for non-sinister reasons—an innocent explanation for the two bloodstains. And there was another possible source of one bloodstain, his lawyers said: menstrual bleeding. A feminine-hygiene product had been discarded in the trash. And, in a previously undisclosed report, medics had stated, "during CPR compressions, the deceased was bleeding from the vagina."

But the county coroner, Dr. Russell Uptegrove, testified he found no sign that Sarah was menstruating, nor did he find any pelvic-area injuries that could have caused a bloodstain.

Uptegrove guided the jury on a head-to-toe tour of Sarah's injuries and his suspicions about them. As photos were shown, Sarah's brother sometimes squeezed his eyes shut and rested his head on his prayer-position hands.

Just about everyone seemed startled when Uptegrove held up a gardening tool that doubles as an autopsy aid: a pair of long-handled loppers—just like the ones sold at Lowe's hardware store for seventeen bucks, he said.

Shudder. Poor Sarah's family, I thought, listening to the gory details about Sarah's body being cut apart.

But it was important for the prosecution to point out that the loppers likely nicked Sarah's liver while the tool was used to snip apart her ribcage. The laceration was noted in the defense expert's autopsy report but Uptegrove's report omitted it.

Now that Uptegrove had addressed the laceration, the defense would have a hard time claiming that the injury resulted from aggressive CPR—and they couldn't claim the damage escaped Uptegrove's notice.

More than in the two earlier trials, Uptegrove exuded confidence.

Among his strongest points: He didn't know what caused bleeding inside Sarah's neck, "but it didn't happen from this endotracheal tube," Uptegrove said, waving the device. "That's a *fact*." Some of the bleeding could have come from the needle that pierced Sarah's jugular vein, he said, but "the blood is not going to defy gravity" and travel to the front of her neck.

Uptegrove laid the cornerstone of the prosecution's case.

Now it was time for defense lawyer Lindsey Gutierrez to chip away at it.

She established that the coroner knew little about medics' techniques, including use of the breathing tube that he showed the jury. And he was unaware of certain studies showing that resuscitative and strangulation injuries can mimic each other.

And now, for the first time, Uptegrove faced specific questions about his examination of Sarah's brain—leading to a stunning disclosure.

Gutierrez asked Uptegrove about microscopic signs of narcolepsy that can be found in part of the brain, the hypothalamus.

Gutierrez: "And, as you sit here today, you don't know whether or not that part of the brain is associated with narcolepsy?"

Uptegrove: "No."

And did Uptegrove take any samples of Sarah's hypothalamus? No.

Gutierrez implied that Uptegrove skipped steps because he was too busy. He performed about 300 autopsies in 2008, the year Sarah died, fifty more than a recommended limit. The National Association of Medical Examiners warns that even a skilled pathologist can be prone to shortcuts and mistakes when the caseload is that heavy.

Uptegrove denied rushing through Sarah's autopsy. He said it took longer than an "ordinary" one. But he didn't record the time it ended.

Uptegrove's testimony plodded along for five hours until jurors were dismissed into the chilly Friday night air. It seemed like the jurors had taken very few notes—causing some observers to wonder how they could keep the tedious medical details straight.

After the coroner alleged homicide, the prosecution could call the Mystery Witness at any time. Widmer Watchers waited as impatiently as children expecting a special visitor: "Is she here yet?"

Monday, January 31. No Mystery Witness. Jurors' pens remained mostly still.

Tuesday, February 1. Still no Mystery Witness. But jurors suddenly seemed to be taking more notes. Had they heard about criticisms of their scant note-taking?

Spectators stopped staring at jurors' note-taking when Sarah's mom, Ruth Ann Steward, went on the witness stand—and her testimony took a surprising turn.

After prosecutors deftly dispelled concerns about Sarah's heart murmur, Ruth Ann shocked the courtroom when she declared: Ryan and Sarah were "hateful to each other." That was the most derogatory description on the record about the couple. Several people made muffled gasps; Ryan was taken aback.

Asked to detail the "hateful" language, Ruth Ann replied, "Just not nice words," implying the words were too awful for her to repeat publicly.

A previous juror commented: Sarah's mom "seemed like a different witness," compared to Trial Two.

How much would the "hateful" characterization sway this third panel of jurors against Ryan? Would Ruth Ann's new testimony help them believe that Ryan and Sarah's public sweetness masked a relationship that had soured in private?

Quite possibly. Especially if they also believed the shocking statements that were about to come from the lips of a stranger.

Spellbinding yet perplexing

As court began on Wednesday, February 2, 2011, Sarah's mom took a seat in the gallery just in time to hear the Mystery Witness: Jennifer Jean Crew.

Jennifer seemed ill-at-ease as she entered, wearing a dark, pin-striped pantsuit. Time froze as all eyes focused on her. Could this 36-year-old woman with long brown hair, streaked with blond highlights, hold the key that would unlock the Widmer mystery?

Prosecutor John Arnold, hands clasped behind his back, acted as a human barrier between the defense table and Jennifer's path to the witness stand. His bodyguard-like stance seemed to project that he was shielding Jennifer from Ryan.

As Jennifer strode past, Ryan glanced at her with a disgusted look on his face—an image captured in a front-page *Enquirer* photo.

Jennifer raised her right hand and swore to tell the truth. Then she spent four hours in the witness chair.

The blogosphere went wild. A live blogger from WCPO-TV, Channel 9, reported that blog "traffic" tripled when Jennifer took the stand.

At first, Jennifer's testimony was firing on all cylinders—then it sputtered like an engine fueled with bad gasoline.

Throughout the trials, Arnold had often bellowed, "OBJECTION!" from the depths of his formidable girth. While questioning Jennifer, he assumed an atypically quiet tone, like a grandfather coaxing a child to ride a bike for the first time.

Arnold got the unflattering stuff out of the way: Yes, she had convictions for misdemeanor theft and "fraudulent practices." Yes, she was being treated with methadone for a prescription painkiller addiction. No, she was not the manager of a "strip club." Instead, she was a *bartender* at a lounge where dancers performed; she managed the dancers' schedules.

Then Arnold began delving into Jennifer's contact with Ryan.

She had watched parts of the *Dateline NBC* episode about Ryan's case on September 18, 2009. Minutes after the broadcast ended, Jennifer typed a message to Ryan via FreeRyanWidmer.com: "God knows that you are innocent … your wife is watching you from heaven and is now your heavenly angel just as she was your angel on earth."

Three days later, Ryan emailed a six-sentence thank-you note. More communication followed. Topics included football—her Raiders and his Bengals. The college courses she was taking. His pets. His court case. Sarah.

While Jennifer testified, she avoided looking at Ryan. He stared at her, but his gaze appeared heavy-lidded and dull, not piercing. He broke eye contact only to quietly confer with attorney Lindsey Gutierrez over his shoulder.

Jennifer described Ryan confiding in her more and more—until one night, twelve days after their first conversation, a phone call from Ryan awakened her, she said.

Arnold: "And tell us what the defendant said, or what you heard when the call began?"

Jennifer: "The defendant was crying."

The *defendant?* Why parrot Arnold's word, instead of saying "Ryan"? This type of unnatural response gave some Widmer Watchers pause about the Mystery Witness.

According to Jennifer, Ryan was so upset, she couldn't understand what he was saying at first. He seemed drunk. Then she made out these words: "I did it. I did it. I killed Sarah. I did it."

The jury didn't know investigators had records of Jennifer giving two other variations of the alleged confessional quote: "I killed Sarah," repeated four times; and "I killed her. I killed Sarah." Odd. Shouldn't a confession's exact words be unforgettable?

And why would Ryan confess to her, of all people? Prosecutors suggested Ryan may have thought it was "safe" to come clean with Jennifer. She lived more than five hundred miles away and he must have doubted she would travel that distance to reveal his secret.

Or, as the defense would later contend, was The Call an elaborate fabrication by someone seeking her proverbial fifteen minutes of fame?

Jennifer stated: Ryan told her that Sarah had discovered he cheated on her while she was out of town with her mom—and that he had been surfing internet porn. The couple began arguing over his cheating, porn-surfing, drinking and smoking. The more they argued, the more Ryan drank.

Ryan thought: *I didn't cheat and we didn't fight. Isn't it convenient that you couldn't give any details about the supposed "cheating" or how Sarah supposedly found out these things? You're just repeating stuff that's been all over the news. And I didn't drink much that night; I had to get up for work the next day. Like I told the police, I drank only four beers.*

Jennifer stated: An angry Ryan retreated upstairs to watch the football game on the bedroom TV, alone. The argument rekindled when Sarah came upstairs to get ready for her bath. Sarah told him their marriage was over; she was leaving him. A shoving match ensued. Ryan punched Sarah in the chest. She fell back and hit her head. Then Ryan blacked out. He regained consciousness and saw that Sarah's hair was wet, and she was on the floor, not breathing. There was water everywhere; Ryan sopped it up, but didn't disclose what he used, nor where he hid the evidence.

Ryan thought: *Here we go again with the stupidity about TV channels—already public info. And I would NEVER hit a woman. Where is any evidence Sarah was punched? Isn't it convenient that you can't say HOW I supposedly drowned her? You just claim I "blacked out." Yeah, right. I've never "blacked out" in my life! What a bunch of bull.*

Jennifer stated: While describing Sarah being assaulted, Jennifer wept and turned to face the jury. Then she said that, during Ryan's 911 call, "he breathed—poof, poof, poof, poof—to make it sound like he was giving CPR."

Ryan thought: *That's just a repeat of what the prosecutors have been claiming since the first trial.*

Jennifer stated: She promised Ryan that she would keep his confession secret, and he implied he would kill her if she revealed it. She pretended to continue backing Ryan, so he wouldn't retaliate and make her his next victim.

On December 2, 2009, Jennifer sent five final texts to Ryan. He never responded. Jennifer stated they had agreed to stop communicating.

Ryan thought: *I sensed something "off" about Jennifer. She sent almost SIXTEEN HUNDRED texts in less than two months. I didn't want to hurt her feelings or make her feel like I didn't appreciate her support. So, I just kind of eased out of it. Maybe she got mad because I stopped answering her.*

Jennifer stated: Six months after her last contact with Ryan, Jennifer revealed the alleged confession. She didn't come forward right away because she was afraid of Ryan—and because she thought it would be a moot point if he was convicted during Trial Two. But after learning about the hung jury and seeing an image of Sarah's mom, Jennifer felt compelled to break her silence: "I saw the sadness and the pain and the hurt …They needed to know the truth."

Confronting contradictions

While Arnold questioned Jennifer, she was compliant, weepy and sometimes spoke so softly that her words were hard to hear. Between sentences, her lips were pressed together, corners downturned. She sometimes pressed her hand to her forehead, as though she had a splitting headache.

When Jay Clark confronted her, it was almost as if someone flicked a switch on her demeanor. She hardly looked up. She shifted uncomfortably. Fussed with her hair. Wiped her nose with a tissue.

Even though Jennifer appeared to be cowering, she would also become insistent, almost defiant. She even pointed out Clark's receding hairline at one point. Spectators' eyes widened when she did that.

Asked about her mental-health history, Jennifer acknowledged she had once been diagnosed with bipolar disorder, but "that was later changed." She also had been treated for depression.

Clark raised questions about her honesty. Instead of sending a picture of herself to Ryan, she passed off a picture of an attractive blond friend instead. She later emailed another photo with a note: "Here is the real me." Jennifer stated she sent the bogus picture because a friend advised her to be cautious.

And the date, time and circumstances of The Call were all in flux.

Jennifer initially gave no date for The Call when investigators from Ohio traveled to Iowa to interview her in June 2010. But she told them The Call came around 2 or 3 a.m., from a blocked number, and lasted an hour or ninety minutes.

After Jennifer got her phone records, no call seemed to fit those criteria. But she pointed to a call on October 26, 2009. At 10:06 p.m. Iowa time. Fifty-nine minutes long. Yes, Jennifer insisted, that was The Call. She knew for sure. Because the next day, October 27th, was her daughter's birthday.

Well then, Clark asked, why didn't Jennifer specify the 26th as The Call date until *after* she saw her phone records?

Jennifer responded emphatically: "I know what day he confessed he killed his wife."

And why did 10 p.m. seem like 2 or 3 a.m.? Jennifer said: "As I stated earlier, I was asleep and I thought the call came in later than it did."

But Jennifer's phone records conflict with that statement. Two text messages went from *her* phone to Ryan's—at 10:03 p.m. and 10:06 p.m.

That proves, unless there's such a thing as sleep-texting, that Jennifer could not have been asleep when Ryan called. His call—The Call, according to her—came at 10:06 p.m., right after her second text.

Those two texts leapt off the page at me while I researched for this book. But neither the prosecution nor the defense asked Jennifer about them during the trial.

Prosecutors had ample opportunity to see those texts; they had Jennifer's phone records months in advance of her testimony. Defense lawyer Clark got the fifty-page document after the trial started, and apparently didn't notice those texts. Ryan said no one had previously pointed them out.

But Clark did attack other "things that make you go 'hmm'"—as he later described—about Jennifer.

One of the strongest: the content of Jennifer's email to Ryan shortly after The Call. "You make me smile when I think there is nothing to smile about," she wrote. ...You are a great person that I would trust with my life and my children's. Can't wait to meet your family. You touch my heart ... I would do anything in this world for you. Love ya."

Those are remarkable sentiments to express to a guy who supposedly just admitted to killing his wife, Clark noted. Jennifer's response: "I sent him that to convince him that I was still right there, that I didn't think that he would hurt me, that I didn't think he would hurt my children."

Clark raised more doubts about Jennifer's statements:

- **Did Ryan's "special ringtone" alert her or not?** Jennifer testified she knew The Call came from Ryan because she heard his "special ringtone." But she had earlier told investigators that The Call came from a "blocked" number. If that was so, the designated ringtone wouldn't ring, correct? No, it wouldn't, she said, but "I thought it was blocked. I thought the number did not appear."

- **How did the Widmer trash end up on the floor?** Jennifer alleged Ryan "freaked out" after realizing that the bathroom trash can had been knocked over as he struggled with his wife, and he forgot to clean it up. But a policeman who collected evidence said the wastebasket was *undisturbed* when he arrived; he said another officer admitted dumping it to look for drugs or other clues about Sarah's unresponsiveness.

- **Was Jennifer's memory reliable?** When Jennifer started a methadone program in March 2009, she wrote this response to a question about whether she suffered blackouts: "There are times when people tell me things that I did or said and I do not remember what they're talking about." Jennifer testified that happened under the influence of painkillers, not during her methadone treatment.

Methadone and painkillers can make people have vivid hallucinations or nightmares that seem real. Jennifer wasn't asked in court whether she had experienced those problems. But she made peculiar claims that either reflected odd coincidences or fantasies mingling with reality.

She said she worked for J. Crew, a clothing company. That name was remarkably similar to hers. And she also referred to another "crew," the rock band Mötley Crüe. That group's morbid ballad about a man killing a woman, "You're All I Need," made Ryan think of Sarah, Jennifer testified.

And, according to Jennifer, an unnamed TV show inspired Ryan's coverup of Sarah's murder. But based on her description, prosecutors identified the show as Forensic Files' *Summer Obsession*. That was the real-life story of a man who tried to disguise the true cause of his wife's death by putting her into a tubful of water.

Summer Obsession aired several times—notably on June 8, 2010, just before Jennifer talked to Ohio authorities about Ryan's alleged confession, Clark pointed out, implying that the show may have influenced her. But Jennifer denied watching the show.

Thus, two pop-culture references—the Mötley Crüe song lyrics and the *Summer Obsession* TV show—became prosecution exhibits against Ryan.

When Jennifer finally stepped down from the witness stand, quite a few folks were scratching their heads, perplexed about what she said—and didn't say.

Evolving evidence

The day after the Mystery Witness testified, Judge Bronson replaced his perfunctory rules reminder to the jurors with an emphatic warning: "It is imperative that you report to the court any breach of the court's instructions."

I told my editor, "Something's up with these jurors." The gag order prevented me from asking about it at the time. Later, I would learn that my instincts were on target.

As the prosecution's case went on, Lieutenant Jeff Braley played less of a role; he was no longer sitting at the prosecution table. But there was a new slant on his testimony. He had previously testified that officers looked for any sign of wet towels that could have been used in a cleanup.

This time, he added: "It wasn't a detailed search where we would open every drawer, every cabinet." That lent credence to the Mystery Witness' assertion that Ryan had hidden cleanup evidence *somewhere*.

But Braley acknowledged that no one at the scene saw any indication that Ryan had been drunk or had blacked out—leaving that claim of the Mystery Witness standing unsupported.

As in the previous two trials, the final prosecution witness was Dr. Charles Jeffrey Lee, the forensic pathologist who largely backed up the coroner.

Defense lawyer Jay Clark elicited new testimony from Lee by asking whether he agreed with passages from medical journals:

- Resuscitation injuries "may be misinterpreted as evidence of inflicted injuries." Lee agreed.

- Neck-muscle hemorrhages have been recorded in people who died during an epileptic fit, possibly caused by neck muscles jerking. Lee declined to comment without reading the entire article first.

- "Apparent 'bruising' of the neck musculature does not always indicate compression of or trauma to the neck in a drowning." Lee agreed.

Then Clark asked whether Lee saw indications that the county coroner had taken extra steps to rule out various conditions for Sarah. Cardiac problems? Neurological problems? Narcolepsy?

No, no and no, Lee answered. Thus, Clark reinforced the defense team's theme: This extraordinary case received only "ordinary" examination.

Yet Lee insisted Sarah's death was rightfully labeled a homicide. He doubted she suffered heart or brain problems, citing "overwhelming evidence to the contrary:" Neck trauma. Blunt-force injury. And drowning.

THE DEFENSE'S CASE

MONDAY, FEBRUARY 7–FRIDAY, FEBRUARY 11, 2011

After eight long days with the prosecution in control, Clark was struggling to get his second wind.

He was physically and mentally exhausted. Even more than after Trial Two. His home life was strained, and he was constantly putting out fires in this nightmarishly quirky case.

But Clark had some razzle-dazzle left. He was planning a stunt that he hoped would spray-paint "REASONABLE DOUBT" like neon graffiti all over the cornerstone of the prosecution's case.

But first, he had to plow through other witnesses.

Testifying for the third time for the defense, Dr. David Smile seemed unwaveringly committed to his belief: All of Sarah's injuries could have resulted from medical procedures.

A respected local emergency room doctor and teacher of first-responders, Smile charged no fee for his services in Trial Three. The implication: He was donating his time in the interest of justice.

Clark also offered testimony to further challenge the Mystery Witness' claims.

Chris Kist, Ryan's college roommate: He was visiting Ryan a couple hours before The Call; Ryan was neither drunk nor upset. He'd never known Ryan to listen to Mötley Crüe. When prosecutors asked whether he was present at the Widmers' home the night Sarah died, Chris shot back: "I don't need to be there to know he didn't do it." The jury was told to disregard that.

Melissa Waller, *Dateline* viewer, from Washington State: Melissa, a 29-year-old married woman, felt a bond with Ryan after watching his story on *Dateline NBC* because her brother, like Ryan, had found his wife dead. On the night of The Call, Melissa ended her phone conversation with Ryan at 11 p.m. Cincinnati time—and she detected no sign that Ryan was upset or drunk. That was six minutes before Ryan called the Mystery Witness, who said he seemed intoxicated.

Shirley Bonekemper, Ryan's former employer: Shirley testified that Ryan was working much of the weekend before Sarah's death—when the Mystery Witness alleged he had cheated on Sarah. Shirley's testimony didn't account for all of Ryan's time that weekend, but it did suggest he had less free time for alleged infidelity.

From the witness stand, Shirley looked at Ryan and identified him for the record. His face looked gaunt. The light was gone from his eyes. He looked worn out from defending himself for the third time.

Shirley momentarily wondered: What had happened to the sweet, innocent young man she had known?

Then she realized—he was gone forever.

Science lesson on a cookie sheet

Toward the end of the defense presentation, it was time for Clark to unveil the surprise that he hoped would prove Sarah's autopsy was botched.

It would be memorable. Even more visually startling than the coroner's gardening loppers. And the accompanying testimony could unlock an acquittal, Clark thought.

For the demonstration, Clark enlisted Dr. Michael Gregory Balko, a Kentucky forensic pathologist.

Board-certified in three specialties, Balko said most of his work was dedicated to "brain autopsies," identifying neurological factors in a person's death, mostly with a microscope.

Balko wanted permission to use an anatomical model of a human brain to explain his work to the jury. "It's not real," Clark said, flippantly adding, "May I approach, judge, with the 'un-real' brain?" Chuckles filled the courtroom.

Minutes later, however, Clark and Balko did display *real brains*—specifically, pig brains. Morbid. But Clark hoped that the demonstration would help the jury to see deficiencies in the Warren County coroner's autopsy of Sarah.

Pig brains are comparable to human brains, except they're smaller, Balko said. He showed the jury two pig brains: one that was preserved and one that wasn't, both courtesy of a meat-packing house that Clark had contacted.

Unpreserved brain tissue has "the consistency of very warm Jell-O," Balko said. To allow meaningful examination, the brain must be soaked in preservative for a few weeks until it becomes firmer, "the consistency of Velveeta cheese," Balko said. Comparing brain tissue with familiar refrigerated foods? Disturbing. But memorable. And easy to understand.

As Balko demonstrated cutting into the pig brains, jurors craned their necks to get a better view. He showed them how precise slices can be taken from the preserved, or "fixed," brain. But cutting into the unpreserved brain caused it to disintegrate into a mushy mess on the surface Balko was using: Mrs. Clark's cookie sheet.

Uptegrove had testified that he took samples from Sarah's *unpreserved* brain. She had been dead less than twelve hours at the time of that autopsy, insufficient time to "fix" brain tissue.

Cutting into unfixed brain tissue would result in missing "at least half the diagnoses," Balko said. That also distorts landmarks used to identify brain sections. That's why, during the second autopsy, Dr. Werner Spitz may have been unable to discern disparate parts of Sarah's brain and take identifiable samples. Once an unfixed brain is cut, "it's impossible to put back together," Balko said.

Uptegrove took "four small pieces" of Sarah's brain tissue, Balko said. None came from brain areas that needed to be checked for evidence of seizures, Balko said, adding that he typically would take *fifteen or twenty* samples when searching for seizures.

Uptegrove testified he had no reason to believe that a neurological malfunction incapacitated Sarah. Balko's reaction: "The brain wasn't adequately examined to make that conclusion."

Balko also said that, in his opinion, Uptegrove didn't take enough tissue samples from Sarah's heart.

Finally, Balko hypothesized that Sarah may have suffered from a specific disorder sometimes found in people born with a cleft palate—as Sarah was.

People with a genetic mutation called Andersen-Tawil Syndrome, or Long QT Syndrome-Type 7, may experience abnormal heartbeats and loss of muscular control; symptoms may not surface for years. Sarah never underwent testing for that, and she had no tests for the "QT interval," the time it takes the heart to recharge. Among about a dozen types of Long QT syndromes, the Long QT-7 seemed to most closely mirror Sarah's characteristics, Balko said. Sufferers may have severe headaches and narcolepsy-like sleepiness—as Sarah reportedly did.

Balko also cast doubt on the coroner's contention that the jugular-vein IV puncture couldn't have caused all of Sarah's neck-chest hemorrhage.

Leaking blood would travel along layers or "planes" of tissue throughout the human body, he said. "Is there a division or pocket that prevents it from going to the back side?" Clark asked. Yes, Balko said, implying that blood from the IV could have pooled into the front of Sarah's neck, causing the suspicious hemorrhage.

Because of too many unknowns in the evidence, Sarah's manner of death was also unknown, Balko said.

Balko's testimony was matter-of-fact, professional, clinical. And seemed to be very credible. Balko, who was paid for his services during Trial One, did not testify in Trial Two. This time, he "capped" his usual fee to testify, something he said he had never done before.

Prosecutor Travis Vieux tried to show that Balko based his opinions on limited information, because he hadn't spoken to Sarah's mother and didn't personally see Sarah's body, for example. But Balko testified he did review a long list of items, including photos and reports from both autopsies, microscopic slides, medics' reports and their written statements. Just as the prosecution experts had.

Balko did well on the stand, but a Trial One mistake came back to haunt him. Vieux pointed out that Balko had misidentified a structure in Sarah's neck in one photograph.

Would Vieux's attacks succeed in discrediting Balko? Or would the pig-brain demonstration prove so compelling that it overshadowed Vieux's criticisms?

CLOSING ARGUMENTS and DELIBERATIONS
MONDAY, FEBRUARY 14–TUESDAY, FEBRUARY 15, 2011

Legal experts thought that the Mystery Witness' testimony compelled the defense to put Ryan on the witness stand to deny the alleged confession.

But Jay Clark told his client: "There's no 'f-ing' way you're getting up there." Ryan acquiesced, figuring his lawyers knew best.

And with that, the longest Widmer trial yet was drawing to a close.

About one hundred spectators came to hear closing arguments. Not a single seat was empty. And, behind the scenes, prosecutors wound up a final changeup pitch.

In a closed-door session, Judge Neal Bronson granted the prosecution's request for the jury to consider an alternative to murder: involuntary manslaughter.

The new charge, which alleged that Ryan unintentionally caused Sarah's death while assaulting her, was revealed during closing arguments. Jurors were unaware that the charge was a last-minute addition—nor did they know that a manslaughter charge was offered to Ryan in the plea deal that he rejected.

Legal experts thought prosecutors must have worried the evidence supporting murder was thin. Why else would they present a manslaughter option to the jury?

Yet publicly the prosecution projected only confidence—and indignation over the loss of Sarah's life.

During closing arguments, even undisputed facts seemed wildly different, depending on which side was doing the talking.

Undisputed fact: Ryan said he was going to lift Sarah out of the tub, then he resumed talking with the 911 dispatcher twenty-nine seconds later.

Prosecution's argument: That half-minute was not enough for Ryan to have lifted Sarah's wet, lifeless body out of a bathtub that was "half-obscured by a door," which swung open from the bedroom, prosecutor Travis Vieux said. Ryan surely lied and feigned his actions. Sarah must have already been on the floor when he called 911. Or maybe her body was never in the tub.

Defense argument: "Twenty-nine seconds is an eternity when you have to sit and wait," Clark said. To make his point, Clark stood still. He went quiet. And so did the rest of the courtroom as twenty-nine seconds ticked away. "Think about how long that was," Clark said. "…And then when he comes back on the phone, listen to his breathing, listen to the effort it takes. He's short of breath.

Twenty-nine seconds is an eternity to move somebody."

And so it went. Back and forth. Things that seemed innocuous to the defense were characterized as sinister by the prosecution. The dry scene. Sarah's dry body. Face-up/face-down. TV channels. Finger streaks. Bruises. All the same points of contention from the first two trials, plus a new one: The Call.

Prosecutor John Arnold spent considerable effort defending the Mystery Witness—and disparaging Ryan for getting into a relationship with her.

"The defense wants you to look at Ryan Widmer as sort of a Boy Scout, the perfect person, and put Jennifer Crew in the lowest gutter you can find," Arnold said. But Ryan was the one who gave Jennifer his personal email address and phone number, then called her. It was his decision to confide in her.

"It was the defendant who called Jennifer Crew that night, shortly after eleven o'clock, local time, Monday, October twenty-sixth—another Monday night, another Monday night football game, just like the night that Sarah died," Arnold said.

That was fairly strong. But it failed to neutralize the powerful blows Clark struck about Jennifer.

A memorable Power Point slide displayed "Jennifer Crew by the numbers," as Clark read aloud:

> 6 last names
>
> 4 convictions for crimes of dishonesty
>
> 1 habitual-offender designation
>
> 895 text messages to Ryan after he "confessed" to her
>
> 2 phone calls to him after he "confessed"
>
> 1 memory that's not very good
>
> 1 bipolar diagnosis
>
> 3 visits from Warren County investigators to talk to her
>
> 5 years addicted to OxyContin
>
> 3 years in a methadone program
>
> 1 picture of a friend
>
> 2 meetings with the prosecution to prepare for her testimony
>
> 0 corroboration

The confession Jennifer described was preposterous, Clark said: Sarah supposedly was angry with Ryan and decided "she's leaving him—right after she takes a bath…That's what you have to believe if you're going to believe (Jennifer)."

That was one of the best zingers of the entire trial.

Clark blamed the case on assumptions. First, police officers mistakenly believed that Sarah was pulled from a tubful of water rather than a drained tub. Then the county coroner called the death a homicide without fully exploring her history of sleepiness.

If a 24-year-old newlywed bride is found dead in her bathtub, "the husband must have done it," Clark said. Investigators didn't take the time and effort to rule out other possibilities before accusing Ryan, he said.

"I'm not trying to tell you I know what happened … but no one bothered to look," Clark said. "There are too many things that are inconsistent with a forcible drowning.…How did a violent life-or-death struggle take place with no water anywhere?"

A verdict of not guilty must be rendered, Clark said, if the evidence left the jurors "not really sure either way"; or if they believed he was "guilty but the evidence falls a little short."

An acquittal would mean justice for both Sarah and Ryan, Clark said, "because Ryan is not guilty of this—and Sarah wouldn't want him punished for something he didn't do."

The final word would come from Arnold.

He implied that, while the defense had style, his own presentation was based on substance. Arnold told the jurors he didn't have "a fancy Power Point presentation" or jokes, like Clark did. And while the pig-brain demonstration was "very interesting," the defense was only raising "unlikely possibilities to try to establish some imaginary doubt."

Jurors should trust the county coroner, "who did the autopsy," instead of an expert who was "second-guessing," Arnold said.

There is "no innocent explanation for orchestrating the 911 call," Arnold said. Ryan's statements—on the 911 call, to the coroner's investigator and to a nurse—didn't remain consistent because "sometimes it's difficult to do that when you're hiding the truth," Arnold said.

"Ryan and Sarah were the only people home that night," Arnold said. "That means he had the motive, he had the opportunity and he had the means."

Arnold argued that evidence showed that Ryan intended to kill Sarah—which is murder. "But if you somehow conclude this was not an intentional act, the judge will explain involuntary manslaughter to you."

With that, the jurors went to sift through mountains of evidence, in search of the truth. And justice.

THE VERDICT

TUESDAY, FEBRUARY 15, 2011

When the jury began deliberations, most people hunkered down for a long wait.

Trial One deliberations had lasted about twenty-three hours; Trial Two, thirty hours. Based on that trend, this jury might spend three or four days reaching a verdict, some people guessed.

Ryan and his close friends and family retreated to the nearby Rittgers law office to wait.

The Trial Three jury began work at midday Monday, February 14, Valentine's Day. The jury deliberated about four hours before adjourning for the night.

When the jury resumed work on Tuesday, the morning passed uneventfully. As did lunchtime. But then a problem surfaced: The courthouse water supply had been cut off somehow. Without working toilets and running water in sinks, restroom breaks for jurors and spectators could become unpleasant.

Judge Neal Bronson decided it would be best to dismiss the jurors. They'd already put in an eight-hour day. They could come back fresh on Wednesday, and the water supply would hopefully be restored.

The judge was chatting with attorney Jay Clark and told him: "I'm going to send them home for the day." Right after that, the bailiff entered the room with news. Not about the water. About the jurors.

"They have a verdict," the bailiff announced.

Clark was floored.

So was young Charlie M. Rittgers. After he got word at his law offices, he walked into a conference room where Ryan sat with his dad, Gary; his stepmom, Kim; and his two brothers, among others.

Rittgers had a bad feeling—and the look on his face showed it. His lips were taut and he kept his eyes down as he said, "They've reached a verdict."

Everyone ran to their cars and drove to the courthouse.

Kim volunteered to babysit an infant in her car while everyone else went inside the building.

Maybe the news would be good this time, Kim thought, trying to set aside the bad vibe she detected from Rittgers.

The jury had been at work for what, twelve hours? Was that really long enough to consider all the evidence?

Maybe they were able to come to a quick decision because there was so much doubt. Not just reasonable doubt, Kim told herself, but a ton of doubt. Maybe the pig-brain demonstration and all the steps the coroner missed just screamed "reasonable doubt" to the jurors, as much as it did to her.

And there were no ominous storm clouds this time. It was windy and a little overcast. Unlike that horrible, stormy night in spring 2009, when the Trial One jury convicted Ryan.

The baby began to cry, apparently sensing Kim's stress. Kim got out of the car and soothingly bounced the infant as she waited for news from the courthouse.

Inside, the tension as thick as ever. But this time, Gary sensed the prosecutors had swagger. They seemed to be smirking, as if they knew they had scored a conviction.

His thoughts spun in circles: If that was so, was it on the murder charge? Or the involuntary manslaughter? Or was his imagination playing tricks? Surely the prosecutors wouldn't know the verdict before it was read—would they?

Gary took a seat directly behind his son. Two minutes later, the bailiff called court into session. Judge Bronson warned spectators would be arrested for outbursts. Then the judge instructed Ryan to stand with his lawyers. Judgment time.

Father and son prepared themselves the same way: Both tilted their heads down, shutting off all senses except their ears.

There would be no mistaking the words that came from Judge Bronson as he read the verdict: "We the jury... find the defendant, Ryan K. Widmer is..."

Ryan took a deep breath. Then he heard:

"Guilty of murder." That dreaded phrase. Again. As awfully clear as it could be.

Ryan folded forward onto the table—as he had done after Trial One. He buried his face in his hands—as he had done after learning his wife was dead.

Gary just looked stunned and tilted his head to rest on the palm of his left hand. Sarah's mom betrayed no visible reaction, as a victim's advocate clutched her arm.

While the judge "polled" each juror to verify that this was the verdict each had reached, Ryan mostly stayed doubled-over, shaking his head in disbelief. His lawyers stroked his back in vain efforts to soothe him.

People in the courtroom looked around at each other. Sobs erupted from spectators—and from Ryan.

When given the chance to speak, he said:

"Judge, I did not do this. I don't know why this has to keep going on. I mean, my life has been ruined—and it's not because of me. I love Sarah. I would never hurt her. Never. And this has gone on for two and a half years now. I haven't had an answer for what happened to her. All I want is an answer … We've had to hire doctors to try to figure out what happened to her, been depleted of money and this just keeps going on and on.

"This is just not right. Not right."

Then he was sentenced to fifteen-to-life. Again.

Outside, Kim was still walking around with the baby when Gary's sister, Joy, came rushing, shouting: "Oh my God, they found him guilty."

Kim's heart dropped to her knees. Then Joy ordered: "Give me the baby. You need to go be with Gary."

Kim was stunned. She felt like she might throw up. But Joy had given her a mission, so she pushed aside her nausea and went to find her husband.

News reporters were clustered around the courthouse door. One videographer spotted Kim and asked his accompanying reporter, "Who is this?" The reporter replied: "She's nobody."

Kim felt insulted. Yet she was also relieved. The news camera would've been pushed in her face if she had been "somebody."

Amid a knot of people streaming from the courthouse was Gary, surrounded by TV cameras.

He collapsed to his knees, sobbing loudly into his hands while another relative hugged him. She used her body to shield Gary, begging the news crews: "Leave him alone."

He eventually got back up, saw Kim and ran to her. They put their arms around each other and wept.

After about five minutes, suddenly Kim wondered: Where was the baby? Who had the baby? She saw that Ryan and Sarah's good friends, Dana and Chris Kist, were holding the little boy.

The baby was safe.

So Kim's thoughts shifted to Ryan. Kim had never felt so sad.

It struck her: Ryan could stay locked up for the rest of his life, and for much of the life of that little baby—who had a special relationship with Ryan.

He was Ryan's son.

That was Big Secret No. 2.

And it was just one of the controversies that would soon surface, fueling debate about Ryan and his case long after he was once again labeled Ohio Prison Inmate No. A599952.

CHAPTER 10
Shockwaves and Sorrow

The post-verdict frenzy felt different this time.

Two years earlier, when the Trial One verdict came, no hint of juror misconduct was in the air—and everyone was stunned when those allegations surfaced.

This time, in 2011, potential juror misconduct was top-of-mind for many Widmer Watchers—and not just because it had plagued the case before.

There was reason to suspect something might be amiss with the Trial Three jury after Judge Neal Bronson's emphatic follow-the-rules warning at mid-trial.

The "he-did-it" crowd was relieved that the case was over—and that Scary Ryan finally would get his comeuppance. In the courthouse hallway, a police officer mused that Ryan would probably be "popular" among rapists in prison. That sparked an impassioned exchange with a TV reporter who was appalled to hear a cop wish sexual assault on anyone.

Sarah's mother, Ruth Ann Steward, witnessed the trial's ending for the first time but declined to address the court.

Prosecutors issued a "justice-was-done" statement on behalf of Sarah's family. Later, the Steward family released a short message thanking prosecutors and requesting news crews to leave them alone.

Ryan's closest supporters, including his lawyers, were too choked-up to talk.

Courthouse deputies hurried everyone out of the building.

Up against a tight deadline—with no time to drive to *The Cincinnati Enquirer's* suburban office—photojournalist Cara Owsley and I ended up at a nearby McDonald's restaurant to snag a wi-fi signal.

While customers ordered fries and Big Macs, Cara and I worked on laptops to chronicle one of the region's biggest news stories in a decade: "WIDMER FOUND GUILTY OF MURDERING WIFE." That was the *Enquirer's* front-page headline the next day.

Before the newspaper landed in readers' hands, news of the verdict had already hit internet, TV and radio.

Coverage saturated Greater Cincinnati more than any court case in memory. The phenomenal popularity of the WLWT-TV Channel 5 live blog had spawned copycats. By the end of Trial Three, at least four live blogs and/or Twitter feeds were rolling, along with coverage from seven TV stations, two newspapers and several radio stations.

Because the coverage was so pervasive and detailed, plenty of people fancied themselves as armchair jurors, believing they knew just about as much about the case as the actual jurors did.

Within minutes of the verdict, people started debating whether Ryan's jurors got it right and followed the rules.

Jurors' post-verdict comments threw gasoline on the furor:

A male juror told a local radio station that Ryan was a "punk," and the jury could tell he was guilty by looking at him.

Juror #8 told me that the jury believed Ryan truly had loved Sarah but something irked him and "he just snapped." Yet legal experts said that description seemed to better fit manslaughter—an unintentional killing—instead of murder, a purposeful killing.

Juror #10 told WKRC-TV, Channel 12, in a videotaped interview: "The evidence, to us, did not prove innocence." This begged the question whether the jury accepted the presumption of innocence.

A suburban newspaper, *The Pulse-Journal*, reported that a juror was troubled by Ryan's decision not to testify—directly conflicting with Judge Bronson's exhortation: "The fact that the defendant did not testify must not be considered for any purpose."

Such statements would have no effect on the case unless jurors signed affidavits admitting failure to understand or follow the law. That never occurred.

In a motion to void the verdict, the defense asserted the jury got it wrong—an opinion shared by 53 percent of *Enquirer* readers in an online poll.

Bitter disagreements over the verdict raged online, and sometimes in person. Many people seemed incapable of having an intelligent, fact-based discussion without name-calling and personal insults. That trend seemed to have worsened since Trial One—not just about the Widmer case locally but also about other topics across America. Online communication seemed to embolden people to say things they probably wouldn't have the guts to utter face-to-face. Ryan's supporters were dismissed as "blind" and "cult" followers. Jurors were labeled "dumb as a box of rocks" and "ignorant." Ryan was denounced as "white trash" and "cryin' Widmurderer."

Some people vented frustrations on Warren County's new head prosecutor, David Fornshell, even though he had no involvement in Ryan's prosecution. He was sworn in two days after Ryan was convicted. County Republicans had appointed Fornshell to fill the final two years of Rachel Hutzel's term after she won election to an appellate judgeship.

Fornshell initially declined much comment. But he would later demonstrate his resolve to preserve the verdict—which was under attack, partly because of concerns that bubbled up at mid-trial and remained secret until afterward.

More Widmer weirdness

With the judge's gag order no longer in effect, Ryan's lawyers unveiled the reason for Judge Neal Bronson's stern words to the jury on February 3: Multiple people had contacted the defense team and warned that the fix was in; jurors allegedly had already decided to convict Ryan, even before the prosecution had finished presenting evidence.

A woman referenced as "S.L." was a close friend of Juror #1, and three of S.L.'s relatives had called Ryan's lawyers and reported that S.L. told them that Juror #1 had stated: "Don't worry about the Widmer case. We have all talked about it and we know he is guilty. He is going to burn in hell."

Aha, critics thought: If jurors already had made up their minds, that would explain why they didn't feel the need to take notes—and why this jury's deliberation, at twelve hours, was by far the shortest among Ryan's trials.

But Juror #8 said those were misinterpretations. He told me that note-taking might have been distracting to some jurors; to him, it seemed others took plenty of notes. And, he said, one juror was blessed with a "total recall" memory that enabled him to accurately remember everything.

The deliberations process was relatively fast, he said, because it was well-organized and methodical.

He said the most damning evidence was the pattern of injuries and non-injuries on Sarah, particularly the neck hemorrhaging.

The jury thought "maybe" the Mystery Witness was telling the truth, that Ryan confessed. But they "discounted" much of what she said, Juror #8 told me.

And Juror #8 saw no sign that anyone had prejudged the verdict.

Unbeknownst to him and the other jurors, Judge Bronson had summoned Juror #1 into his chambers on February 2, after the Mystery Witness testified. Attorneys from both sides listened as the judge explored concerns from the defense.

Juror #1, an older woman, was put under oath. In response to Judge Bronson's questions, Juror #1 said: She had not discussed the case with anyone; the jurors had not discussed the case; no one had predicted the verdict nor stated what consequences anyone should face.

Those answers satisfied Judge Bronson. He allowed Juror #1 to stay on the jury.

After the trial, more worries swirled around the same juror's online activities. A supporter of Ryan made troubling discoveries on the Facebook social networking site: Two of Juror #1's sisters had "liked" Facebook pages about Ryan while his trial was in progress.

Those postings, along with Juror #1's, were publicly available. One sister "liked" a link about FreeRyanWidmer.com; the other sister "liked" a page titled, "Ryan Widmer guilty and he should be." (sic)

Because Facebook automatically notifies users of their friends' "likes," Ryan's lawyers contended that Juror #1 may have been exposed to her sisters' Facebook postings, especially because Juror #1 had visited Facebook shortly after one of the posts was made.

Also of note: On February 4, two days after Judge Bronson questioned her, Juror #1 went on Facebook and posted a YouTube video titled, "Bath time is fun!"

The video's content was innocuous— a child and a dog playing in a bathtub. But why would a person post a *bathtub* video while serving as a juror in a *bathtub* drowning trial? Ryan's lawyers said the "bath time is fun" video may have popped up as a "recommended" video to people who searched online for "Ryan Widmer" and "bathtub"—or it may have been linked to the prosecution's banned Widmer re-enactment video.

Across the nation, some judges had been advising jurors on high-profile trials to stay off social networking sites, so they wouldn't stumble upon information that could taint them.

That wasn't done in the Widmer case.

Judge Bronson, then in his early 60s, had openly joked that he knew little about digital-age communication. He made frequent inquiries about any such breaches, and he trusted jurors to report those.

His order forbade jurors from *researching the case* and from *communicating about it* by any means. But the order did not restrict jurors from using social media for other purposes.

In seeking acquittal or a new trial, the defense complained about jury problems—but stopped short of directly alleging juror misconduct. Instead, the defense argued that Ryan's right to a fair and impartial jury had been compromised on two fronts:

- Juror #1 was "biased" and was improperly allowed to remain impaneled.

- "The jury was misdirected," and shifted the burden to the defense. Based on Juror #10's public statement, "at least one juror was waiting for Ryan to prove his innocence."

A month after Ryan was convicted, those concerns were aired in a hearing that started off cursed—and then went wacky.

Juror #1 had been subpoenaed. But her father's funeral was that day, so she was excused. In an affidavit, she denied making the "burn-in-hell" statement to her friend, S.L.

S.L. was also unavailable to testify because she was terminally ill.

But S.L.'s sister testified, despite prosecutors' objections to her second-hand information as hearsay.

Had the woman's sister, S.L., told her about Juror #1's alleged "burn-in-hell" remark?

Her reply stunned everyone: *She had been smoking pot and was upset and "high" on the night of the alleged disclosure, so she was unsure what S.L. stated.* Gasps and nervous giggles erupted in the courtroom.

Defense lawyer Jay Clark asked: Then why had she called his office to alert him to the statement—and repeatedly discussed it with him? The witness replied: "Because I thought maybe that was what she said ... I kept thinking about it, and I couldn't with certainty, with my hand before God, say that."

The witness dissolved into tears as her testimony ended. Wide-eyed spectators looked at each other in bewilderment.

Shifting gears, Clark contended that, at mid-trial, extra steps should have been taken to address the Juror #1 concerns, instead of solely taking her at her word.

Clark thought he had asked the judge for more action—such as interviewing other jurors, dismissing Juror #1 or granting a mistrial. But the judge didn't recall such a request. And prosecutors said it was too late to seek those remedies after Ryan was convicted.

Next, the hearing explored Juror #1's mid-trial Facebook activities, which weren't disclosed during the trial. Prosecutors objected to Clark's attempts to explain the mechanics of Facebook to Judge Bronson. And it seemed Clark's explanations were lost on Judge Bronson anyhow.

Clark raised Juror #10's "prove innocence" comment as a sign of a runaway jury. Prosecutors pointed out, that same juror later claimed the defense was "twisting" her words; she insisted that she had presumed Ryan innocent and considered all the evidence, which proved his guilt to her.

Prosecutor John Arnold did not disguise his displeasure: "This case has sort of become 'open season' on jurors." He urged the judge to uphold the verdict, saying there was no credible evidence that the jurors violated rules. It was time to put this case to rest.

Clark retorted: "The justice system isn't set up so the state can finally be done with something." Clark also said he wasn't looking for trouble. He said he had an ethical obligation to explore concerns brought to his attention, but "Mr. Arnold doesn't want the jurors to be held accountable for anything."

About seventy-five people attended the hearing, many of them wearing white to symbolize innocence for Ryan. They left disappointed, knowing that the hearing—and maybe Ryan's best shot for a reversal of the verdict—had tanked.

The next day, the public got a second helping of Widmer Weirdness, served up by another juror—one who expressed some surprising views.

New theory, old theory

Juror #3 went on the air with radio station 700 WLW for more than ninety minutes, trying to dispel any notion of jury improprieties, or that the verdict was unjust.

As Juror #3 also appeared on the station's webcast, he was dressed head-to-toe in green camouflage and he spat tobacco juice into a plastic bottle.

All the jurors followed the judge's instructions conscientiously, he said—and he asserted that the only "misconduct" was that "Ryan Widmer did kill his wife."

The two bloodstains on the carpet and the condition of the bathtub—marred with those finger streaks yet lacking identifiable fingerprints—proved that the scene was "staged," Juror #3 said. After considering all evidence, including deciding whether every witness "was lying or not lying," the jury voted one time—a unanimous, instantaneous guilty.

Solely based on the 911 call and the physical evidence, "any common-sense person would convict him," Juror #3 said.

Then Juror #3 described his unique interpretation of Ryan's 911 call: "The dog was barking at the beginning. And there should be no reason for him to be barking if she's in the tub, because that's the natural place for the master to be. …That tells me that she was laying on the floor and that's the reason the dog was going crazy."

As I listened to the radio, I couldn't fathom how Juror #3 had come up with "The Barking-Dog Theory of Homicide."

The radio station's phone lines lit up with callers wanting to talk to the juror, mostly about his theories. Among the exchanges:

Did the jury actually deliberate over the dog barking? "Yes, sir, we did." Yet no one on either side of the case had claimed that the dog's barking had evidentiary value.

How did Ryan kill his wife? "I think he either drowned her in the tub or the toilet; we're not for sure." Yet during Trial Three, no one had claimed Sarah was drowned in the toilet.

Without testimony that Sarah was drowned in the toilet, how can you theorize that was what happened? "Drowned is drowned," Juror #3 said, so the exact scenario didn't matter.

How did Ryan manage to kill Sarah yet walk away without a scratch or other mark on him? Juror #3 declared Sarah's nails were "short" because of her work as a dental hygienist—a description that's debatable based on photos of her. He thought Sarah may have been incapacitated and that her hands were otherwise occupied. "You would be puttin' your hands on the bottom of the tub to get out," he said.

Theories aside, Juror #3 got some facts wrong—most notably about the county coroner's examination of Sarah's brain.

Juror #3 stated the coroner "tested all areas in the brain" for evidence of narcolepsy or seizures—which was incorrect. The coroner testified he did not know that the hypothalamus plays a role in narcolepsy; other witnesses testified more samples were needed to rule out seizures.

Two callers picked up on this discrepancy. They challenged Juror #3's understanding of the facts. But he didn't budge his position.

Serving as a juror was enjoyable, Juror #3 said, because "it intrigued my mind."

And, he said, "I paid close attention to every detail."

Déjà vu

When Ryan was first convicted in 2009, it was more of a shock to him because he didn't understand the court system then—and he didn't think it was possible to be convicted on a few misspoken words and a bunch of thoroughly-disputed evidence.

After going on trial two more times, he braced himself. "I knew that the wrong thing could happen," he said.

He described what it was like to be convicted—twice: *Both times, it was the same when I heard the word, "guilty." First, I can't believe it. But then I realize it's real. And it's horrible. It just slams me in the stomach. I don't remember having any thoughts other than the questions: "How?" and "Why?" Over and over. Both times.*

But there was one big difference in 2011. Ryan felt a new layer of agony, knowing that he was leaving behind his young son—the baby whose birth hadn't been publicly revealed yet.

During Trial Three, news reporters and live bloggers had heard rumors about Big Secret #2—Ryan's new girlfriend and their baby. And the prosecution had even filed a document that made an obscure reference to a woman who moved to Ohio to be with Ryan. But reporters were unable to get anyone to confirm the rumors, partly because of Judge Bronson's gag order.

In May 2011, two and a half months after Ryan's Trial Three conviction, a birth announcement was made—via *Dateline NBC's* nationally televised broadcast.

At the time, I was like many people: aghast. Had Ryan cheated on his wife with this woman? Maybe the prosecution's theory about that was on target. What kind of guy gets a woman pregnant while he's facing a fifteen-to-life prison term? And what kind of woman gets mixed up with a guy like that?

Some people felt a little less shocked after the lawyer heading Ryan's appeals, Michele Berry, pointed out the circumstances of Ryan's involvement with Sarah #2, a New York woman who started corresponding with him after the 2009 *Dateline* broadcast about his case. Ryan's wife had been dead for more than a year when he met Sarah #2, and he was sad and lonely, Berry said. But many still dismissed Berry's statements as damage control for a phony "grieving husband."

Ryan admitted: Yes, it was industrial-strength stupid to get into an intimate relationship while awaiting a murder retrial. But he had rediscovered happiness.

Ryan had survived enough stress to kill a blue whale. His wife had died. He was arrested for murder, tried, convicted, then freed—only to face being tried all over again. All the while, he was dealing with his mother's alcoholic rantings.

Sarah #2 was among hundreds of people who wrote to Ryan after *Dateline* first aired his story in September 2009. After Ryan wrote his customary thank-you note to her, they stayed in touch. Just as he did with virtually anyone else who continued contacting him.

When Ryan's online communication with strangers—particularly women—was revealed, older generations were disturbed. But people in their 20s were more inclined to see it as normal social interaction.

Ryan, who was 27 when the saga began, never imagined his socializing could produce messy entanglements such as those with the Mystery Witness and Sarah #2. "I never intended to have a relationship with her or anyone else," Ryan said.

Around Halloween of '09, Sarah #2 had become aggravated with a situation in New York, where she lived. So, she decided she needed a little getaway. Why not go to Ohio and meet Ryan? Sure, Ryan said.

It didn't strike him as odd that a woman would want to travel to meet him. In hindsight, Ryan realized he should have been leery. "But, at the time, I was just grateful for anything that anyone was willing to do to support me," Ryan said. "I didn't question it."

When Ryan met Sarah #2, he was smitten. She was fun to be around. And attractive. Her attention made Ryan feel good again, and it was a welcome diversion from his court case.

The following month, around Thanksgiving, Sarah #2 returned to Ohio to attend a FreeRyanWidmer.com fundraiser. She and Ryan spent time alone. And that's when "one thing led to another," as Ryan put it, blushing during a prison interview.

Ryan said he thought Sarah #2 was unable to conceive a child. So Ryan was stunned when she contacted him in December 2009 and revealed she was pregnant. They both panicked. But Sarah #2 and Ryan decided to make the best of it.

Ryan confided solely in his twin brother at first. Months later, he shared the secret with a few others, including his mom. Ryan thought he'd be acquitted in Trial Two. Then he'd be able to share the happy news freely, with no fear of repercussions.

But after the hung jury, Ryan realized he needed to tell his lawyers about his impending fatherhood. They were surprised, but not upset, he said. They told him they would deal with it, and that his relationship with Sarah #2 was of no legal significance to his case.

A few weeks before the baby's due date, Sarah #2 rented an apartment near Ryan's mom's house in summer 2010.

So that health insurance would pay for the birth, Sarah #2 had to fly back to New York. When she returned to Ohio, she stepped off a commuter airplane and handed Ryan his 2-day-old son at Cincinnati's Lunken Airport. He instantly fell in love with the little boy. The one who was named after him. The one who had eyes like his, staring back at him.

Ryan couldn't stop smiling. He had wanted to be a father before he turned 30—and he got his wish. Even though the circumstances were far from ideal. Even though he would have preferred having a baby with his wife, Sarah. Even though the prosecution had just dropped its Mystery Witness bombshell.

None of that mattered because Ryan loved his son—and because he saw the birth of his son as a sign from God: Trial Three would find him acquitted. Then he, Little Ryan and Sarah #2 would move out of Ohio and start a new life together.

When Ryan was convicted again in Trial Three, that fairytale scene shattered like a snow globe crashing onto a tile floor.

Being ripped away from his baby made the clank of the prison's metal doors seem that much louder and colder. Ryan couldn't even make himself look at Little Ryan's picture at first. But within several weeks, staring at photos of his boy steeled his resolve: He would never stop fighting to reverse his conviction—to get out and to be with his son again.

No matter what anyone might think about his hookup with Sarah #2, Ryan said he would never stop loving—and missing—the former Sarah Steward, his wife.

In honor of that, Ryan got a new tattoo. He enlisted "Slick Rick," a fellow prisoner known as a tattoo artist. Using a guitar string as a makeshift needle, Slick Rick inscribed "Sarah," in blue cursive on Ryan's left ring finger, taking the place of the wedding band that Ryan had kissed when he was first convicted in 2009.

Granted, other people might think that the Sarah tattoo represented his new girlfriend. Ryan didn't care. He knew what the tattoo signified to him: a testimonial to his unending love for his wife—and to his insistence that he would never have harmed her in any way.

"She'll always be my wife," he said.

Headlines kept coming

Just two days after the court hearing that featured the pot-user witness, Judge Neal Bronson rendered his decision:

- **About Juror #1's alleged "bias:"** While commending Ryan's lawyers for their "zealousness," he said their contentions had impugned the integrity of Juror #1 and had implicitly cast aspersions on all the other jurors, too. No proof was presented that anyone actually heard Juror #1's alleged "burn-in-hell" remark, nor that any juror had violated any rule. He made no specific mention of the controversy over Juror #1's mid-trial Facebooking.

- **About the sufficiency of the evidence:** Very few facts in the case were "uncontroverted." Thus, it was the jury's responsibility to decide which facts to believe, how much weight to give the facts and what conclusions to draw. That's the risk that a defendant takes when he exercises his right to a trial by jury, the judge said.

The judge declared: "MOTIONS DENIED."

Ryan ruminated over his decision to forgo a "bench trial"—trial by judge. He had chosen a jury trial based on legal advice: It would be riskier to entrust his fate solely to *one* person—the judge—versus trying to find at least one sympathetic person among twelve jurors.

After his first conviction by jury, Ryan wondered whether a bench trial would be better. But his legal team warned that changing course could backfire. Judge Bronson most likely would recuse himself. And that would put Ryan at the mercy of an unknown judge—one who might be less experienced and possibly less inclined to take a principled but controversial stance on a murder case.

In 2001, Judge Bronson rejected a jury's death sentence for a state prison inmate who strangled his cellmate. The judge took that action because he learned that jurors had been improperly exposed to photos he had banned from the trial.

Ryan said he was never able to "read" how Bronson was leaning in his case. And even after Judge Bronson retired from the bench in 2013, he told me that he would not comment on the Widmer case while appeals were pending. Those were still in progress as of this writing in 2018.

Normally, after a verdict and an initial appeal, even high-profile murder cases tend to fade from public view.

But spinoffs of the Widmer case kept making news.

Sometimes referencing the Widmer case, judges would warn jurors about outside experimentation or even nonchalant browsing on Facebook and other social media. Legal scholars said the case showed why new rules were needed to clamp down on jurors in the digital age.

Then, *Dateline NBC* revealed that Ryan had granted his first post-conviction interview to that show—and that he, his new girlfriend and baby would be part of a two-hour episode, "The Bathtub Mystery."

The first time *Dateline* broadcast Ryan's story, it became the most-watched *Dateline* episode of the 2009 season, coast-to-coast.

Dateline would air the 2011 update in early May, a "sweeps month," when TV viewership is tracked for ratings that determine advertising income.

Viewers were clamoring to hear what Ryan would say during the *Dateline* program, his first public statements other than tearful declarations of innocence when he was convicted.

Dateline saved Ryan's interview for the program's final few minutes.

After denying that he killed his wife, Ryan made statements that further damaged public perceptions of him; the headline on one news article described him as "defiant."

I cringed when I heard Ryan accuse Ruth Ann Steward, his wife's mom, of being "a liar" when she testified that he and his bride had been "hateful to each other."

Ryan apparently didn't care—or was unaware—that it seemed like a cheap shot. But many of his supporters didn't blame him for lashing out, considering how dramatically her testimony changed.

Ryan faltered when he tried to describe Sarah's position as he found her in the bathtub. Then he made an accusation that sounded outlandish: The medics and police were in cahoots against him. When *Dateline* reporter Dennis Murphy pointed out that police and fire first responders don't even work for the same agency, Ryan replied, "They clearly do when they get up there to testify, because they're clearly coached into what to say."

Critics said: "No wonder this guy didn't take the witness stand!" His claims sounded desperate and baseless. His demeanor seemed shifty; his eyes darted away from the camera at key moments.

Ryan's supporters responded that it was unfair to judge him on edited video. Some also felt that he was entitled to vent frustrations.

Appellate lawyer Michele Berry said her client didn't really mean he thought Sarah's mom was a liar and that there was a conspiracy to entrap him.

Rather, Berry said, Ryan had made a clumsy attempt to express that memories can change as time passes, and it seemed that Ruth Ann and other prosecution witnesses "reconstructed their memories," perhaps subconsciously, to fit the prosecution's mold.

The new prosecutor, David Fornshell, was highly critical of Ryan's performance on *Dateline*.

And Ryan's mom, Jill, was embarrassed that people across America knew about the baby and about Sarah #2.

Shortly after the *Dateline* episode aired, Jill ranted on Facebook. She accused Sarah #2 of being "a user" and asserted Ryan "is in prison where he needs to be."

Jill's close friends saw the Facebook posts as "symptomatic of how delusional she had become," her friend, Suzanne Richmond, said.

Suzanne formerly worked for Jill at Luxottica, and Suzanne had grown to respect Jill tremendously. Jill was a goal-oriented woman who would have seemed hard-nosed if not for her silly sense of humor and caring heart—traits that Suzanne also saw in Ryan.

Suzanne's friendship with Jill deepened after they no longer worked together—and especially while Ryan was being prosecuted and convicted. "A lot of superficial relationships fell apart, and she needed friends; I wasn't going to let her down," Suzanne said.

Jill was "very approachable," and was such a skilled communicator that she could be blunt yet diplomatic at the same time. Suzanne agreed with most people: Ryan didn't inherit that skill from his mom. And it showed with his *Dateline* appearance, Suzanne thought, although she thought editing may have made him look worse. But mostly, watching *Dateline* made Suzanne angry—because it made her relive everything she had seen Jill endure.

After *Dateline* aired, some people had Widmer fatigue. But I remained Widmer-intrigued. I had a huge list of questions to ask Ryan in case I ever got an interview.

Persistence paid off. I became the first Cincinnati-based reporter to land an interview with Ryan. I had made no promises except this: I would give Ryan the chance to more fully tell his story, and I would listen with an open mind.

There were no restrictions on the questions. I could ask anything I wanted to.

As the interview date approached, *Enquirer* photographer Cara Owsley and I discussed how odd we felt. We both had been absorbed with Ryan's case for almost three years, yet we had never been allowed to talk to him. Cara joked that she would be able to recognize the back of Ryan's head anywhere because she had spent so many hours staring at it.

Ryan was then housed at Warren Correctional Institution, in the same county where he was tried and convicted. Cara and I were escorted into a small concrete block room, where we met Ryan. After a little introductory chit-chat, we dove into the questions.

One that *Enquirer* readers kept asking: Why didn't he testify? Yet even before I asked Ryan that question, I could sense part of the answer—based on this convoluted sentence:

"I'm sitting here talking to you today off of not one fact that should point to my guilt of anything," he said a few minutes into the interview. What? "Off of not one fact?"

I stopped him and asked for clarification. His second try came out clearer: "I feel like the facts of the case point toward my innocence, not towards guilt."

He answered many questions clearly. But I quickly perceived that he often groped for the right words. He was mostly matter-of-fact and expressionless—demeanor that wouldn't play well to a jury. His flat affect didn't lend itself well to TV sound bites, either. But that wouldn't matter much for a printed article. He just needed to be understood well enough that I, the reporter, could tell a compelling story accurately.

Ryan spent more than two hours fielding questions from me during that first interview on May 31, 2011.

Layers of editors sliced the resulting story before it ran in the *Enquirer* almost two weeks later. The front-page headline declared, "Widmer: I'll never give up." At the time, I didn't know that Ryan's cousin, Sean Cronin, the football coach, had inundated Ryan with "NEVER GIVE UP" flyers when Ryan was put behind bars.

Although the article was lengthy, many details that Ryan shared were never printed in the newspaper.

But his story remained imprinted in my memory—tucked away like a forgotten reference book, waiting to be rediscovered.

Investigating the detective

Lieutenant Jeff Braley's credibility crisis had lain dormant while the Widmer case was pending. But the day after Ryan was convicted, it was revived. Officials in Hamilton Township, where Braley worked, hired an attorney to dig into his allegedly fraudulent personnel records.

The timing of the probe seemed suspect to Ryan's supporters. Now that the trial was over, any possible dirt on Braley would be useless to Ryan's lawyers—except maybe in appeals, which are almost always long shots.

But officials said the township simply took the first opportunity to act. The township trustees' regularly scheduled meeting occurred right after Judge Neal Bronson lifted his order prohibiting certain parties from public comment or discussion about "the character, credibility or reputation" of anyone tied to the Widmer case.

Attorney R. Douglas Miller spent about three months investigating Braley's personnel history. Braley had admitted that two documents in his personnel file contained false assertions that he earned a master's degree and held certain jobs. But he said someone else may have forged the records to sabotage him during the Widmer case.

In June 2011, Miller released his report. He had found no evidence that anyone else had altered Braley's records. But a state handwriting analyst had declared that the handwriting on the records appeared to be Braley's—and Miller found a new concern about Braley.

"Numerous" people said Braley claimed he had belonged to the U.S. Army's elite Special Forces. And, "it was everyone's understanding" that was why Braley was chosen to lead the police department's new tactical team around 2001—when Braley was not yet commissioned as a police officer.

Braley denied claiming he served the Special Forces. But, the investigator said, "considering the fact that a civilian with no actual military Special Forces experience was put in charge of the (tactical) team, one would tend to conclude that the statements were indeed made."

Two days after the investigator's report was issued, advocating possible discipline, Braley resigned from the township police department, citing "many current events."

Braley also had just gotten bad news from a federal appeals court: A federal lawsuit, alleging that he and other officers conducted an unlawful raid in 2007, was allowed to proceed.

The lawsuit alleged civil-rights violations, including allegations that police fabricated reasons to raid an "underage drinking party"—which turned out to be a father-son birthday celebration attended mostly by middle-aged people.

On August 10, 2007, nearly two dozen cops swarmed the property of Ted and Mary Pritchard just as Ted, who was turning 52, was blowing out the candles on his birthday cake in the back yard. Startled partygoers scattered; police chased and arrested some of them.

Later, the Pritchards received an anonymous letter with some important information, possibly from a police officer who wanted to clear his conscience: It said officers had conspired to unlawfully raid the Pritchards'.

The Pritchards were stunned when they learned what happened. A Hamilton Township officer's wife was at her home in Butler County, many miles away from the Pritchards' when she made a noise complaint about the Pritchards. She claimed she heard "yelling and screaming" from their property. "It sounds like a big ol' party," she told a dispatcher.

Court testimony later revealed that Braley planned the raid based on an unverified tip that teens were going to be drinking at the party. Braley took no steps to corroborate the tip. He met with the department's top brass to plan a raid, and they enlisted help from state liquor agents; township officers were lined up to work outside their regular hours that Friday night.

The Pritchards' lawyer, Konrad Kircher, alleged that the raid was conducted partly for political reasons, under false pretenses.

Braley and his colleagues denied the allegations, and said they had "probable cause" from the noise complaint and from Braley's assertion that he spotted someone drunk and yelling loudly.

Both of those seminal events happened just before midnight, when state liquor agents intended to leave if there was no action.

In January 2012, a federal jury decided that officials, including Braley, committed more than forty counts of civil wrongdoing, including conspiracy to violate the Pritchards' rights. In a settlement negotiated while jurors deliberated, the township accepted the jury's findings and paid $350,000 in damages.

Just after that verdict, WLWT-TV Channel 5 interviewed Mary Pritchard. She said she had followed news coverage of other cases involving Braley—and her own experience made her wonder about the Widmer case: "Was everything on the up and up?"

Because the Pritchard case concluded almost a year after Ryan was convicted, Ryan's jury had no knowledge of it. Neither did many people who heard Ryan's seemingly preposterous conspiracy claim on *Dateline*.

Ryan's appellate lawyer, Michele Berry, filed actions in several different courts, making multiple claims against Braley.

Berry said Braley had a "penchant for manufacturing facts to further his career," and she argued his involvement may have tainted the Widmer case. He supervised evidence-gathering, quickly got charges filed against Ryan and, Berry said, may have played a role in the coroner's decision to rule Sarah's death a homicide.

But the coroner denied Braley told him how to rule Sarah's manner of death. And Prosecutor David Fornshell brushed aside Berry's contentions.

Fornshell caustically predicted: Attempts to secure a fourth trial would probably continue for the duration of Ryan's prison sentence.

Coroner faces more scrutiny

Soon after Ryan's trial ended, the Warren County coroner would find himself facing off against one of Ryan's lawyers again.

Despite the trial outcome for Ryan, attorney Lindsey Gutierrez's tough cross-examination of Dr. Russell Uptegrove was impressive enough that she was hired to help in another case that centered on Uptegrove's work.

Besides being Warren County's coroner, Uptegrove conducted dozens of autopsies for other counties. One involved the death of 45-year-old Tom Rogers at a Middletown, Ohio, wastewater treatment plant where he worked. Rogers died in 2008, the same year Sarah Widmer drowned. Uptegrove ruled Rogers' death was an accident, caused by exposure to poison gas. As a result, Rogers' employer, United Oil Recovery Services, and several company executives faced criminal charges for his death.

When the case went to trial before a judge in Butler County, next door to Warren County, Gutierrez again grilled Uptegrove.

She alleged that Uptegrove failed to give due consideration to other possible factors in Rogers' death: Obesity, an enlarged heart and a mixture of drugs in his system, including toxic levels of a painkiller.

In May 2011, the trial ended with a judge acquitting the company and its executives, saying he was unable to convict based on "speculation."

Uptegrove stood by his work, saying he had years of experience and was competent despite lacking board certification. And Uptegrove said it was not his role to decide whether anyone should have been criminally charged. While that's true, Gutierrez said, "he definitely played a large part" in charges being filed in both the Rogers and Widmer cases.

Gutierrez also alleged that Uptegrove had a pattern of quick judgments and skipping steps. Uptegrove said it was unfair to hyper-focus on a few cases, considering that he had performed thousands of autopsies. Given that volume of work, Uptegrove said, there were bound to be times when people disagreed with his rulings.

That made me wonder: Had Uptegrove ever acknowledged a mistake and changed a ruling? Not that he could think of, he said at the time.

Ironically, another tragedy intertwined the Widmers with Uptegrove. Almost five years after Ryan Widmer found Sarah and dialed 911 to say, "I think she's dead," his twin brother, Ayran, called 911 and reported, "I think my mom's dead."

In fact, Ayran knew that his mother was dead. It was obvious based on her grotesquely discolored skin. It was a horrifying thing to see, he said, "especially when it's your mom."

It was July 29, 2013. Ryan had been in prison for more than two years at this point.

Ayran had become concerned about Jill because no one had heard from her in several days. He headed toward his mom's house to check on her.

Jill had built the house, valued at more than $300,000, in 2001, when life was good. Her career at Luxottica was nearing its zenith. The home was situated in the Fairways of Crooked Tree, a pleasant, prestigious Mason subdivision.

After Ryan was convicted, she sank into a deep depression. She became hermitlike and would not answer the door. The home that welcomed so many happy get-togethers had become Jill's prison. She left occasionally to visit the prison that held her son.

Jill rarely contacted even good friends, including Suzanne Richmond. The last text Suzanne received from Jill was on Suzanne's birthday, July 22, 2013. That also was the day Ayran had last texted his mom—and it was the same day that Luxottica fired Jill because of her drinking problem, Suzanne later learned.

A week later, on July 29, Ayran was outside his mom's house. Signs of neglect were everywhere. Bushes were overgrown. A faded autumn-themed wreath still hung on the door. Ayran knocked. No answer. He went around back and found the rear door unlocked. He opened it, and Jill's two dogs came rushing to him.

After Ayran calmed the dogs, he encountered a scene disturbingly reminiscent of one that had shaken Ryan three years earlier. Just as Ryan had spotted only his mom's legs protruding from behind a couch, Ayran also initially saw only Jill's legs, sprawled along the kitchen floor.

Ayran rushed to her and exclaimed, "Mom, mom!" But Ayran got no response. He could tell she had been dead for a while. Possibly for days. The scene was disgusting and heartbreaking. Jill was dead on the floor, surrounded by trash, dog feces and all manner of clutter, including dozens of wine bottles.

Ayran had known her condition was going downhill. "She had kind of, in a sense, given up on life," he said later.

But he was unprepared for what he found. Shaking, he called 911.

For a moment, he worried: Would he fall under suspicion?

One of the dogs at the scene was C.J., the French bulldog that played a starring role in Ryan's marriage proposal to Sarah—and could be heard barking as Ryan called 911 to report Sarah had drowned.

As police arrived and took photographs, Ayran spotted a familiar face: Doyle Burke, the coroner's investigator who had testified against Ryan.

Ayran was less-than-thrilled to see Burke at the scene of their mother's death, considering the damage Burke's testimony had done to Ryan.

Burke offered his condolences. But to Ayran, the words rang hollow.

And the whole family resented the fact that Uptegrove would rule on Jill's death because she had died in the county where he was coroner. To the Widmer family, Uptegrove was largely to blame for Ryan's prosecution—and, indirectly, for Jill's demise.

As news of Jill's death spread, some people blamed Warren County authorities for the stress that killed her. Others said Ryan could have saved his mom a lot of money and heartache—and even her life—if he would have just owned up to his crime.

But those people didn't know Ryan, and the bond he had with Jill, Aryan said.

"Especially with the relationship that Ryan had with my mom—we always felt like he was her favorite—he would have admitted it if he had done it," Ayran said. "There's no way he would have put her through all of that, especially not after they offered him a plea."

Ryan's dad contacted the Correctional Reception Center in Orient. Ryan was summoned to an office where a prison chaplain delivered the bad news.

Ryan wanted to go to his mom's funeral. But after the Widmers learned they would be stuck paying thousands of dollars for security to watch Ryan, everyone including Ryan decided it was too costly.

Ryan also was distressed to learn that Uptegrove would be doing the autopsy on his mom. But there was nothing he could do about it.

When Uptegrove was done with his work, Ryan and his family thought the contrast was remarkable when they saw how long it took for a ruling in Jill's case versus Sarah's.

Uptegrove issued a preliminary "homicide" ruling the morning after Sarah's death; he signed her death certificate three days after she died.

In Jill's case, Uptegrove initially listed "pending" for both the cause and manner of death. It took two and a half months for the death certificate to be updated with the manner—natural—and cause, "complications of chronic ethanol abuse."

Jill appeared to have foreseen her own demise.

While Ryan was awaiting Trial Two, she sat down at her computer and typed a letter.

Her words seemed like hyperbole then, but now looked prophetic.

"If he goes back to prison, I will die."

CHAPTER 11
Epilogue

"The Widmer curse."

That was the phrase Cincinnati legal expert Mike Allen coined to describe consequences of the Widmer case.

Reflecting on his decades-long career—as a police officer, judge, prosecutor and defense lawyer—Allen couldn't think of another case that had wrought so much drama and misery.

Ryan's mom, Jill Widmer, was dead at age 55—a casualty of the case that broke her heart as much as alcohol abuse had wrecked her body.

Rachel Hutzel, the county prosecutor who spearheaded the case against Ryan, had also died. Allen, a friend of Hutzel, said some considered her a victim of the Widmer "curse." Hutzel passed away of cancer in August 2012, about a year and a half after she began serving as an appeals court judge. She was 56.

Jeff Braley, the lead detective on the case, lost his career; he sought a fresh start by moving out of state.

Braley's former police department began requiring more police experience and better screening for new hires. Those changes were made after Scott Hughes became chief in 2016, long after the Widmer case, to better prepare officers for challenging situations.

Sarah's mom, devastated over the loss of Sarah, sold her Ohio home in 2016. She moved south, nearer to her son. I received no response to requests to interview her and another relative of Sarah for this book.

Ryan's family struggled to recover financially and emotionally, after throwing a half-million dollars toward his defense.

Ryan's dad and stepmom, once empty-nesters, were helping Sarah #2 take care of Little Ryan. She and Big Ryan split during the second year of his incarceration, but Little Ryan still sometimes visited his dad in prison after that.

Growing up with his dad behind bars, Little Ryan didn't quite seem to understand why the dad he loved couldn't be with him every day, couldn't watch him play baseball or come play catch.

The ripple effects spread from the original tragedy—Sarah's death—and enveloped everyone who cared about her and about Ryan. The case even made a lasting impact on strangers. The tragic tale gripped their hearts. The mystery tortured their minds: If Ryan killed Sarah, *why* did he do it and *how* did he do it? If he was innocent, what really happened to Sarah, and how could the authorities have missed it?

I heard rumors that prosecutors might be holding back some information, but I was unable to find out whether that was true. They declined interviews.

As Ryan's appeals lawyer put it, "a perfect storm of things gone wrong" landed Ryan in prison—starting with Braley.

Attorney Michele Berry blamed Braley for laser-focusing on a hunch that Sarah's death was a homicide, blinding him to other possibilities. "This is a case of shooting an arrow and drawing a bullseye around (the spot) where the arrow landed," she said during a December 2015 hearing in a Dayton, Ohio, federal court.

Errors in Ryan's case violated his rights, Berry said: The judge shouldn't have forbidden the defense from assailing Braley. Testimony about the tub markings lacked a scientific foundation and constituted "junk science." Police illegally seized the tub—so evidence arising from it shouldn't have been allowed and his first lawyers should have fought to exclude it.

Berry also argued that the prosecution should be ordered to release Sarah's DNA so it could be tested for Long QT Syndrome. Sarah had specific symptoms suggestive of that disorder, which can cause sudden paralysis—and has been connected to drownings.

And, above all, "the manifest weight of the evidence" did not support a conviction, Berry argued.

A prosecutor from the Ohio Attorney General's Office contended that Berry's issues were mostly "state law claims," not federal law claims, and that the federal court must defer to state court rulings. "Actual innocence" cannot be considered a constitutional-rights violation, the state prosecutor said.

As of this writing in 2018, Berry was still waiting for a federal judge to rule on her arguments. The chances didn't look good. A magistrate judge, who heard the arguments, recommended that the judge reject Berry's claims.

Post-verdict arguments seemed moot for folks who believed the verdict was just. For them, the matter was settled: Ryan was in prison, where he deserved to be for killing his wife. End of story. They thought the justice system worked, even if it disgusted them that it took three trials—followed by seemingly endless appeals.

But thousands of others were disquieted. Some were unsure if Ryan killed Sarah, but they thought the evidence didn't prove it "beyond a reasonable doubt." Others were convinced that Ryan was innocent, wrongfully convicted.

Many in both categories say the Widmer saga permanently shattered their faith in the justice system.

As the ten-year anniversary of the case approached, the "Free Ryan Widmer" Facebook group remained solid, with more than 6,000 members. The group continued to attract a few new followers—and random detractors—whenever the case popped up in the news: another appeal was shot down, *Dateline NBC* aired a rerun of Ryan's episode, or the Widmer case was referenced in other criminal cases.

Each news blurb reminded me of the many untold aspects of the Widmer tale— important points that were never explored. They were lost as reporters rushed to meet deadlines, under gag-order restrictions, then pursued the next big story.

The hidden Widmer facts were stored in the recesses of my memory, buried amid reams of legal documents and locked in the minds of people connected to the case.

Dredging them up would require a deep dive into the Titanic-sized Widmer wreckage—a plunge that my curiosity and my conscience compelled me to take.

Why Ryan's Story remained untold

Many people sneered at Ryan for tearfully protesting his innocence after passing up three chances to take the witness stand. I might have been among them, if my work experience hadn't changed my perspective.

Lots of people have told me that if they were wrongfully accused of a crime, nothing would prevent them from testifying. Nothing.

As a rookie reporter, I thought the same thing.

But a few years into my twenty-seven years in journalism, I realized that deciding to testify isn't as simple as it seems. It's one of the most complex and delicate decisions an accused person can make.

Protesting your innocence doesn't mean a judge or jury will believe you—and even your best effort to tell the truth can backfire.

Jurors and spectators scrutinize everything the accused person says or does, even if he just sits in court and doesn't testify. Everything is magnified and subject to interpretation. If a defendant cries, jurors might think he's putting on an act; if he doesn't cry, he's "cold-hearted."

Poor grammar, imprecise word choices and awkward sentence construction might make someone seem guilty too.

That's why defense lawyers often warn their clients that testifying presents a "damned-if-you-do, damned-if-you-don't" dilemma.

Although jurors are routinely warned against attaching any meaning to a defendant's decision not to testify, jurors often cannot shake the natural human desire to hear the defendant declare, "I didn't do it."

People also may subconsciously assume that failure to testify signals that the accused is afraid his guilt will be laid bare on the witness stand.

And if the accused does deny wrongdoing, those denials typically are greeted with spadesful of skepticism. We've all heard people protest their innocence, only to recant after being caught in a web of their own deceit.

And whenever a defendant testifies, a prosecutor can pounce on the slightest inconsistencies, hesitations or forgotten details.

The danger, defense lawyers say, is that an innocent, fallible human is every bit as capable of making those "mistakes" as a guilty one is—especially under the stress of sitting in the witness chair.

So, on principle, I understood *why* any defendant might have a hard time deciding whether to testify.

And that was before I knew anything about Ryan.

I later learned that, in everyday, non-stressful situations, what Ryan meant to say was often different from what he actually did say—even at his job. While he got high marks for following instructions and sticking to deadlines, a 2007 evaluation said: "communication is an area that Ryan could really improve."

On the rare occasion when Ryan would get emotional, his communication glitches would flare up. His words didn't come out right when he proposed marriage to Sarah—and they got jumbled up the night she died, too, his friends said.

A communication expert from Atlanta "worked with him and worked with him" in advance of Trial One, attorney Charlie Rittgers said. Yet the expert failed to get Ryan to communicate well enough to testify.

Rittgers thought that might not matter. He thought there was "reasonable doubt all over this case," and therefore it was possible—even probable—to win an acquittal without Ryan's testimony.

Two subsequent defense teams made the same determinations.

Almost a decade later, Ryan told me he remained puzzled: "I never understood fully why they felt I'd be a bad witness."

But, trusting his lawyers' advice, Ryan stayed off the witness stand and gave no media interviews—until after he was convicted.

And that's why the full version of Ryan's Story—his detailed account of the night his wife drowned—was never told. Not to the public. Not to a jury. Not even to the police.

He would have told police what happened if given the chance, Ryan and Rittgers insisted.

If Ryan's Story had come out, maybe he could have explained the seemingly sinister circumstances surrounding Sarah's death.

Or perhaps his explanations wouldn't have mattered. Not when the police at the scene were struck with such powerful suspicions. As Lieutenant Jeff Braley told Dateline NBC: "Something was screaming to me: Something's bad wrong."

The 911 call did it

So what, exactly, was Ryan's Story? And would it be plausible?

To find out, I challenged Ryan: Put me on your prison visiting list. Allow your lawyers to give me any information they have; let me see their documents and let them talk freely with me. Answer every question I throw at you. And know that, if I catch you in a lie or a contradiction, I will call you out on it. And I will not shy away from revealing it.

Ryan had no problem with any of that; he said he had nothing to hide.

And I challenged myself: Get documents that tell the whole story—court records, the entire police investigative file, Ryan's diary, his personal correspondence. Read the trial transcripts—all 6,000 pages. Examine all the photos from the scene and from Sarah's autopsies. Re-read dozens of news articles. Consult blogs and other online sources. Ask Ryan and others to fill in the gaps. Compile Ryan's Story from interviews and records. See which aspects of his verbal version match the records and which don't. Then get out of the way and let the story tell itself—until a conclusion emerges.

When I first reconnected with Ryan in January 2017, he said: "You are absolutely right, I have so much to say ... Every day I wake up, I can't understand how this has all happened and how it is still going on." He had been in prison more than six years at that point.

In one of our first conversations, he told me that the 911 call was one of the main reasons he was locked up.

But that's all he said about it.

Extracting the deeper meaning behind that statement required lots of follow-up questions. And so it went with many other questions I asked. But I never got the feeling that Ryan's vague, cryptic answers were purposely evasive.

He would always say, "Let me know if you need more." And that became a running joke—because it seemed that I always did need more.

Each question and answer lifted away a wisp of the fog enshrouding the case, shedding new light on old records that told only part of the story—and, perhaps, revealing a little more of the truth.

○ ○ ○ ○ ○

This is what Ryan told me about the 911 call that started it all—and ultimately helped lead to his conviction:

When Ryan called 911 at 10:49 the night his wife died, Monday, August 11, 2008, he didn't take time to consider what he was saying. His words just came out.

Afterward, he didn't recall precisely what words he had used during the call. His diary says he finally listened to a recording of it months later. Some things he heard surprised him, including the "face-down" description. Ryan insisted that was a misstatement.

He told me that, when he first found Sarah, she was floating face-up, her blue eyes staring up at the ceiling—an image he'll never forget. He told the same thing to his lawyers before he knew he was being charged. That description is corroborated in his lawyers' initial notes, handwritten on August 13, 2008, two days after Sarah died: "Found her on (her) back... Foaming blood coming out of nose." He told me that same version when I first interviewed him in prison in 2011. His account remained consistent in 2017 and 2018.

Ryan told me that he didn't know why he said "face-down" to the dispatcher and, apparently, to several other people.

I sensed how that might have happened. Ryan is a smart guy, and I had noticed that his thoughts sometimes seemed to move faster than his ability to articulate them; he would combine two thoughts into one. Hence, "jump *the* gun" and "jump *to* conclusions" became, "*jump to a gun*," in my first interview with him in 2011.

And, when Ryan spoke about Sarah's position in the tub on the 911 call, he may have been thinking Sarah's face was *down* below the water and *down* under the water. But it came out wrong: "face down," which most people would interpret to mean that her face was flipped toward the bottom of the tub. And that was not how he found her, Ryan insisted on multiple occasions.

For investigators and prosecutors—strangers to RyanSpeak—the "face-up/face-down" discrepancy seemed to be a careless lie, an early indicator of Ryan's guilt.

But even if Ryan had lied about which way Sarah was facing, what would such a lie accomplish? It wouldn't change the fact that she had drowned. In fact, saying she was "face-down" created *more* suspicion than if she were "face-up," the normal position for a bather.

Therefore, Ryan had nothing to gain if he had lied about that. And it seemed believable that any person could misspeak under stress—especially Ryan.

So I accepted this aspect of Ryan's Story—while still wondering about many others.

Why she was dry

Ryan's Story actually begins before he called 911. That's when he took steps that might account for Sarah's skin feeling dry or "not overly moist" to first-responders.

Here's what Ryan told me about those crucial moments, just before and just after he called 911—which concurred with records such as the 911 recording, his diary and his lawyers' documents.

When Ryan found Sarah unresponsive in the bathtub, his first instinct was to get rid of the threat—the water—and to try to rouse her. He automatically reached down and pulled the drain plug. Tick-tock, tick-tock went the clock, as the water level began to drop, gradually exposing parts of Sarah's body to the air that would begin drying her wet skin.

Ryan pulled her torso toward him, getting her into a semi-seated position, which removed her head and shoulders from the water. Tick-tock, tick-tock.

He tried to elicit a reaction. "Sarah, Sarah," he said, patting her face and chest. Tick-tock, tick-tock.

Realizing Sarah needed more help than he could give, Ryan went back into the bedroom to retrieve his cellphone so he could dial 911. Tick-tock, tick-tock. More time passed.

He came back into the bathroom. But the call suddenly disconnected. That was a common problem for people living in and near the Widmer's semirural neighborhood, where cellphone signals could be spotty.

Within seconds, Ryan grabbed Sarah's phone from the bathroom countertop, dialed 911 again—and that time, the call went through.

After reaching the dispatcher, Ryan dropped to his knees again, holding Sarah at the side of the tub. He stayed there, beside her, while he described the situation for the dispatcher—starting with the words that provoked suspicion: "My wife fell asleep in the bathtub and I think she's dead."

One minute into the call, the dispatcher asked whether Sarah was still in the water. "The water's completely drained," Ryan said.

The dispatcher directed Ryan to get Sarah out of the tub, to unlock the doors so medics could enter the house, then to begin CPR. Ryan reported he was following those directions.

Five minutes into the call, Ryan yelled, apparently to the first-arriving officer, "Come up here, please hurry up."

Sometime after that—perhaps twenty seconds later—the officer would have had his first chance to touch Sarah and to notice that her skin felt dry.

Would Ryan's Story "fit" with that timing?

That would depend on two factors:

1. How much time it took for the tub to drain while Ryan tried to rouse Sarah, sat her up and began his 911 calls—which no one estimated during any of his trials.

2. How long it would have taken a body to air-dry in the Widmer home that night—which jurors tested at home themselves even though they did have trial testimony to consider. A defense expert said it took his body seven minutes to air-dry at his home.

Absent any trial testimony about the first factor, I resorted to my own unscientific experiment to estimate the bathtub-draining time. I filled my bathtub to the overflow valve, the level Ryan described when he found Sarah, and pulled the stopper.

My tub was empty in about two minutes—an intriguing result, considering this sequence:

While the Widmers' tub drained, perhaps a minute and a half passed while Ryan accomplished all of these actions: trying to get Sarah to react, propping her up into a seated position, then scrambling to call 911 from two different phones.

During the 911 call, another minute elapsed before he told the dispatcher that the water had drained from the tub.

By that point, about two-and-a-half minutes had elapsed; sufficient time for the tub to drain, based on my experiment.

About four minutes later, the officer's voice is heard on the call.

By then, about six-and-a-half minutes had elapsed since Ryan started draining the tub—close to the seven-minute span that it took for Dr. Michael Gregory Balko's skin to air-dry, as he testified in Trial One.

But would that seven-minute drying time have been accurate in the Widmer household that night? That's unknown because investigators had failed to note humidity, temperature and other conditions—and the defense-hired engineer was never allowed to testify about the air-drying times he calculated from weather data and other sources.

Ryan had no clue that dryness would become THE issue—until prosecutors opened Trial One by emphasizing the dryness of Sarah and the bathroom. Right away, Ryan could see they were trying to imply that Sarah was never in the tub.

To him, the truth was simple: Sarah was not wet because he had emptied the tub before she was removed. Just as he had told the 911 operator.

As for the "dry" condition of the bathroom, Charlie Rittgers, Ryan's first lawyer, had argued that the bathroom's dryness was a testimonial that Sarah's drowning was silent, not violent. No splashed water meant there was no struggle.

And there were some signs of wetness that could fit with Ryan's Story: the crinkled pages of a magazine on the floor outside the tub, droplets of water photographed on the bathtub stopper and the carpet samples taken from under Sarah's body. So perhaps the back of Sarah's body was still wet when Ryan placed her on the floor.

Ryan was stunned when the prosecution advanced various theories, alleging the dryness proved that Ryan drowned Sarah in the sink or toilet—and that the stains on the floor proved Ryan had spun Sarah.

To him, those theories were outlandish: "I felt like no one would ever believe what they were trying to say."

And, Ryan told me, that's why it was incomprehensible for him to be convicted.

Actions and reactions

What about the apparent contradictions that Coroner's Investigator Doyle Burke noted when Ryan talked to him at the hospital where Sarah was taken?

Ryan's lawyers, through their questions, implied that Burke may have misunderstood Ryan—or may have made note-taking errors.

Burke made no audio recording, and only wrote a couple hundred words summarizing his questions and Ryan's answers.

These fifty-two words were among the most damning for Ryan:

I asked why he drained the tub and he said that when he called 911 they said to pull her out of the tub, so he did, and he pulled the drain plug also-

I asked if he pulled her out before, or after the 911 call and he now stated, after-

Ryan told me—and had told his lawyers—that he was trying to convey that he had lifted only Sarah's head and shoulders at first—*and then her entire body.* Had Burke misunderstood whether "pulled her out" referred to *part* of Sarah or to her whole body? Ryan's lawyers tried to imply that during his trials—but jurors either failed to get that point or just didn't buy it.

○ ○ ○ ○ ○

What about Sarah's body position, both in the tub and out of the tub?

A lot of suspicion swirled around that. Prosecutors described Sarah, face-down, streaking her hands along the back of the tub, then Ryan spinning her body on the carpet to alter the scene.

According to Ryan's Story, he found Sarah face-up, with her head at the faucet end of the tub. Ryan told me: He had no idea how she got there, but that was where he found her.

Did she collapse as she tried to step in or out of the tub? Had she been rinsing her hair under the faucet, then felt woozy? Just about anything was possible, Ryan said. Even if Ryan had testified, those questions would have remained unanswered, he said: "I was not in the bathroom, so there was no answer I could give (about what happened to Sarah) and that's what everyone wanted."

He said it was ridiculous that people thought it was "suspicious" that he found Sarah at the "wrong" end of the tub. If someone wanted to "stage" a drowning, wouldn't it make more sense for a suspect to claim that the victim was "right where she normally should have been," at the reclining end of the tub?

If Ryan found Sarah as he described, with her head near the faucet and *away* from the bedroom, how did she end up on the carpet the other way around, with her head pointed *toward* the bedroom?

Ryan described a series of movements that investigators apparently never envisioned.

After the 911 dispatcher told Ryan to remove Sarah from the tub, Ryan had to maneuver around cramped quarters. The door leading to the bedroom opened inward, toward the bathroom. When that door was open, it blocked about half the tub, leaving the faucet end of the tub accessible.

Facing the faucet end of the tub where Sarah was, Ryan stepped into it with his right foot. He kept his left foot on the bathroom floor, for leverage.

Ryan reached into the just-drained tub. Sarah was still slippery, he said. He got a grip on his second try, scooping her into his arms. One of his arms cradled her upper back; the other, the backs of her knees.

While holding Sarah, Ryan pivoted toward his left foot. He lifted his right knee to step out of the tub and onto the floor. His back was now toward the tub, alongside that closed door.

○ ○ ○ ○ ○

At this point, I interrupted Ryan. I was having trouble picturing these actions in the tiny bathroom I had toured six years earlier.

I asked whether the door impeded him while he tried to remove Sarah from the tub—and did he then have to use the back of his body to push the door back into place against the tub, as he carried Sarah?

His response: "I don't know for sure, and I don't want to tell you wrong."

Ryan easily could have lied about that, just to agree with me; saying yes to my question would have made his story more plausible. Yet he told me that he just didn't know.

Just as Ryan's lawyer, Charlie Rittgers, had tested Ryan's honesty, so did I. Repeatedly. So far, he passed the test. Still, I reminded myself to watch for slip-ups.

○ ○ ○ ○ ○

Carrying Sarah, Ryan took a couple steps forward. With his torso turned sideways, his left shoulder led the way as he squeezed through the three-foot space separating the cabinets and the bathtub.

As Ryan approached the doorway connecting the bathroom with the bedroom, he was losing his grip on Sarah.

She dropped "slightly," according to Ryan, her head striking the bathroom floor. She was now lying between the cabinets and the door, opened against the tub. Her head was near the doorway but her body was still in the bathroom at that point.

Ryan pulled Sarah into the bedroom, just far enough to make her torso accessible for him to do CPR.

Sarah was now positioned with her upper half on the bedroom carpet and her lower half still in the bathroom.

To get Sarah there, Ryan would have walked only a few steps while carrying her, then took a few more seconds to pull her part-way into the bedroom. Those actions easily could have been accomplished during the twenty-nine seconds that elapsed during his 911 call.

After Ryan told the 911 dispatcher that Sarah was now on a flat surface, the dispatcher told Ryan to go unlock the doors for the emergency crews.

When Ryan returned upstairs, he was panting. He knelt next to Sarah's left side and started trying to do CPR—and that's when he made breathing sounds that some people said sounded fake on the 911 call. The breaths were too loud and too fast.

During Trial Three, Ryan's lawyer, Jay Clark, suggested a possible reason: the phone was propped on Ryan's shoulder, so he could listen to the dispatcher. And the dispatcher must have surmised that Ryan was doing that, Clark said, because after those loud breaths, the dispatcher said, "Ryan, go ahead and put the phone down and try CPR for me." Ryan responded, "Okay, yes I am... Come on, Sarah, come on."

Ryan put the phone next to Sarah's head and tried to remember what he had learned in CPR training. He wiped bloody froth from her mouth and tried to breathe life back into her—a memory that made him shudder as he recounted it for me years later.

Ryan responded to skeptics who thought he never tried to help Sarah with CPR: "None of those idiots have ever had to do that on someone they love. I had to, and I was doing what I thought was the way to do it. If I would have blown into the phone, it would have sounded not like it did."

That last phrase was classic RyanSpeak—unusual phrasing, but still understandable.

As I reflected on the face-up/face-down contradictions, the "pulled-her-out" ambiguity, and all the rest, I wondered: Wasn't it stretching the limits of credulity for one person to either misspeak or be misunderstood that many times?

Still, I reminded myself: In fairness to Ryan, I still hadn't caught him being dishonest. There would be plenty more chances for that.

○ ○ ○ ○ ○

While Ryan was making the CPR attempt—or feigning it—Steve Bishop, a Warren County sheriff's deputy, was on his way to help. He happened to be near the Widmers' neighborhood when he heard a dispatch about a reported drowning.

When Bishop arrived, he opened the front door and yelled, "Sheriff's Office!" He had to yell a second time before he heard a response, "Up here!"

C.J., the dog, was barking. Bishop was afraid the dog would attack. So he stopped part way up the stairs. Ryan assured the officer that the dog wouldn't bite him; Ryan led him to Sarah.

What happened next?

There are two different stories—Bishop's and Ryan's.

When Bishop testified, he adamantly asserted that Sarah's body remained stationary until medics prepared to transport her to the hospital.

If Ryan had testified, he would have claimed that Bishop told him to move her body.

One can only guess how a jury would have sorted out that conflict.

○ ○ ○ ○ ○

Months after I first heard the verbal version of Ryan's Story, I was crouched down in the basement of attorney Jay Clark's office building, digging through his Widmer case files for the second or third time. Something caught my eye: A typewritten document with a faded purple Post-It note stuck to the front, labeled "Ryan's Notes."

I pushed myself to my feet and stood there, reading it. *Wow. These appeared to be Ryan's own words, describing everything that had happened the night his wife died, and even the weekend beforehand.*

This was even more compelling than Ryan's diary, which was contained in the first set of records Clark loaned me.

Finding Ryan's notes was like discovering a diamond in a Dumpster. Among thousands of papers I had already reviewed, this six-page document might be the most valuable yet; it could refute Ryan's Story—or powerfully reinforce it.

A personal account of an event, written or recorded at the time of an incident or just afterward, is some of the best "evidence" a researcher can get. A contemporaneous record tends to be more vivid and more credible than one created later, after memories fade and agendas shift.

But when and why had the notes been created? The document was undated but there were two clues: the purple Post-It note and two holes punched into the top of it—characteristic of documents that Ryan's first lawyer, Charlie Rittgers, kept in two-pronged folders.

I took a picture of the front page and emailed it to Rittgers' secretary, asking: "Do you recognize this?" She did. That was her handwriting, and those were the notes that Ryan had created for Rittgers back in 2008, shortly after the case began.

That answer authenticated the document; the notes were created just after Sarah's death—when Ryan had no knowledge of the prosecution's case against him. And when he thought that only his lawyers would see it, never imagining that it would be seen by someone like me. That context increased the likelihood that the contents could be accurate and truthful.

Before I put much stock in the notes, I wanted to see Ryan's reaction to my discovery. Would he be afraid that I might find something embarrassing—or a major conflict with his story?

His reaction: "Oh yeah, I guess I do remember writing something like that. I had forgotten all about it until you mentioned it. I hope it helps you." No jitters. No loss of eye contact.

The notes revealed nothing that conflicted with Ryan's Story. Nor did I find any conflict with a similar document Ryan created two years later, "Ryan's Timeline of Events," dated March 17, 2010.

As weeks and months passed, I'd ask Ryan questions; he'd answer. I'd compare his answers with records; then I'd review more records and ask more questions.

So far, his responses and the records reinforced each other.

One example: In trial transcripts, medics testified that they had trouble keeping Sarah's head from moving out of position during resuscitation efforts. Ryan's notes, created before he knew what the medics would testify about, said he had the same difficulty: "Her head would not stay straight up. Each time I gave compressions...I had to readjust."

Still, Ryan could have fabricated his notes and his timeline to dupe his lawyers. If so, he would have a hard time keeping his story straight years later, wouldn't he?

"Hateful" description was powerful

To experienced crime investigators, "victimology," studying the victims, is just about as important as scrutinizing the suspects.

That requires gathering information about personality, activities, associations, relationships, education, phone records, financial records—anything that might provide insight as to why the alleged crime happened. Investigators also try to probe the psychology of the victims, the suspects and how they interacted. All of that helps ensure a solid case and valid conclusions.

But it would have been virtually impossible for investigators to have completed many of those steps within the two-day span before Ryan turned himself in to face the murder charge.

Investigators hadn't interrogated Ryan, except for a four-minute interview with the coroner's investigator. And I found no record of any meeting with Sarah's family until *after* Ryan appeared in court; that's also when her mom met with the coroner, according to her testimony.

That's where the problems began, Ryan said—caused by a lack of information and a plethora of assumptions about Sarah, the scene, and him.

"They never truly cared to know me," he said. "They just made up who they wanted me to be."

Once the case went to trial, it became a battle of portrayals: The prosecution's Scary Ryan versus the defense's Innocent Ryan.

If defense witnesses had been permitted to testify more freely, they would have described Ryan as responsible, considerate, conscientious, even-tempered, and a dog-lover who didn't have a mean bone in his body.

They would have told the jury that Sarah was a small but mighty fireball who could hold her own if confronted. And, if Ryan had attacked her, she almost certainly would have gotten in some licks—instead of leaving Ryan completely unscathed and no defensive wounds on her.

They would have said that, considering the available evidence, they couldn't picture a guy like Ryan suddenly "snapping" and killing the love of his life.

Yet that was exactly what the Trial Three jurors imagined. After learning the evidence. After seeing Ryan's stoic courtroom demeanor. After hearing inflammatory testimony from Sarah's mom. All of it fit the Scary Ryan mold.

A juror, Heather C., told me it bothered her to see Ryan betray no emotion when Sarah's autopsy photos were shown. That bugged her, she said, even though she knew that Ryan may have been inured to the images after seeing them repeatedly. Sarah's family "couldn't even look at them," Heather said.

Heather didn't know how Ryan had reacted during his two prior trials: He had shielded his eyes from the autopsy pictures—the behavior of a guilty man, some jurors and spectators declared. *See, he cannot even stomach the consequences of his own crime. Guilty conscience.*

Same situation, two opposite reactions from Ryan—both interpreted by others as "guilty" behaviors. Indeed, it did seem that everything he did, or did not do, was magnified through a lens tinted "guilty."

In his 2011 interview with radio station WLW, Trial Three Juror #3 claimed Ryan laughed while Sarah's mom, Ruth Ann Steward, testified. But Heather said she didn't remember seeing that—and Ryan said he never did it.

If Ryan had been caught on camera laughing at Ruth Ann, that image surely would have been broadcast. But I thought Juror #3 may have detected some type of reaction from Ryan when Ruth Ann made her surprise declaration that he and Sarah were "hateful to each other."

That testimony had a visceral impact on Ryan—and on Heather.

Ryan, normally unflappable, talked faster and more emphatically when I asked about the "hateful" statement. He said it was a mischaracterization of playful teasing; no one else who had seen his interaction with Sarah described it that way.

Heather said Ruth Ann's "hateful" description helped her envision Ryan getting angry enough to kill Sarah, when coupled with all the other odd circumstances.

But Heather and the other jurors were unaware of how the tone of Ruth Ann's testimony had evolved since Trial One.

Another statement from Sarah's mom—about Ryan checking on Sarah's credit-card purchases—was evidence that Ryan was "controlling," Heather said, another factor that enabled the jury to picture an argument that ended in murder.

No other witness alleged knowledge of an argument between the couple—except Mystery Witness Jennifer Crew. And the jury disbelieved Jennifer's testimony, Heather said: "It was a waste of almost a whole day."

Surprises about Sarah

As Ryan was the prime suspect in Sarah's death, there was no meaningful investigation of two other "suspects" that surfaced during Ryan's trials: Long QT Syndrome and narcolepsy/cataplexy—sleepiness and loss of muscular control.

No one tested Sarah for those two disorders, before or after her death.

Although Sarah had some symptoms that suggested narcolepsy, Sarah seemed to have more factors in common with Long QT Syndrome, a heart-rhythm problem.

Otherwise healthy people may have Long QT without knowing it—and some research links the disorder to a higher risk of drowning. A Mayo Clinic article on the topic said, "An unexplained drowning of a young person might be the first clue to inherited Long QT syndrome in a family."

Some patients may remain symptom-free for decades.

Specifically, Long QT Syndrome-Type 7 is known to afflict people with certain bony abnormalities, such as cleft palate, as a Trial Three expert mentioned. Anyone looking at Sarah would never guess that she had been born with that defect. It was repaired during infancy—a fact Ryan didn't even know until it surfaced during his case.

By itself, a cleft palate is viewed as a harmless malformation. But did Sarah exhibit other possible signs of Long QT-7?

Quite possibly, based on photos of her.

In a side-view wedding photo (pictured in this book), Sarah's ear did appear lower than normal—below eye level, where most people's ears sit. Low-set ears are among the possible traits listed for Long QT-7.

That photo also seems to reveal another feature sometimes seen in confirmed Long QT-7 cases: a small lower jaw.

Besides bony abnormalities, the other two main features of Long QT-7 are heart-rhythm abnormalities and bouts of paralysis, *most often in the legs.*

Reading that gave me chills; it clicked with a new piece of information about Sarah—a strange behavior she reportedly exhibited the night she died.

As Sarah headed to take her bath around 10 p.m., Ryan's notes say, "she came over, gave me a kiss, told me she loved me. I told her I loved her most. She walked to the bottom of the stairs, turned on the upstairs light and..."

Then something odd happened, according to Ryan's notes.

"...she walks on her tippy toes as she often did."

"I said, 'Hey, what are you doing walking on your tippy toes?' She said, 'I love you, check the doors before you come up.'"

Walking on tiptoes?

That had never been mentioned during any of Ryan's trials. Nor at any time afterward. Maybe Ryan's lawyers overlooked this detail or didn't perceive it as relevant to a murder case.

To me, the toe-walking stood out—more than the sleepiness, the headaches, the stomachaches that plagued Sarah. This was specific, not general; it was unusual, not common.

After reading about the "tippy toes," I did an internet search and found instances of people reporting toe-walking before seizures—also on the list of Sarah's suspected conditions.

Ryan said no one had ever asked him about Sarah's toe-walking before I noticed it in his notes in late 2017. But he couldn't remember much about it. And he hadn't remembered writing that detail in his notes.

Ryan couldn't estimate how many times he saw Sarah walk on tiptoe, nor could he identify any specific circumstances associated with it. He didn't think he had ever asked Sarah about that behavior—until the night she died. And she didn't answer his question about it.

Had anyone else seen Sarah walking on her tiptoes? Yes, according to one of Sarah's friends.

Dana Kist must have thought I was crazy when I called her out of the blue and asked. But she responded, yes, she had seen Sarah doing that, at the office where they worked and at her apartment. Dana never asked Sarah about the toe-walking. She assumed it might have been related to a knee injury that required surgery some years earlier.

After I told Dana that Sarah's unusual walking could have been an indicator of something serious, Dana, a nurse, agreed that it seemed disturbing to imagine Sarah walking so strangely right before she drowned.

○ ○ ○ ○ ○

Ryan's notes described another sequence of events that could pinpoint the moment when something went terribly wrong for Sarah.

About twenty minutes after she went upstairs to take her bath, Ryan was finishing his third beer of the night. He changed TV channels to watch Michael Phelps swim in the Olympic finals.

It was between 10:20-10:30 p.m... I heard a slight noise come from upstairs but did not think anything of it as I figured she was getting out of the tub, or she had dropped something.

By 10:49 p.m., Ryan was on the phone with 911, reporting Sarah was unresponsive.

○ ○ ○ ○ ○

In people with Long QT-7, muscular impairment may happen without warning, often when the person's blood is low in potassium. Low potassium can also affect heartbeat—and can lead to sudden death.

So what were Sarah's potassium levels when she died? Witnesses testified they found no such readings in Sarah's autopsy records—another crucial unknown in the case.

Whether Sarah may have had a hidden medical problem was something that juror Heather C. said she "worried and wondered" about. But based on the evidence that was presented in court, she voted guilty. Nothing else seemed logical or reasonable, she told me.

But now she wondered aloud: "God, I hope there wasn't stuff that would have changed my mind in the opposite direction."

No "aha!" moment

During the trial, I mused that a short, attractive blonde in the back row of the jury box looked like an older version of Sarah.

That juror was Heather. And when I met her six years later to interview her for this book, she told me that her fellow jurors noticed her resemblance to Sarah, too. Heather was only about a half-inch taller than Sarah, who stood five-foot-one, and Heather would make a good stand-in for her, the jury decided.

So, during deliberations, Heather knelt down on the floor, next to the tub. She hovered her hands above the finger streaks inside the bathtub. And, she said, the visual effect was convincing: "If you were trying to catch yourself, those streaks fit perfectly," lining up with her own hands.

It felt "creepy" for Heather to picture Sarah struggling and dying in that tub.

Heather marveled that people were "still nuts about the case" years after it happened, and that a quasi-celebrity glow would still surround her when people found out she had been a Widmer juror. Shortly after Heather started a new job, a colleague exclaimed, "I didn't know you were on that jury!" Heather replied, "Well, it's not like I wear a sign that says 'Widmer Juror' on it."

But for a while, it almost was like wearing a sign in the small community where she lived and worked. Live bloggers had given away many details about Heather—her occupation, the sports teams she followed, the fact that she wore a poncho to court. People easily figured out that Heather fit that description.

She hated serving on that jury. She hated the pressure that came with knowing someone's life was in her hands. She hated seeing the autopsy pictures and thinking about Sarah dying and her family suffering.

"It was a horrible experience, and I'd never want to do it again," she said.

If Ryan won an appeal, it would be hard to take, she said, because she was convinced of his guilt. Every so often, she'd get a text from a friend: "Oh, he's appealing again." Good grief—during three trials, thirty-six jurors had considered his case, and all but six or seven had judged him guilty. Wasn't that enough to show that the evidence was convincing? "Are we just going to keep going on until he gets the result he wants?" she wondered aloud.

During jury selection, defense lawyer Jay Clark seemed to disbelieve Heather when she denied having an opinion about attorneys. Other than working with a lawyer on a will, she had no real experience with them, she said.

But Clark "kept badgering me," she said. Finally, Heather got fed up and shot back something like: "I'm starting to have an opinion," based on the way Clark was questioning her. Then he backed off. But that left a bad taste in her mouth. "I did not like him," she told me, repeatedly.

Heather said she didn't have a preconceived opinion about Ryan's innocence or guilt, either. As a mom focused on raising two sons, she paid little attention to crime news. She had heard that the Widmer case involved a drowning in a bathtub, and that there was a lot of public drama over it—but that was about all she knew when she was drafted for jury duty.

When I asked what evidence was most persuasive to convict Ryan, Heather immediately cited the 911 call—and many things on it. "The whole call was shady," she said.

The position in which Ryan described finding Sarah wasn't believable. "How do you get face-down with your head toward the spigot?"

Why didn't he get her out of the tub?

And surely Sarah wouldn't have been face-down in the tub while Ryan was draining it, right? (Heather didn't know Ryan had consistently asserted Sarah was face-up in statements to his lawyers.)

The dry condition of Sarah's body when first-responders arrived at the Widmers' home was another big factor. "We don't know how long it was before 911 was called... she could have already been laying there," Heather said.

The dry condition of Ryan's body bothered her, too: "How'd he get her out of there, perform CPR, carry her and lay her down and not get wet?"

The jurors were also very suspicious about the two bloodstains. Because of those, "we thought he moved her, but we didn't know why," Heather said. "That was always an unanswered question."

There were lots of those, she acknowledged.

○ ○ ○ ○ ○

There was an intriguing possible answer to one of Heather's unanswered questions: Was there any explanation for the bruise on the right side of Sarah's forehead, near the hairline?

Jurors never got to hear about this: Sarah reportedly fell a few days before she died.

Investigators' notes, written in October 2008, say a neighbor mentioned that someone reportedly "had seen Sarah fall on a rake" while doing yard work. But the neighbor "did not know who made the comment."

During Trial Two, in 2010, Ryan's lawyers tried to get information about that on the record. They asked the Widmers' next-door neighbor, Mandy Antonczak: "Were you aware about a fall that she had in the front yard?" Yes, Mandy answered. But the judge forbade her from answering further. I was unable to find out anything more about it.

○ ○ ○ ○ ○

Heather listed many other reasons she convicted Ryan—things I had heard from other jurors: The bruising on Sarah's head and neck, the "fake-sounding" CPR breaths, Ryan offering the "falls-asleep" explanation for how she drowned instead of focusing on asking for help.

Heather said she expected a big, damning revelation would slap her in the face and help her decide the case. "But there never was that 'aha!' moment," she said.

Heather wasn't among the jurors who theorized Sarah was drowned in the toilet, nor did she attach any significance to the fact that the Widmers' dog was barking—as Juror #3 had.

Yet Heather said she was unable to come up with a scenario depicting what happened in the Widmers' bathroom. "I'm not God," she said, "and I wasn't there." (Ironically, that statement was similar to one that Ryan made to protest his innocence.)

In response to criticisms about the Trial Three jury reaching a decision in twelve hours—about half the time it took the Trial One jury to convict—Heather responded, "It wasn't like, 'Let's just get this done.'"

The Trial Three jury went through the 911 call numerous times and reviewed testimony of the witnesses. Then the foreman decided to take a vote; Heather thought the vote might be nine to convict, three to acquit, based on the conversation. "But we took our first vote, and the foreman read them off—all guilty," Heather said. "It was kind of eerie, because we said, 'Did that really just happen? Did we all agree on that?' And he said, 'I guess we are finished.'"

Afterward, Heather wept to her husband on the phone, releasing emotion that had built over the course of nearly a month.

Upon reflection, Heather said the lead detective "definitely jumped the gun," and "it didn't seem like they looked elsewhere for any other causes." But she didn't think those issues affected the evidence that was found against Ryan.

As Heather and I ate lunch at a Warren County restaurant, she agreed with me that sometimes two people can look at the same thing and see it differently—especially in the Widmer case. To illustrate she understood my point, Heather placed a salt shaker on the table between us. The shaker had a label on it. Lots of words were printed on one side; on the other, a big letter "S," for salt.

"So," Heather said, "you could describe what you're seeing from your side, I could describe what I'm seeing on my side. And we would both be right—but we also would both be wrong."

Very perceptive, I thought.

In that vein, I told her I was aware of facts that the jury didn't know—and I wondered if those facts would have changed perceptions of the case. Heather said she often wondered "how much that goes on in court, that the jury is not privy to," because of the numerous objections and hush-hush conversations between the lawyers and the judge.

"But," she said, "all you can do is go with what they give you."

Sealing Ryan's fate

Because there were so few pieces of undisputed physical evidence and so many ways to interpret each fact, I thought it might be impossible for a jury to reach a unanimous conclusion.

Especially after two mistrials.

Yet the Trial Three jurors managed to convict Ryan—even without a motive or a specific scenario.

When I asked Ryan's lawyer, Jay Clark, how that happened, he replied bluntly: "I did a shitty job picking a jury."

Clark said he should have more thoroughly grilled potential jurors. I doubt that would have gone over well with Heather, who said Clark's questioning irritated her.

Clark thought more questions from him might have smoked out people who were unwilling to accept "we don't know what happened" as a legitimate alternative to murder.

"People don't want to leave it unexplained, why a twenty-four-year-old woman just drops dead, drowns in the bathtub," Clark said. "But I think the jury got it way wrong. I think they ignored very sound scientific evidence that Ryan could not have done what they said he did."

To reach the guilty verdict, the jury had to either disbelieve or disregard virtually every expert who testified for the defense, including Dr. Chandler Phillips, the human-factors expert.

"The jury didn't listen to the evidence given by the people who didn't have a dog in the fight. Chandler Phillips didn't care who won or lost. His testimony was that the injuries Ryan and Sarah had—or didn't have—couldn't have happened in that bathroom during a struggle," Clark said. "If they're not going to believe Chandler Phillips, they're not going to believe Ryan Widmer... just another reason it would not have helped to put him on the witness stand."

Clark said he liked and respected Judge Bronson: "He always gave both sides a full and fair opportunity." But, in Clark's opinion, the judge erred when he blocked the defense from questioning Lieutenant Jeff Braley.

"I think it deprived Ryan of the ability to let the jury consider the character of the person who was pushing the whole thing against him," Clark said. "The case started with Braley and it took on a life of its own from there."

Braley was at the scene, thinking "something's bad wrong." Then, the next morning, Braley was at the autopsy. Clark's question: "You think it doesn't influence what the coroner sees—or doesn't see—if Braley is standing there saying he thinks the husband killed her?"

He noted Braley didn't even sit with prosecutors during Trial Three, a signal that the questions swirling around him were becoming a liability for the prosecution: "They tried so hard to distance themselves from Braley after embracing him."

As the husband of a police officer, Clark understood policework better than the average defense lawyer. And he thought that investigators, starting with Braley, reached erroneous conclusions about Ryan. Police training programs warn that faulty conclusions often result from "confirmation bias"—accepting information that fits a theory or a belief while rejecting or misinterpreting anything that doesn't fit.

"I think they all did that," Clark said, referring to investigators as well as jurors. And, he said, it all started with the mistaken assumption that Sarah was pulled from a water-filled tub, not an empty one.

Reflecting on the guilty verdict, Clark became convinced that many people who had bad impressions of Ryan—or were closed-minded to non-sinister interpretations of the evidence—had kept their opinions to themselves.

By the luck of the draw, that group was disproportionately represented in Ryan's jury pool—and landed on the jury, Clark said.

The Widmer case was, in many ways, the biggest of Clark's career. And he had lost. That's an occupational hazard for a trial lawyer, he said: "Sometimes you lose cases you should win, and sometimes you win cases you should lose."

The loss hurt, he admitted, because he wholeheartedly believed that the outcome was wrong—legally, morally and factually.

"The truth never changes," he said. "We never caught Ryan changing his story, embellishing what happened—and they (prosecutors) can't say that about all their witnesses."

"For those jurors who are saying, 'He did it, but we don't know how he did it,' how can you say that, based on the evidence you were presented?'" Clark said. "That goes against the presumption of innocence … and if you cannot articulate for me how the defendant killed his wife, you're not basing your decision on the facts."

If that was what happened, Ryan never had a chance.

Hidden perspectives

Juror Heather C. had said: Little things added up to murder.

Clark and Ryan had said: Little things were blown out of proportion—and the big picture was being misperceived as a result.

Same facts, different perceptions. Just like Ryan reacting or not reacting to the autopsy photos. Just like the salt shaker that looked different on Heather's side than it did on mine.

The salt shaker example showed that Heather was logical. Yet her statements left me wondering, just like Clark: How do you convict someone of murder without being able to describe how the crime was committed, in a way that fits all the known facts? How is that proof beyond a reasonable doubt?

In rare cases, suspects have been convicted of murder even when their victims' bodies were never found. But as far as I could recall, those cases almost invariably included physical evidence that linked the killer to the victim's body, or at least to the death scene.

In the Widmer case, there were only *opinions* and *arguments* that Ryan had laid hands on Sarah—no physical proof directly connecting Ryan to Sarah's body. Ditto for the drowning scene.

Maybe any such evidence had washed away with the bathwater. Or maybe that evidence never existed because there was no struggle between Sarah and Ryan—and Sarah instead succumbed to a medical problem that interfered with normal walking, as Ryan observed that night.

Ahh, the two-sided salt shaker came to mind again. Almost every shred of evidence, every circumstance, could be seen two different ways: suspicious or not suspicious.

Even the "fecal stain" near Sarah's head was a point of contention. It was suspicious under the prosecution's Spinning Sarah Theory and innocuous, according to the defense's claim: the stain was actually partially digested food—a possibility, based upon a scientist's testimony and a photograph.

Based on jurors' comments, the non-suspicious interpretations failed to resonate with jurors—to the point where it seemed as though the defense team had been merely whispering, while prosecutors and their witnesses were speaking through a bullhorn.

The prosecution had pounded, pounded, pounded an idea into jurors' minds: dry, dry, dry equals murder, murder, murder.

Ryan's lawyers may have stood a better chance if they had used repetition for effect, too: It was a natural reaction for Ryan to prop Sarah into a seated position, out of the water. Then the tub drained, drained, drained, as Sarah dried, dried, dried.

Or maybe nothing would have overcome the jurors' inclination to believe the people in authority—an often-cited flaw in the criminal-justice system.

Jurors tend to allow *opinions* of coroners and other government employees to masquerade as *facts*.

They expect prosecutors, police, medics, coroners—paid with taxpayers' money—to be honest, conscientious and competent. People seem to feel a *need* for these trusted public servants to be not only technically correct, but to be morally and legally *right*.

For most people, the authorities are white knights crusading against the dark knights, defense lawyers who will say and do anything to "get their guy off," including paying experts to deliver made-to-order opinions.

But few things in life are that black-and-white—especially not in the murky world of criminal justice, where forensic science often collides with politics, personalities, psychology, news media and pop culture.

Prosecutors and defense lawyers both hire experts—busy, highly educated and well-paid professionals—who could be earning a paycheck instead of testifying in court. And while some experts have indeed been exposed as unscrupulous, most surely covet their professional reputations too much to jeopardize them.

Yet research has shown that jurors tend to dislike *and* to distrust experts who are both prestigious and highly compensated.

Among forensic pathologists, Dr. Werner Spitz, who testified for Ryan, was off the charts in both categories. Did his testimony backfire? Possibly, because jurors apparently rejected or otherwise didn't absorb his testimony.

The same could be said for the testimony of Dr. David Smile, despite many credibility-boosting points: He testified in mostly plain language. He was a board-certified, experienced emergency room doctor who testified for the defense for free. And Smile said virtually all of Sarah's injuries could have resulted from medical intervention.

That opinion was incompatible with a guilty verdict. So were the opinions of Dr. Chandler Phillips, the human-factors expert, and Dr. Michael Gregory Balko, the brain pathologist.

In the end, the jurors seemed to value prosecution experts' opinions like 14-karat gold ingots—while tossing aside the defense experts' opinions like tarnished scrap metal.

Possibilities and probabilities

Ryan thought he was unbelievably lucky to have married a sweet, beautiful, bright young woman. Yet that was where their misfortune began—whether an unknown marital crisis sent Ryan over the edge or a hidden health problem doomed Sarah.

What were the chances that an even-tempered guy would suddenly go berserk and commit a mortal sin against the woman he loved?

Likewise, the odds seemed "vanishingly small," as one prosecution witness put it, that a 24-year-old woman with no significant medical history would suddenly, inexplicably drown in her own bathtub, alone.

However, just as buying more tickets gives a lottery player more chances to win the jackpot, each odd symptom and trait could have increased Sarah's chances of suffering from a medical problem that remained undetected.

Sarah's cremation—a decision Ryan said he made because it was practical and less expensive—destroyed any chance that additional evidence could ever be recovered from her body. Ryan, who wasn't sure whether he consulted with Rittgers about cremating Sarah, regretted that decision because of the consequences: It left prosecutors in control of the sole remaining possible sources of Sarah's DNA—such as the bloodstained carpet samples. The prosecution has been court-ordered to preserve all such evidence. But prosecutors have refused to turn over any DNA to the defense for genetic testing. Their argument: Even if Sarah's DNA tested positive for Long QT or some other disorder, that wouldn't exclude homicide as the manner of her death.

Legal analyst Mark Krumbein takes issue with that stance. "If she had a condition that could have led to her death, wouldn't you want to know that?" he said. "Considering all the things she seemed to have in common with Long QT, I don't think that ignoring that potential is dealing with it in a fair way."

Visiting Ryan, "the killer"

Without a proven diagnosis for Sarah, new evidence or a legal error that persuades a judge to throw out Ryan's conviction again, the law says Ryan shall remain "a convicted killer."

For many who know him, that term seems incongruous; it fits nothing they see in him, and no evidence in his trials persuaded them otherwise. They wish the jury somehow could have seen the Ryan they know: naïve and trusting, a little shy with people he doesn't know well, easy-going and unlikely to get agitated.

Friends Dana and Chris Kist love seeing Ryan. But they hate the process of visiting him—and leaving him afterward.

It's a surreal experience for middle-class, law-abiding people to walk past rows of razor wire, to go through metal detectors and other security checks, then set foot into a world they cannot understand.

"Somehow, he has managed to deal with everything better than any of us have," Dana said. The couple, who introduced Ryan and Sarah to each other in 2006, have visited Ryan about once every other month since he was convicted in 2011. For most of that time, Ryan has been imprisoned at the Correctional Reception Center in Orient, Ohio.

That's where I met with him about a dozen times for this book.

The visiting room is about triple the size of an average living room. Visitors are escorted out of the main building by a uniformed guard, through the prison yard to a second building where the visiting room is located. They pause at a window to display picture ID's and fluorescent-ink hand stamps to a second guard, then they're allowed to enter the visiting room.

Inside, another guard sits on a raised platform behind an old, carved wooden railing, staring at a computer screen and scanning the room. That guard decides where each visitor will sit among the rickety metal chairs with maroon cushions, each marked with a number. About two dozen inmates might be welcoming visitors on a given day.

After a few minutes, visitors half-forget they're visiting someone in prison. They share funny stories, discuss current events and updates on their personal lives—normal conversations in abnormal surroundings.

But it wasn't always that way for many of Ryan's friends and relatives. They went through an awkward adjustment period, when they didn't quite know what to say to him.

Sharing good news from their daily lives—vacations, family celebrations, cookouts—might make Ryan more depressed. And sharing their complaints— stress at work, traffic congestion, a sick child—seemed unworthy of kvetching about, compared to being in prison for murder.

Yet visitors started to see that Ryan liked hearing about their ups and downs; it made him feel included in their lives and allowed them to vent. After the way his case destroyed his mom, Jill, "I don't think Ryan wants anyone else to ruin their life because of the situation he's in," his twin brother Ayran said.

Ryan's former co-worker Lori Worley hated to admit that she distanced herself from Ryan because she couldn't handle his situation.

"When he was convicted, it was like someone put a knife through my heart," she said. "For a while after that, I couldn't even talk to him because it was too hard on me. But then I realized I need to get over myself, and just be there for him to talk to."

A few months later, she steeled herself and signed up for prepaid email and phone services that allowed Ryan to contact her; Ryan put Lori on his visiting list.

The two of them rarely talked about Ryan's legal case or its consequences to him.

"Does he ever talk about how hard it is to be where he is? No—never," Lori said, "because he doesn't want to make it harder for me to deal with."

When Lori was diagnosed with breast cancer in April 2016 and began chemotherapy, she'd tell Ryan about her ordeal. "And Ryan always made it about me, not about him," she said. "He's kind of an old soul for his age."

Since 2012, Lori has talked to him almost every week—nearly three hundred times. "I don't know how they haven't sucked the life out of him. But he still finds it in his heart to care about other people."

Visitors can stay for an hour or two, or all day, 8:30 a.m. to 3:30 p.m., weekends. Each person can visit a maximum of four times per month.

Ryan's visiting list has almost always been filled to the limit: fifteen names. At times, he has had to temporarily remove some visitors to make room for new ones. He appreciates the many people who have consistently visited him, including Mollie Mihalik, the redhead who became like his second mom; she still drives a vehicle with a "Free Ryan Widmer" bumper sticker on it.

Visitors can bring up to twenty bucks—in fives, ones and coins—to buy vending-machine food for themselves and for Ryan. He loves Mountain Dew, microwaveable cheeseburgers and baked Lay's potato chips—junk food that seems special compared to prison meals.

Ryan is reluctant to talk about the food he gets and other details of prison life. The way he sees it, complaining doesn't help and could make things more unpleasant for his visitors.

Ryan's visitors say they are heartbroken to leave and return to "the outside," leaving him stuck "on the inside."

○ ○ ○ ○ ○

During the time that he has been "down," as prisoners call it, Ryan learned to cope by staying busy.

Ryan has worked in prison jobs as a teacher's aide and a law library clerk, earning about twenty-four bucks a month to buy snacks and toiletries from the commissary.

Ryan is allowed to special-order boxes of food and personal items twice a year; his supporters take up collections to pay for those. Pop Tarts and canned Skyline Chili never tasted so good.

He participates in a foster-care dog program, caring for animals until permanent homes can be found for them. He has a regular schedule for physical exercise and for emailing, calling and visiting friends and relatives.

He longs for more contact with his son, who lives far away with his mother. But Ryan is happy whenever his dad, Gary, shares updates on how Little Ryan is doing in school and in sports.

Within the prison system that controls virtually every aspect of his life, Ryan has taken charge of the few variables that are under his control. He has devised a structure that helps him keep his sanity.

He distances himself from conflicts among other prisoners. And he has learned to watch his back, to always be aware of his surroundings. Anyone who visits Ryan for any length of time will notice that his eyes dart around the visiting room—something he didn't do before he was imprisoned, his brother Ayran said. Otherwise Ryan still seems pretty much himself, maybe a little more mature and a little more articulate as time has passed.

When I asked Ryan what he misses most about being "on the outside," Ryan replied: "What *don't* I miss?"

As I tried to figure out the Real Ryan, I asked him: "What would you like people to know about you?" He replied that I should ask people who know him. That reminded me of what his boss, Shirley Bonekemper, told me. When she asked him to describe his best qualities for a job promotion, his response was, "What do you want me to say?"

After a bit of prodding, Ryan told me: "I'm a good person. Not even pertaining to what I'm accused of, and what I'm in here for. I've always strived to do the right thing. Like even with school. I never even wanted to get bad grades. There's not a violent bone in my body. Nor have I ever contemplated breaking the law. It's not even in me to, like, steal something … And I would never lay a hand on a woman."

Ryan told me that, regardless of how he's portrayed, or what people perceive about him, he knows what the truth is: He wasn't in the bathroom when his wife drowned; he did nothing wrong.

Although he doesn't like talking about himself, he occasionally grants media interviews because he figures that any attention on his case is potentially good. Maybe it could reach "someone out there" who has information that could change everything, he said.

○ ○ ○ ○ ○

I might have encountered one of those people.

As I was wrapping up research for this book, I tried to reach a person who witnessed some things the night Sarah died. I was unsure whether I even had a correct phone number but thought, "It can't hurt to try."

My call was returned when I least expected it, while I was cooking dinner one Wednesday night. I grabbed a yellow legal pad and a pen, then explained that I wanted to hear recollections of the Widmer case for this book, a ten-year retrospective.

The conversation continued on condition that I withhold the person's name.

The Unnamed Witness initially made observations I had heard before. But just when it seemed that the interview would provide no new information, I asked about certain circumstances—and got a response that shocked me. The Unnamed Witness told me that no investigator had ever asked the question I was posing, then made a revelation that differed from anything I had read in thousands of pages of documents.

My hands shook so badly I could hardly scribble notes and my pen wasn't working right. While scrambling for another pen, I asked the witness to repeat the statements. There was no mistaking what I heard. But I could not use it unattributed. It was too potent.

Two days later, on a Friday afternoon, I met the Unnamed Witness at a coffee shop. But I was unable to get an on-the-record confirmation. I became convinced that the Unnamed Witness showed up mostly out of curiosity, to get information from me. I obliged.

The witness agreed to meet me for lunch the following week, on a Sunday, but didn't show up. My texts and phone message got no response. Maybe the witness got cold feet after realizing the information might be helpful to Ryan, whom the witness believed was justly convicted.

As investigators know, the first thing out of a person's mouth is usually the truth; that's one reason I remain convinced that what I heard on the phone was accurate.

Maybe the Unnamed Witness will experience a crisis of conscience and come forward someday, just as Trial One juror Jon C. did, when he revealed the jurors' wet-dry experiments despite his belief that Ryan was guilty.

If that happens, a court would have to decide what impact the new information would have, if any.

Trying to get it right

In a justice utopia, jurors would be able to eradicate biases and prejudices as effectively as the agents in the *Men in Black* movies used a "flashy thing" to erase people's memories.

Jurors would fully understand principles such as the presumption of innocence, the defendant's right to remain silent and reasonable doubt. They would disregard "gut feelings" that a person is guilty, based on appearance, demeanor and unanswered questions. Their decisions would be based solely on facts, devoid of emotion.

And they would resist the temptation to try to "solve the mystery" in a baffling case like Ryan's.

But that's not reality.

Instead, jurors often are so determined to reach the "right" verdict that they may become overzealous, said Thaddeus Hoffmeister, an Ohio law professor who studies juries.

The Trial One jurors' wet-dry experiments reflect that phenomenon, Hoffmeister said. They got themselves into trouble when they tried too hard to figure out a key question that was barely addressed during testimony: how long it would have taken Sarah's skin to air-dry.

When I asked Hoffmeister to analyze why the Trial Three jurors convicted Ryan, he said they were presented with dueling scientific evidence. To convict Ryan, they had to "ignore" the defense experts' testimony, even though it was scientifically valid, Hoffmeister said.

When prosecutors sought to move the trial because of pretrial publicity, Hoffmeister, who attended some of Ryan's court proceedings, wrote an affidavit supporting the move. Hoffmeister worried whether a fair and impartial jury could be seated in Warren County because of pervasive publicity and "the entrenched opinions that many potential jurors are likely to have."

Even if jurors can set aside their opinions, mistakes can happen if they misinterpret the facts or the law. Yet even badly flawed verdicts often survive appeals, said legal analyst Mark Krumbein.

"As long as there's some evidence to hang their hat on, it's hard to throw out the verdict, even if the jurors come up with some illogical or bizarre interpretations of the evidence or the law," Krumbein said. "There's usually nothing that the defendant can do."

It's hard to say how often jurors reach the wrong decision. But in a 2007 Northwestern University study, jurors reached incorrect verdicts in about one of every eight cases, compared to the verdict that judges in those cases believed was correct.

Among hundreds of cases I covered as a reporter, I thought "the system" usually got it right. In a scant handful of cases, I confronted authorities about possible miscarriages of justice. But never once did I hear a prosecutor, police officer or a coroner admit: "Whoops, we were wrong."

Prosecutors do sometimes "*nolle prosequi*" cases—drop charges. But that rarely seems to happen in high-profile cases, Krumbein said.

"Nobody cares or notices if that happens when it's a shoplifter or a guy who punched someone in the face," Krumbein said. "The worse the crime, the more people pile on. They want to solve it, they want to punish the person and their peripheral vision is gone."

Often, these thoughts are subconscious, below the surface—and the authorities may be unaware of how profoundly such "target fixation" can affect a case, Krumbein said.

"And," he said, "if any shortcuts are taken, it's okay—because they're convinced they're doing the right thing."

Tell that to more than 2,200 people who were cleared of crimes they didn't commit; they collectively *wasted sixteen hundred years* in U.S. prisons, according to the National Registry of Exonerations in mid-2018.

Untold thousands of other prisoners assert that they are innocent but stand little chance of "proving" they were wrongfully convicted, based on misleading or misinterpreted evidence—the situation Ryan claims to be in.

"It's so easy to charge and to indict somebody. And once that happens, you're facing an uphill battle," Ryan said. "From then on, the assumption is that you 'did it.' How do you fight against that?"

Holding onto hope

For the past decade, Ryan's cousin, Sean Cronin, has continually worn a white bracelet on his right wrist. In fading black letters, it says, "Free Ryan Widmer... An Innocent Man."

While Sean has coached football at the University of South Florida and other places, countless coaches, players, recruits and parents have asked him about the significance of the bracelet. He struggles to respond because it's hard to explain Ryan's case and all the thoughts and feelings connected to it.

The bracelet makes Sean think of happier times, the carefree days when the Cronin boys—Sean and his two brothers—would hang out with the three Widmer boys—Ryan, Ayran and Kyle—like six brothers.

"Sometimes, it has brought me to tears, just thinking of how things are now and how things were then, back when the six of us were out playing wiffleball, just naïve to the world," Sean said.

The Widmer case "changed the entire family dynamic," Sean said, because everyone reacted differently. Personalities changed. Mental health became unstable. Once-prayerful people lost their faith in God. "Every one of us knows he's innocent—and we feel this void and this sadness whenever we get together, knowing there's no reason why he shouldn't be there with us," Sean said.

Sarah's family surely feels similar resentment over her absence—a dilemma for which Sean expressed compassion: "They could either believe that Ryan, a guy they trusted, did something to Sarah—or accept the alternative: That no one may ever know what happened to her. What's harder to deal with? I don't know."

The bracelet makes Sean think about the justice system. "People assume the system works. I don't assume that's true anymore. I know better than that. I have seen how perceptions, not evidence, can make a person seem 'guilty,' to the police, the public and the jury," Sean said.

"If this happened to Ryan, who was middle-class and could afford a lawyer, it could happen to anybody," Sean said. "What if he was too poor to afford a good lawyer, and the death happened in a poor neighborhood where it wasn't 'shocking?' In Ryan's case, there was so much attention because it was 'shocking' that he was a college graduate who lived in some suburb. But what if he wasn't? No one would have cared."

The bracelet makes Sean think about ways the justice system could be improved—and that maybe Ryan's case could be a catalyst for those changes, which have been advocated for years. "There are no checks-and-balances, not like you were led to believe in school," Sean said. The work of police, coroners and prosecutors should be subject to more oversight, other than the scrutiny of defense lawyers, he said—and the culture needs to change so that the authorities aren't afraid to admit mistakes.

Sean longs for the day when he can take off that "Free Ryan Widmer" bracelet— the day when Ryan will be set free.

He hopes that will be before Ryan's first parole eligibility date in July 2025. By then, Ryan, who was 27 when Sarah died, will be almost 45 years old. And the State of Ohio will have spent about $400,000 to keep him locked up.

Sean has dreamt of Ryan's release ever since he wrote him a letter that ended: "I can't wait until this is all over and we can go to a lake somewhere, have some beers and talk about what an unbelievable circumstance you have overcome."

All about the unknowns

Over the years, my opinion of Ryan's guilt or innocence vacillated. Just when I thought my mind was made up, another game-changer would surface.

The weirdness of it all made me wonder whether Ryan was guilty. The alternative—that a medical disorder struck Sarah in the tub—seemed unlikely based on information presented in court.

Yet I wondered: What were the facts that *didn't* come out in court? Would those have presented a different picture?

I thought about missing pieces in any story I covered, thanks to a wise journalism professor at Kent State University who said: "Always remember that what people *don't* tell you may be more important than what they *do* tell you."

Professor Bruce Larrick molded me at a time when journalism students still used typewriters, not computers. Many things have changed. But his advice never steered me wrong. He honed my natural curiosity and encouraged me to think more critically, to always wonder: What are the missing statements, the missing facts, the unknowns?

In the Widmer case, the list of unknowns was long—the tests that *weren't* done, the testimony that Ryan *didn't* give, the injuries that *weren't* explained on Sarah, the injuries that *weren't* found on Ryan.

Topping all of that, I wondered what the authorities *weren't* stating publicly, especially in light of their own actions.

They acted with lightning speed to rule Sarah's death a homicide and to indict Ryan, before any real investigation could have been done—begging the question: Had accusations been made prematurely?

Then prosecutors took steps that seemed to project a lack of confidence in the strength of their case:

- The head prosecutor decided against personally handling the case and delegated it to two assistants.

- Prosecutors suddenly changed the Bill of Particulars in the midst of Trial One, alleging Sarah was drowned somewhere other than the bathtub.

- They distanced themselves from the lead detective—literally and figuratively.

- They offered Ryan a plea deal.

- Then, at the last minute, they added a manslaughter option for jurors to consider.

Those events left me disquieted.

I considered other unknowns: Did prosecutors have some secret evidence that wasn't admissible in court? Was there an "X Factor" that made them so determined to get a conviction—and that convinced Sarah's family of Ryan's guilt?

Or was the whole case built on a shaky foundation? Had tunnel vision prevented authorities from seeing the ideal—to pursue justice, not just a conviction?

What things were Ryan's lawyers holding back? What was Ryan himself holding back?

These questions and others ricocheted through my mind like metal balls bouncing off bumpers in a pinball machine. Nothing seemed to abate my uneasiness over the Widmer case—not even my departure from full-time journalism.

My worries intensified in light of events that happened after Ryan was convicted.

Jeff Braley, the lead detective, resigned in the wake of an investigation that raised concerns about his honesty.

Then Braley was embroiled in the controversial court case over the Pritchard raid that happened in 2007, a year before Sarah's death.

Additional questions about the county coroner's methods and conclusions surfaced in the United Oil case.

"If those things had come up before the trial—instead of after—that could have been a big help to the defense," attorney Mark Krumbein said. "The stars did not align for Ryan Widmer."

When I resolved to re-examine the Widmer case from top to bottom, I tried to approach it the way jurors are supposed to start: with the presumption of innocence.

At the same time, I remained vigilant, looking for answers to the unknowns— just as I always had.

To assess the credibility of Ryan's Story, I applied a two-part litmus test:

Did Ryan's Story remain consistent?

Although Ryan made conflicting statements the night Sarah died—well-documented during his trials—I found no directly contradictory statements after that.

Did Ryan's Story track with undisputed physical evidence?

- He stated he drained the tub and did *not* struggle with Sarah. That could explain why Sarah and the scene were dry.

- He stated that Sarah's head was near the faucet and he had to pivot to get her out of the tub and through the narrow space between the tub and the cabinetry. That could explain how Sarah's head ended up pointing the opposite direction, toward the bedroom, when first-responders arrived.

- He stated that, after Sarah was on the floor, he performed CPR on her, and wiped bloody foam from her mouth. That corresponds with three "fingertip" streaks found on the carpet in the hallway, a spot where officers saw him crouched down, listening as medics worked on her.

- His simple explanation for the movement of Sarah's body—to get her out of the doorway, creating room for medics to work on her—corresponds with the two bloodstains and with the narrow doorway. Granted, that statement conflicts with the testimony of the deputy who arrived first on the scene. But questioning implied that the deputy's memory might not have been the best. An evidence technician testified that the deputy told him he had dumped the Widmers' bathroom trash to look for evidence. But the deputy testified he didn't recall emptying the wastebasket.

The deeper I dug, the more it looked like Ryan's Story was explaining many circumstances that were otherwise inexplicable.

And the more it looked like Ryan's conviction was based on those unknowns.

Analyzing it all

As I reflected on the events that preceded Ryan's conviction, a stream of "what-ifs" possessed me, such as:

What if Sarah had insisted that her doctor test for disorders related to her strange sleepiness?

What if Sarah had answered Ryan when he asked why she was walking on her tippy toes?

What if a more highly trained police officer had been in charge of the investigation?

What if Ryan had immediately removed Sarah's whole body from the water-filled tub?

What if the coroner had delayed his ruling until he was able to more extensively review the whole situation? What if he had waited until Sarah's brain was preserved, and taken more samples for testing?

Each of those variables could have affected everything else that followed, and the unimaginable stress and strain for everyone involved.

Even if Sarah's family had responded to my interview requests, nothing I can write would adequately express the depths of their grief and turmoil. Likewise, even though many other people spent countless hours answering my questions, my attempts to comprehend and to convey their experiences seemed inadequate.

I don't know what it's like to lose a loved one in such a sudden, tragic and controversial manner.

I don't know what it's like to decide whether to convict someone of murder—and then have your decision scrutinized.

I don't know what it's like to have a relative thrown in prison, nor what it's like to be imprisoned.

But talking to many people—and reviewing all the knowns and unknowns of the case—did lead to one abundantly clear conclusion.

And it wasn't the "easy" one that I had envisioned.

When I started working on this book, I half-hoped I would find a glaring inconsistency, exposing Ryan as a liar and a justly convicted killer. That would tie up everything in a nice, neat package. I could write a conclusion something like, "Despite all the fuss, it sure seemed like Ryan's jury got it right."

Instead, this was the ironic conclusion that became apparent:

The case began when Sarah was submerged—and that is what happened to the love, the hopes, the dreams that she and Ryan shared. That is what happened to their families and to everyone the case touched.

And that, I fear, is also what happened to the truth.

Acknowledgments

After decades of writing news articles on deadline, I thought writing a book would feel leisurely, carefree.

That's not quite how it went.

At times, I felt like a sprinter trying to finish a marathon. I often felt "gassed," and I still had miles and miles to go before reaching the finish line.

Eventually, I found my stride: dig-think-write, rethink-rewrite-dig.

But just when it felt like I was making steady progress, life's demands would interrupt the flow; I would lose my mojo.

Through it all, my best buddy, my husband Michael, was there to lift me up, to cheer me on, to dust me off, to wipe away the sweat and grime and tears; to set my head straight.

Without Michael, I never would have left the starting gate. At his urging, I left my full-time job so I could write this book, while continuing to work three part-time positions. "You can do it," he said, over and over. So did his mom, Betty—until the day she died. I regret I was unable to finish it before she passed away at the start of 2018.

Michael spurred me on, saying he knew his mom believed in my ability to convey powerful messages—and in my dedication to doing the right thing.

I thank, honor and love Betty and Michael, along with my sister Sandy Peate, for the long hours they spent reading and discussing various drafts of this work.

I'm incredibly indebted to my former *Cincinnati Enquirer* colleague, Peter Bronson, for his mentorship—and for his editing this book with a scalpel instead of a machete.

Thank you, Peter, for the many hours you spent coaching me. Thank you for giving me the confidence to write more freely than I ever had before. Thank you for teaching me to hear my own "voice" better and, more importantly, to trust it.

I would also like to acknowledge my former *Enquirer* editor Jim "J.R." Rohrer for helping to create journalistic magic during the third Widmer trial in 2011 and for the many hours we spent talking about the case, even years later. I'd like to acknowledge the professionalism of other *Enquirer* staffers who worked alongside me while the case was pending, especially photographers Cara

Owsley, Stacey Doose and Glenn Hartong; and to those who encouraged me to write a book on this case "someday," including J.R., Jennifer Baker, Paul Daugherty and Mark Curnutte.

Special thanks to Martin Yant, a Columbus, Ohio, private investigator and journalist who also is a tireless advocate for truth and justice. I have admired Marty ever since he opened my eyes to an egregious case in Dayton, Ohio, in 1996.

Thank you to Mollie Mihalik for shepherding me through the prison-visitation process—and to Ryan Widmer for accepting me as a visitor, for entrusting me with his full story and for answering every nit-picky question to the best of his ability.

Thank you to talented graphic artist David Juergens for the incredible cover design, and to photographer Kelsey Moffitt for caring enough to set the right tone with images shot on a very windy day. Thanks also to proofreader Jane Wenning and to book designer Andy Melchers for their attention to detail.

I appreciate every person who listened to my excited—and sometimes frustrated—chatter about my progress on this project.

I'd also like to express gratitude to the following individuals who dedicated time, effort, encouragement and resources to make this book better than it would have been without their help:

Mike Allen, Michele Berry, Shirley Bonekemper, Heather C., Jay Clark, Jackie Cronin, Kevin Cronin, Sean Cronin, Debbie Cupp, Kathy Edwards, Mark Godsey, Lindsey Gutierrez-Quillin, Brooke H., Thaddeus Hoffmeister, Konrad Kircher, Chris Kist, Dana Kist, Mark Krumbein, Nancy Petro, Abbey Vontsolos Reynolds, Charlie H. Rittgers, Charlie M. Rittgers, Farrah Rudd, Debbie S., Marilyn Schnebelt, Dawn Stinson, Jeff Suess, Jennifer Thompson, Brent Turvey, Mike Vaccarriello, Julie Phillippi Whitney, Ayran Widmer, Gary Widmer, Kim Widmer, Lori Worley.

To many others I may have overlooked, I am grateful.

Made in the USA
Lexington, KY
01 August 2018